AF426158

# A BICYCLE TRIP
# OF LONG AGO

# A BICYCLE TRIP OF LONG AGO

From Saint Paul, Minnesota
to New York, Boston, and back
in 1915

A Daily Journal of the Trip

by

## LEON W. SCHROEDER

1980

*A reproduction of the original
privately-issued book*

Copyright ©2023 Diana Gilley/Schroeder Family Press
All Rights Reserved

Published by Schroeder Family Press
Medford, Oregon

Created and produced by
Lucky Valley Press
www.luckyvalleypress.com

Source material by Leon W. Schroeder, 1980

This book and its contents are protected under International and Federal Copyright Laws and Treaties. No part of this book may be reproduced or transmitted in any form or by any means, electronic or mechanical, including photocopying, recording, or by any information storage and retrieval system without express written permission from the publisher.

Softcover ISBN: 979-8-218-18554-1
Hardcover ISBN: 979-8-218-19097-2

Printed in the USA on acid-free paper

# A NOTE ABOUT THE BOOK AND THIS NEW EDITION

This is a reproduction of a book written and produced by Leon W. Schroeder in 1980 as a typewritten, 8.5 x 11-inch, 310-page, privately-issued hardcover volume. Only a dozen copies were created.

Mr. Schroeder pasted his own original photos onto the typed pages, along with documents, press clippings, and thumbnails made from 1915 postcards.

In this reproduction, every attempt has been made to maintain clarity in the photographs. Some images in the original book were faded photocopies of previous images and some photographs are dark. Those, and the small photographs of 1915 color postcards, often do not reproduce well.

The paper in the original book varies in brightness and in many places the paper is smudged or handworn. (The upper right edge is darker from being touched many times). No attempt has been made to remove these variations in shading.

The 1980 original was printed only on the right-hand pages, with page numbers in the upper right corner. We have retained those original page numbers in the upper right.

In the original, the contents of every page was shifted far to the right, very close to the right edge. To create a visual balance on the two-sided pages of this new book, the contents of each page has been centered, and the surrounding blank area of the original has been slightly trimmed.

Otherwise nothing has been altered, modified, or omitted. All text and images in this reproduction appear in their original size.

Regarding the cost of living, $1.00 in 1915 would be worth about $29 in 2023.

*−David Gordon*
*Lucky Valley Press, 2023*

*This page, the two preceding pages, and the front and back cover were newly created for the 2023 edition.*

*All other material in this book is solely from Leon W. Schroeder, 1980.*

# A BICYCLE TRIP OF LONG AGO.

## A Daily Journal Of The Trip

By

Leon W.Schroeder

LEON W.SCHROEDER   1915   HARWOOD E.TEMPLE

I dedicate this book: to my Mother who reluctantly let me take the trip; to Harwood E.Temple my stead-fast companion on the trip; to the hundreds of kind and helpful people we met whose generosity made the trip possible and last but not least to my wife,Lena,who helped me write the story of the trip.

All rights to this story or any part there-of reserved by the author.

San Carlos,California 1979

## ST. PAUL
### TO
## NEW YORK
#### ON BICYCLE

LEON SCHROEDER
1010 FAIRMOUNT AVE.
ST. PAUL, MINN.

MY CALLING CARD

### BOYS TO PEDAL TO GOTHAM

**Leon Schroeder and Harwood Temple Expect to Make Expenses by Selling Postcards.**

Leon Schroeder, 1010 Fairmount avenue, and Harwood Temple, 758 Lincoln avenue, 18 and 17 years old respectively, will mount their bicycles in front of the Court House at 6 A. M. Monday and begin a two months' trip to New York City and return.

They expect to make expenses by selling St. Paul postcards. A twenty-pound kit will carry the baggage of each, for they are not anticipating accommodations de luxe.

Neither of the boys has made long rides before, but they will begin with easy stages until they become accustomed to the road. Chicago, Cleveland, Buffalo and Albany will be visited.

### Lads to Pump Their Way to New York City

**Leon Schroeder and Harwood Temple to Boost St. Paul on Long Trip.**

Leon Schroeder, 16, 1010 Fairmount ave., and Harwood Temple, 17, 758 Lincoln ave., will leave St. Paul June 28, at 6 a. m., for a bicycle trip to New York city.

They will pay their expenses by selling postcard views of St. Paul.

The boys will carry a tent and cooking utensils, and will camp wherever night overtakes them. They expect to make the trip in two months, over a Southern route. They will return over another route, leaving the East early in August.

They asked for the co-operation of the Association of Commerce in their efforts to advertise St. Paul.

ST. PAUL, MINNESOTA  NEWSPAPERS  JUNE 1915

Note:

The pictures in this book were taken by me while on the trip, except for some photographs of 1915 post cards.

PREFACE

This is the true story of a 3,627 mile bicycle trip made
in 1915 with single speed bikes.My cousin Harwood E.Temple and
I made the trip during the summer vacation when we were in high
school in Saint Paul,Minnesota. The story is a day by day account
of the trip and also reflects conditions that existed in the
United States at that time.

The story is compiled from the diary I kept of the trip,
the letters I wrote home,the many newspaper accounts of the trip
and other records,all of which I still have.

The trip was from Saint Paul,Minnesota to Chicago,Pittsburgh,
Philadelphia,New York City and Boston and return by way of Albany,
Buffalo,Cleveland,Toledo,Chicago,Dubuque,Iowa and Saint Paul.The
distance traveled was about six hundrd miles farther than from
New York to San Francisco.

We carried all of our equipment on the bikes and paid our
expenses by selling post card views of Saint Paul at five cents
each which we were able to obtain for one cent each or for five
dollars a thousand.

A thousand miles of the journey was on dirt roads and with
the heavy and frequent rains that summer they were mostly mud and
water. We had to walk and push the bikes hundreds of miles because
of this condition. At that time the roads pretty well followed
the contour of the ground resulting in many steep hills that could
not be negotiated with single speed bicycles so we had to walk up
a great many of them. This was also true when we crossed the
Alleghany and Appalachian mountains of southern Pennsylvania.

### PREFACE

There were nearly two thousand miles of mostly loose rock roads which were very hard on the tires. We had many punctures and tire blowouts. A set of tires only lasted an average of nine hundred miles.

The trip took 102 days of which about 30 were spent in large cities, stopping at places of historical interest or visiting relatives along the way. In spite of the poor roads,the heavy and frequent rains,and much tire trouble we averaged about 50 miles a day when actually traveling.

The trip was a very rewarding experience and well worth the difficulties of the journey. We enjoyed visiting the small towns, the large cities,the many things of historical interest that we saw and also the opportunity to visit with relatives in far away places. We also met hundreds of wonderfully kind and hospitable people who treated us with kindness and help along the way.

Note:

We each wore out four sets of tires,and the bikes had to be completely overhauled twice,once at Chicago on the trip East and again at Chicago on the return journey.

Harwood's nickname was "Happy" or "Hap" for short and I will usually refer  to him by his nickname.

San Carlos,Calif. 94070
1979

## CHAPTER ONE

The Decision To Go          Preparation For The Trip

In 1914 a friend of mine belonged to a St.Paul,Minnesota hiking club. They practiced all Spring for a major hike in the month of August,from St.Paul to Duluth,Minnesota,a distance of 165 miles.

A few days before the start of this trip,my friend invited me to go along. I decided to go although I did not have the advantage of the preliminary training.

The first day out, my cousin Harwood Temple rode along with us on his bicycle. He carried some of the gear for the group and at every opportunity he kept asking me to take a bicycle trip with him the following summer. He said he wanted to go back to Massachusetts where he had previously lived, so he could visit his friends there.

This seemed like a big undertaking to me and I was not the least bit interested as I had never ridden a bicycle. He kept bringing up the subject, so to satisfy him I said we would talk about it when I got home. With that he said good-bye and rode back to Saint Paul.

About that time my brother John caught up to us on his motorcycle and after giving us an exhibition of speed he left and we continued on our way.

We reached Duluth in five and one-half days, averaging 30 miles a day. We were glad to reach our destination as our feet were covered with blisters and it was very uncomfortable walking. I have told about the above hike because the idea of a bicycle

CHAPTER ONE

trip to the East Coast was first brought up while on that walk.

It was several days after I returned home before my feet
healed and then Harwood (Hap) and I continued our evening walks.
He never failed to bring up the subject of a bicycle trip. At
first I was not interested but the more I thought about it the
more interested I became.

The people I talked to all said it was foolish to even con-
sider such a trip because of the condition of the roads, the
chance of accidents and the possibility of sickness. They also
doubted if we could stand the hardships of such a trip. This only
served to increase my interest as it would be a challenge and I
was about ready to accept the challenge, come what may.

It was in November, 1914 when Hap and I were on one of our
evening walks that we discussed at length the possibility of such
a ride. We knew full well that if we undertook the trip we would
have to successfully complete it, otherwise we would be the laughing stock of all those who said "I told you so".

We knew that we could not expect any financial assistance
from or from other relatives and as we didnt have any money of
our own, this presented a problem. We decided to first get permission from our parents to go and if granted, to work out the
problem of finances afterward.

That night before I left Hap, I agreed to take the trip with
him if permission was obtained. There I was, agreeing to take a
bicycle trip which we knew would be over 3,500 miles long when I
didnt even know how to ride a bicycle and without any money to
pay our expenses.

CHAPTER ONE

But then, that was all part of the challenge.

I asked my Mother if I could take the trip and she said I could, providing I passed in all my studies(she probably thought I would forget all about it long before the following summer).

The next evening Hap came over and I laid out a tentative route for the trip which was as follows: St.Paul to Chicago,Pittsburgh, Gettysburg,Washington, Philadelphia, New York City and Boston. Thence returning home by way of Albany, Buffalo, Cleveland Toledo, Chicago, Dubuque,Iowa and St.Paul.

The problem of financing the trip was discussed. Our first thought was to work our way, but we discarded that idea as not practical. In the first place work was scarce and even if we could find work,which was doubtful, we figured it would cost us a minimum of one dollar a day just for food and lodging plus other expenses. As the rate of pay was ten cents an hour, it would be necessary for us to work at least ten hours a day just to pay our daily expenses. This wouldn't leave much time for riding our bikes.

We finally decided that we would try selling post card views of St.Paul at 5¢ each which we could buy for 1¢ each or for $5.00 a thousand and that is the way we left it.

With the tentative route and the financing taken care of (we hoped) we went about the business of preparing for the trip. Hap's duties were to be as follows: repair all punctures and tire blowouts and also to make all repairs necessary on the bikes. I was to determine the route we took, do the cooking, handle the publicity and make arrangements for a place to camp or other place to spend the night.

CHAPTER ONE

We then met every Thursday evening at our house. In one of the first meetings we decided to leave the St.Paul Court House at 6 A.M. on June 28,1915, one week after school let out.

We each got a large box to store our equipment in, as we got it. With the above matters taken care of, the next problem was to raise the money to buy new bicycles and the other gear needed. This wasn't easy at 10¢ an hour as the bikes alone would cost more than $25.00 each. We made out a tentative list of the necessary things to take, all of which would have to be carried on the bikes.

On December first we each deposited a dollar in the bank and each got a pocket savings bank to take home for our savings.

During the Christmas vacation we got jobs shoveling snow which provided a little money. A few days before Christmas there was an 'ad' in the paper for Western Union messenger boys to work the night before Christmas. I got the job and all through that bitter cold night,I delivered messages and other articles, sometimes having a hard time finding the right address. I took a parcel out to the Mayor's house and at about 12:45 A.M. I had to deliver a cardboard carton of chop suey out on the bluff. After a long cold wait a street car finally came along and I started for my destination.

The chop suey was warm and had a bad odor and before long the carton started to leak and the contents ran all over my clothes. I didn't know what to do as I was afraid I would lose all of it. I found a newspaper and wrapped it around the carton

CHAPTER ONE

and this kept most of it safe. At last I reached the street but
couldn't find the house number shown on the package. I hunted
around in the cold and finally got some people out of bed and
they told me there was no such number.

I went back to the chop suey restaurant and told the man
about it and he said "somebody must have played a joke on me"
but the joke was on me and I didn't like it at all. He gave me
a nickel cigar (I didn't smoke) and I went back to the W.U. office.
It was now time to quit so after a long cold wait for a street
car I finally got home at 4 A.M. This was an example of the work
we did to earn money.

It was soon New Years day and we took fresh hope as the time
for the trip seemed a lot closer. I worked every Sunday at my
Uncle's light grocery store in Minneapolis. For this I got $1.25
plus 25¢ for lunch. I usually spent 5¢ for coffee and a roll and
saved 20¢ which took care of my carfare from home.

So far we hadn't accumulated much money and time was flying.
I watched the "help wanted ads" every day and on January 4th
there was an ad for a high school boy to work afternoons. I went
right down town and got the job. It was a shoe repairing and
clothes pressing establishment. I was to work five afternoons a
week and all day Saturday. For this I was paid $3.00 a week. My
duties were to wait on the trade and run errands when necessary.
After the first week I was allowed to use the cash register but
I didn't like the job and the days went pretty slow.

After a while I worked at this place three evenings a week

CHAPTER ONE

in addition to the afternoons and all day Saturday. It was getting
pretty hard, I went to school in the morning(school let out at
1 P.M. and studying had to be done at home) worked every afternoon, three evenings and all day on Saturday. The pay was raised
to $4.00 a week which helped some. I continued to work at my
Uncle's store in Minneapolis on Sunday.

I then had two evenings a week to myself and on one of them,
Hap and I ushered at the Orpheum Vaudeville Theater. We didn't get
paid for this but we got to see the show free after seating the
customers. We usually walked home after the show and planned our
trip.

Meanwhile I passed in all my studies and all was going well.
My "hope" box was slowly being filled with equipment.

Day after day passed slowly and with the coming of Spring I
bought a second hand bicycle for $3.00 so I could learn to ride.
I rode my bike to school and this saved fifty cents a week carfare.

We continued our planning and by the first of April we had
made up our minds about the bikes we would use, so we each drew
money out of the bank and sent a money order for fifty dollars and
thirty cents to the Mead Cycle Co. at Chicago for two of their
Crusader bicycles. This was a big day for us as it looked like we
would be more sure of taking the trip.

Two days later my Mother told me I couldn't take the trip.
She said I would have to stop working so that I could do the work
around the house. I was frantic and so was Hap when I told him.
He proposed that we cancel the order for the bikes and he would
buy a lathe instead.

CHAPTER ONE

Things looked pretty bad but I didn't want to give up on the trip after planning on it for so long. I told him to wait for a few days and I would try to get my Mother to change her mind. I talked to her but she was firm and in desperation I told her I would quit my job if I could take the trip.

Finally she said if I had a definite amount of money and if I passed in school I could go. With this compromise I quit my afternoon and evening job, working only on Saturday and Sunday.

There was still one big obstacle standing in the way, Hap had to get another approval to go and so far it was not forth-coming and time was running out.

Our single speed bikes arrived in due course and we assembled them at the depot and rode them home, mine was light gray and Hap's was brown. I decided not to ride mine and put it in the attic for safe keeping.

When we first decided to take the trip we planned to tell people about it, have it put in the newspapers and also get a letter from the Mayor of St.Paul. We figured we would get the reaction of people and we might get some helpful suggestions.

We told our friends, relatives and others about the trip and it was amusing the way they took it. Some laughed outright, others smiled and said nothing while others thought we were a little off in the head for even considering such an unheard of trip. Others just shook their heads and said they doubted if such a trip was possible. A few, who didn't want to hurt our feelings went along with the idea when talking to us but in talking to others they said we could not make it. The opinion of all those

CHAPTER ONE

we talked to was that we could never pay our expenses by selling
post cards even if it was possible to make the trip, which they
doubted.

According to most people we would get rheumatism or other
sickness from sleeping on the ground. My Mother said our legs
would give out and she doubted if we would even get as far as
Chicago. My brothers said we would never make it to New York. A
very few admitted that we might make it to New York but that we
would get tired and come home on the train. One of the amusing
responses was the woman who said  "why go so far, if the boys want
to ride a bike, they should go out to Como Park(in St. Paul) there
are so many pretty things to see there"

It looked like the cards were stacked against us. The trip
would be a real challenge and something to be proud of, if we
were successful, so we were more than ever determined to go.

So day after day we endured the laughing,the head shaking
and the warnings of possible accident or sickness. In spite of
this we continued our planning for the trip and continued to tell
people about our plans.

There were one or two who thought we were not attempting an
impossible task and they encouraged us which helped us through the
long period of waiting.

One of the conditions of my Mother's final approval was that
we make the trip a little shorter and not go to Washington. I
promised to do this but the balance of the trip remained the same.

After I stopped working afternoons we took practice trips

CHAPTER ONE

on old bicycles. We took several short trips up to 22 miles in length. The longest trip was 47 miles. We left home about noon and got as far as Hastings when it started to rain. We went to a show and started for home at 5 P.M. We each bought a yard of oil cloth and cut holes for our heads and arms and this kept us reasonably dry. It was still raining and we ran into muddy roads on the way. We stopped at a farm house and bought some bread and milk at 10¢ each. We reached home about 9 P.M. We were pretty tired but we had gone 47 miles in part of a day which encouraged us to feel that we could average about 50 miles a day on our proposed trip.

Each day now seemed longer than the last as we were getting anxious after our long wait. With the coming of June we set about with the last months preparations. We now had our equipment down to a point so that we could handle everything on the bikes. Our equipment was as follows: a small tent in two pieces that clipped together and we each carried half of it, we each had one blanket and a piece of oil cloth to put on the ground at night and to be used to keep the blankets dry when traveling. In our knapsacks we had necessary toilet equipment and a supply of post cards to sell. (See end of chapter for complete list)

We each left $25.00 with our parents for purchase of post cards which they would send to us along the way, as we needed them.

There was still one big obstacle that could put an end to the trip and that was the additional permission Hap had to get in order to go. This was finally granted and now we had clear sailing ahead.

## CHAPTER ONE

At last school was out and we had just one week before the take off. We called on the Mayor of St.Paul and he gave us a letter of introduction to take along. We bought the rest of our equipment and on June 26th all was in readiness to leave on June 28th.

We took a short ride on our bikes on the 26th with our knapsacks and while it was rather uncomfortable, I said nothing. I worked in Minneapolis on Sunday the 27th but came home early. Then I went to bed which proved to be my last night at home for 102 days.

# City of Saint Paul

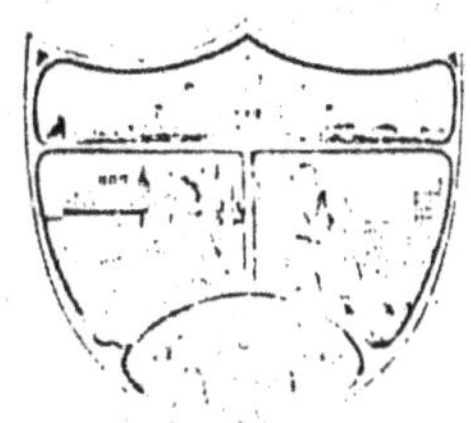

## Mayor's Office

WINN POWERS, MAYOR
L C HODGSON, Secretary to the Mayor
ELIZABETH NELSON, Assistant Secretary

June 25,1915

TO WHOM IT MAY CONCERN:-

Leon Schroeder and Harwood Temple of this city are
starting on a trip to New York City,and I take pleasure
in saying that these boys are honest and reputable,
of good parentage and both are high school students
of our city.  I commend them to the  kindness and courtesy
of all with whom they may come in contact.

Respectfully

Winn Powers

Mayor

## CHAPTER ONE

### LIST OF EQUIPMENT FOR BOTH OF US

All carried on the bikes      Articles we wore shown *

| No. | Article | No. | Article |
|---|---|---|---|
| 2 | Bicycles (single speed) | 2 | Bath towels |
| 2 | Knapsacks | 2 | Tooth brushes - Tooth paste |
| 1 | Canvas tent in 2 sections | 1 | Tire pump |
| 1 | Cyclometer | 1 | Tool kit |
|  | Road guides | 1 | Tire repair kit |
| 1 | Ammonia gun | 3 | Films (to start) |
| 1 | Grill |  | Supply of cards (to sell) |
| 1 | Cooker | 2 | Pieces mosquito netting |
| 2 | Razors |  | Needle and thread - Pins |
| 1 | Schedule |  | $2.00 cash for each of us |
|  | Maps - Handkerchiefs | 1 | Bottle of liniment |
| 2 | Cups - Soap  2 Plates |  | Misl. Rope,string, Matches |
| 2 | Blankets  (1 each) | 1 | Hand axe  Knife,fork, spoon (2) |
| 2 | Pieces oil cloth | 2 | Note books 2 Bicycle locks |
| 2 | Trousers guards | 2 | Pencils  2  $1.00 watches |
| 2 | St.Paul to N.Y. signs | 1 | Camera  1 Bike lamp |
| 1 | Book on things to see | 1 | Pair of socks for each(extra) |
| * 2 | Army shirts (one each) | * 2 | Pair khaki trousers (1 each) |

* Bathing suits (1 each for underwear)

| | | | |
|---|---|---|---|
| * 1 | Pair of shoes for each | * 2 | Caps (1 each) |
| * 1 | Pair of socks for each | * 2 | Coats (1 each) |

## CHAPTER TWO

### SAINT PAUL,MINNESOTA TO CHICAGO,ILLINOIS

June 28th,1915 The First Day  (Monday)

St.Paul,Minnesota to Cannon Falls,Minnesota.

At last, after eight long months of waiting, it was Monday, June 28th, the day we planned to leave.

Imagine how I felt, when upon getting up at 4 A.M. and looking out the window found that it was raining hard. Looked like we might have to postpone our long awaited start.

I called my cousin Harwood on the phone and after discussing the situation at length, we decided to leave as planned regardless of the weather.

Then the eleventh hour preparations went forward at a fast pace and in a short time I was ready to leave. After bidding my Mother good-bye and taking one last look at our house, I was on my way to Harwood's house. (I will usually refer to him by his nickname "Hap").

Hap was not quite ready but soon we said good-bye and were on our way in the rain which by now had let up a little. We rode down Summit Avenue to the business area and reached the Court House at 5:45 A.M.

Hap quickly attached a cyclometer to the front wheel of his bike so we could keep track of our mileage. We will take the main road from Minneapolis-Saint Paul to Chicago and had a B.F.Goodrich road guide to show us the way.

There were three to see us off, Carl Temple, brother of Hap, Lawrence Zachrison, a friend of mine from Johnson High School and Mr. Albrechton, a friend of Harwood.

## CHAPTER TWO

The First Day (Cont.) St.Paul,Minn. to Cannon Falls,Minn.

We were now ready to begin our journey, we each had two dollars (for a 102 day trip), a supply of Saint Paul postcards that we hoped we could sell to pay our expenses, and a letter of introduction from the Mayor of Saint Paul.

The Start   6 A.M.   June 28th, 1915
St. Paul Court House

It was drizzling but promptly at 6 A.M. we mounted our bikes, said good-bye to Mr.Albrechten and rode down Wabasha St. to Seven Corners where we said good-bye to Carl Temple, Lawrence had his bike and was going to ride a short distance with us.

We were soon on the High Bridge over the Mississippi River. We stopped at the middle of the bridge to wave to our Mothers who were on the hill at Avon and St.Clair Sts. overlooking the river. They were waving a white sheet for us to see.

By now it had stopped raining and after crossing to the West side of the river we struck a good gravel road and were soon in Wescott, ten miles from Saint Paul. After visiting with Lawrence for a few minutes and then taking his picture with me in the back-

CHAPTER TWO

The First Day  (Cont.)  St.Paul,Minn. to Cannon Falls,Minn.

ground, we said good-bye and he headed for Saint Paul.

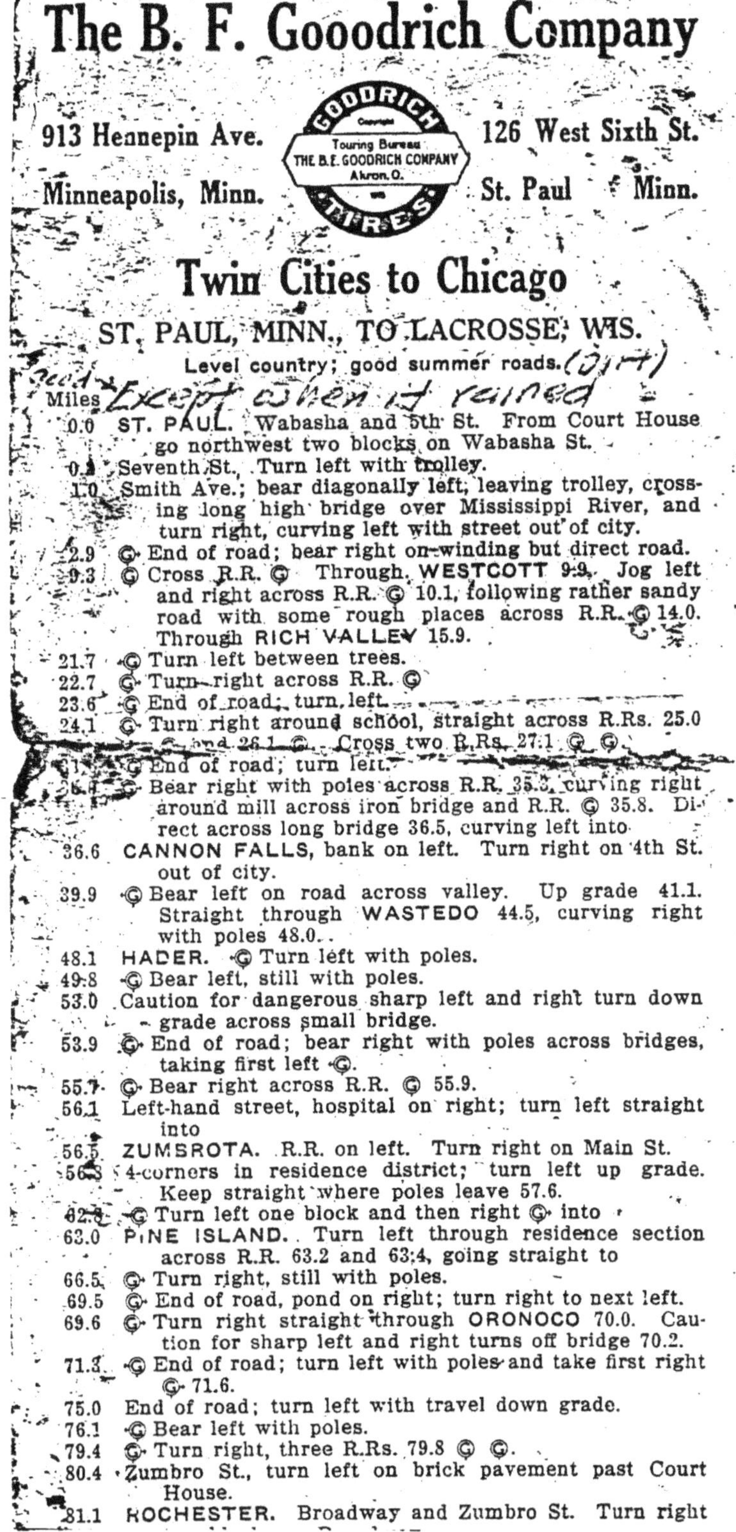

# The B. F. Gooodrich Company

913 Hennepin Ave.          126 West Sixth St.

Minneapolis, Minn.          St. Paul    Minn.

*Touring Bureau*
*THE B.F. GOODRICH COMPANY*
*Akron, O.*

## Twin Cities to Chicago

### ST. PAUL, MINN., TO LACROSSE, WIS.

Level country; good summer roads. (Dirt)

Miles *Except when it rained*

0.0  ST. PAUL.  Wabasha and 5th St.  From Court House go northwest two blocks on Wabasha St.

0.1  Seventh St.  Turn left with trolley.

1.0  Smith Ave.; bear diagonally left, leaving trolley, crossing long high bridge over Mississippi River, and turn right, curving left with street out of city.

2.9  Ⓖ End of road; bear right on winding but direct road.

9.3  Ⓖ Cross R.R. Ⓖ  Through WESTCOTT 9.9.  Jog left and right across R.R. Ⓖ 10.1, following rather sandy road with some rough places across R.R. Ⓖ 14.0. Through RICH VALLEY 15.9.

21.7  Ⓖ Turn left between trees.

22.7  Ⓖ Turn right across R.R. Ⓖ

23.6  Ⓖ End of road; turn left.

24.1  Ⓖ Turn right around school, straight across R.Rs. 25.0 and 26.1 Ⓖ. Cross two R.Rs. 27.1 Ⓖ Ⓖ.

Ⓖ End of road; turn left.

Ⓖ Bear right with poles across R.R. 35.3, curving right around mill across iron bridge and R.R. Ⓖ 35.8. Direct across long bridge 36.5, curving left into

36.6  CANNON FALLS, bank on left.  Turn right on 4th St. out of city.

39.9  Ⓖ Bear left on road across valley.  Up grade 41.1. Straight through WASTEDO 44.5, curving right with poles 48.0.

48.1  HADER.  Ⓖ Turn left with poles.

49.8  Ⓖ Bear left, still with poles.

53.0  Caution for dangerous sharp left and right turn down grade across small bridge.

53.9  Ⓖ End of road; bear right with poles across bridges, taking first left Ⓖ.

55.7  Ⓖ Bear right across R.R. Ⓖ 55.9.

56.1  Left-hand street, hospital on right; turn left straight into

56.5  ZUMBROTA.  R.R. on left.  Turn right on Main St.

56.8  4-corners in residence district; turn left up grade. Keep straight where poles leave 57.6.

62.8  Ⓖ Turn left one block and then right Ⓖ into

63.0  PINE ISLAND.  Turn left through residence section across R.R. 63.2 and 63.4, going straight to

66.5  Ⓖ Turn right, still with poles.

69.5  Ⓖ End of road, pond on right; turn right to next left.

69.6  Ⓖ Turn right straight through ORONOCO 70.0.  Caution for sharp left and right turns off bridge 70.2.

71.3  Ⓖ End of road; turn left with poles and take first right Ⓖ 71.6.

75.0  End of road; turn left with travel down grade.

76.1  Ⓖ Bear left with poles.

79.4  Ⓖ Turn right, three R.Rs. 79.8 Ⓖ Ⓖ.

80.4  Zumbro St., turn left on brick pavement past Court House.

81.1  ROCHESTER.  Broadway and Zumbro St.  Turn right

A Typical 1915 Goodrich Co. Road Guide

## CHAPTER TWO

The First Day  (Cont.)  St.Paul,Minn. to Cannon Falls,Minn.

Good-bye Lawrence

While in this town it started to rain real hard and beyond
was a dirt road and the mud was five or six inches deep. We soon
found that it was impossible to ride through the mud and water
so we walked and pushed the bicycles most of the way. Even while
pushing the bikes the mud would pack solid between the wheels and
the mudguards, the wheels would no longer turn so we had to stop
repeatedly and dig the mud out with a stick before we could
proceed.

We were only about twelve miles from St.Paul when my rear
tire blew out while I was pushing the bike. Hap repaired it in
just 17 minutes and we were on our way. People we met along the
way said, "Better go back home boys, you will never make it".
It did look rather discouraging and we hated to see our new bikes

## CHAPTER TWO

The First Day  (Cont.)  St.Paul,Minn. to Cannon Falls,Minn.

get all covered with mud but it couldn't be helped.

We rode through Rich Valley with a short stop on the main street. We met many horses and wagons along the way,particularly in the small towns. The roads were poorly marked and in most cases had no directional signs at all. What few signs there were had in most cases been placed by the B.F. Goodrich Rubber Co.

Twelve Miles From St.Paul

The First Tire Blowout

(Many More To Follow)

CHAPTER TWO

The First Day (Cont.)  St.Paul,Minn. to Cannon Falls,Minn.

We ate our lunch in a farmer's yard and rested for about an hour down near a stream. The next town we came to was Hampton and in leaving there we took the wrong road as there were no markers along the way.

When we reached Vermillion we discovered our mistake as we were headed back toward St.Paul. By this time we had gone fifteen miles out of our way. After obtaining new directions we cut across country on a very muddy road, walking most of the way. We followed a terrific rainstorm all afternoon, we could see it pouring about half a mile ahead of us. The storm was moving South same as we were and while we didn't get very wet, the heavy rain played havoc with the dirt roads ahead of us. After a while we came to a very muddy newly worked road that took us back to our right road again. We walked about ten miles through mud and water about five or six inches deep that day and we were covered with it.

We stopped to eat supper at the side of the road under some trees about two miles North of Cannon Falls,Minn. I got out our little cooker and set up the portable grate. As there was a farm house a short distance away I bought some milk and we had a good meal of coffee, sandwiches and other food left over from our noon lunch. After eating we played catch with the indoor baseball we brought along.

The sun started to shine and we were hopeful of a pleasant second day. We then rode into Cannon Falls, arriving about dusk. We rode down the Main street which was not paved and muddy.

CHAPTER TWO

The First Day (Cont.)  St.Paul,Minn. to Cannon Falls,Minn.

At the Peoples' State Bank we turned and crossed the Cannon River which was about a block away. We asked permission to pitch our tent in the yard of the first place we came to. The lady was very friendly and said we were welcome to camp there. The man of the house (J.Ford) brought us a lantern and helped us put up the tent. He then brought us a large horse blanket to sleep on so we would be comfortable. He let us put our bikes in a shed out of the weather and we locked them up.

When we got back to the tent we found two dishes of popcorn and some flowers in the tent. Some girls were having a party in the house and they left the presents for us.

That night as we lay in the tent on the hard ground, even with the horse blanket, it was a lot different than in a soft, warm bed at home. We didn't mind it, as we were quite comfortable and were happy to at last be on our long anticipated journey. We talked about the adventures of the day, the hardships encountered didn't bother us, as we knew in advance that the trip would be a difficult one. The kindness and help of the people who let us camp in their yard more than offset the troubles we had during the day.We had traveled our fifty miles that day but we were only about thirty six miles from St.Paul.

One thing we didn't know that night was whether or not we would be able to sell our postcards, as we hadn't tried to sell any the first day. Unless we could sell the cards we would be without money to pay our expenses and we had to have the expense

CHAPTER TWO

The First Day (Cont.)  St.Paul,Minn. to Cannon Falls,Minn.

money in order to continue the trip.

Cannon Falls was a small town at the falls of the Cannon River from which it got its name. The falls furnished water power and it was a milling center in the early days. The Cannon Valley Mill was located there and there was considerable farming in the vicinity.

Helen Ford

The girl who lived in the house

where we camped.

CHAPTER TWO

The First Day (Cont.) St.Paul, Minn. to Cannon Falls, Minn.


VIEWS OF CANNON FALLS, MINN.

STREET SCENE.    CANNON FALLS, MINN.

CANNON VALLEY MILL.    CANNON FALLS, MINN.

## CHAPTER TWO

### SAINT PAUL, MINNESOTA TO CHICAGO, ILLINOIS

June 29th,1915  The Second Day  (Tuesday)

Cannon Falls, Minnesota to Rochester, Minnesota.

We were up early, both of us slept fine and were not cold, thanks to Mr. Ford's horse blanket. I went to town and bought some corn flakes and bread for breakfast. I also bought a tooth brush as I had lost mine the day before. We still had some money left of the two dollars we each had when we left St.Paul but we could see that it wouldn't last much longer.

FIRST BREAKFAST, CANNON FALLS, MINN.

CHAPTER TWO

The Second Day (Cont.) Cannon Falls,Minn. to Rochester, Minn.

When I got back to the tent I prepared breakfast while Hap
took the tent down. Mr. Ford brought a bench and two chairs down
to the tent so we had the comforts of home for our meal. He also
brought water and a pitcher of rich milk. Our first breakfast was
a good one and we enjoyed it. I took a picture of Hap at the
breakfast table and also one of Helen Ford. We washed the mud off
our bikes and after the girl took our picture we were on our way,
first thanking the Fords for their kindness.

We went back to the business district and took the road to
Zumbrota. Just out of Cannon Falls we came to a long steep hill
and as it was too much for our single speed bikes, we walked and
pushed them to the top. At the top was a sign with the speed laws
of the town. In those days 10 miles an hour was the usual posted
speed limit through the towns. It was not raining but the road
was still muddy and we rode at the side of the road where we
could.

When the road was too muddy to ride on, there were times
when we could ride in the rut made by an automobile tire. The mud
in the rut was compacted by the weight of the car which helped
some. At that time automobile tires were only about three inches
wide and this narrow rut didn't provide much opportunity to ma-
neuver the front wheel. We had to watch carefully for if the rut
suddenly deepened the pedal would strike the ground and that had
a tendency to tip the bike and on several occasions we landed in
the mud and water.

## CHAPTER TWO
## SAINT PAUL, MINNESOTA TO CHICAGO, ILLINOIS

THE MAIN ROAD

ST.PAUL, MINN. TO CHICAGO, ILLINOIS

CHAPTER TWO

The Second Day (Cont.) Cannon Falls,Minn. to Rochester,Minn.

The country through which we were riding was a farming area with well kept houses and barns. There were numerous rolling hills from which we had a beautiful view of the surrounding countryside.

We soon descended into a valley and soon crossed it. We stopped at Wastedo, a very small town and while there helped a woman burn some rubbish and she in turn let us use her bench for our lunch. The next town was Hader, where we stopped long enough to buy some pop at the only grocery store in town. We drank it as we rode on our way to Zumbrota.

We reached the town of Zumbrota about noon and it seemed to us that we were a long way from home. We bought meat,potatoes, bread,etcetera for a good noon meal. We went up the street where we could sit down and rest awhile at the edge of the road. A man was painting a house across the street and came over to talk to us. I finally got up enough courage to get out my cards and asked if he would care to buy one? He looked them over and asked how much we wanted for them. Hap and I had debated whether or not we would sell two for five cents or for five cents each. I finally said they were five cents each, he bought one,which was the first card we had sold on the trip. This set a precedent and after telling Hap we could get five cents each for them, that became the price of the cards for the balance of the trip.

Zumbrota was a nice small town about the size of Cannon Falls. One of the things of interest there was an old covered wagon bridge in the Fair grounds. This bridge was built in the early days and once spanned the Zumbro River.

## CHAPTER TWO

The Second Day (Cont.) Cannon Falls,Minn. to Rochester,Minn.

On our way out of town we ate our lunch on a vacant lot in the residential district. I got permission from the owner of the lot to build a fire and later she gave us some butter for our toast. Hap soon had a fire going, I got some condensed milk in town and we had a regular feast of roast potatoes, meat and toast prepared on my grill.

After eating Hap took off his shoes as his feet were sore from so much walking. I shaved in the meantime and we rested until about 2 P.M. Hap started off ahead bare-footed and I was not far behind.

We soon came to a very muddy road and again we had to walk. As we walked along we passed an auto stuck in the mud. The right rear wheel was buried in the mud up to the axle, but as we could not be of any assistance we moved on.

We didn't stop in Pine Island and continued on to Oronoco where we stopped to rest and get a drink of water at a pump in a church yard. In this area every farm house, church and school house had a well and pump in the front yard, this was also true of the houses in the small towns. We found this to be the case throughout Southern Minnesota where we rode. It was late in the afternoon when we started for Rochester, fifteen miles away. We soon came to a gravel road and it was smooth sailing all the way to Rochester. The road was lined on both sides with large trees and was very beautiful and we continued on without stopping until we reached the city. People in automobiles along the way wished

CHAPTER TWO

The Second Day (Cont.) Cannon Falls,Minn. to Rochester,Minn.

us good luck and one little girl started singing: "Its a long

way to New York City".

WHITE WATER ST.

ST.CHARLES,MINN.

THE EVER PRESENT WATER PUMP.

CHAPTER TWO

The Second Day (Cont.) Cannon Falls,Minn. to Rochester,Minn.

There were a few automobiles on the road this close to the city but for the most part they were horse drawn vehicles, especially in the small towns.

We were feeling pretty good and the miles went by rather fast. It was dark just outside the city so I lit the light on my bike but it didn't do much good. We came into the city on Zumbro street and as there was a band concert down town, the streets were filled with people. We stopped in front of a bakery and I sold two cards to a man who insisted I write my name and address on both of them.

A crowd collected and asked all about the trip. I think we were beginning to enjoy the attention we were getting. We bought rolls and milk for our evening meal and then started in quest of a place to camp. After being turned down by one man we got permission from a man across the street. We were very tired but managed to get the tent up by using a clothes pole to support it. After eating we went to bed on the hard ground which was rather damp. By now we knew that we could sell the cards so that was one problem out of the way.

Rochester is located on the Zumbro River at an altitude of about 1180 feet. It is the home of the world famous Mayo Clinic and thousands of people come here from all over the world for medical treatment. The city has many fine hotels and restaurants. Our "hotel" was a tent and our bed, the hard ground but we didn't mind it.

CHAPTER TWO

The Second Day (Cont.) Cannon Falls,Minn. to Rochester,Minn.

VIEWS OF ROCHESTER

PUBLIC  PARK

HOTEL  LOBBY

COUNTRY HOME

BROADWAY, LOOKING SOUTH

ROCHESTER,MINNESOTA

A  BICYCLE  TRIP  OF  LONG  AGO.

CHAPTER TWO

SAINT PAUL,MINNESOTA TO CHICAGO,ILLINOIS

June 30th,1915 The Third Day  (Wednesday)

Rochester,Minnesota to Winona,Minnesota.

We were up at 8 A.M. and after packing up our belongings
we rode down to the business district. Hap bought some tape for
tire blowout repairs and also some cotton for his shoes due to
his sore feet. We then went to the post office and wrote home
to let them know that we were alive and well. While there we
were interviewed by two reporters from the local newspaper, they
said they would put an article about the trip in the paper.

I went into a produce house and a lady there bought five
cards from me at five cents each, this was my largest sale so
far.

After buying some eggs and a loaf of bread we headed out of
the city.By now we were saddle sore from so much riding so we
folded our bath towels and put them on the seats and this made
riding a little more comfortable.

Ahead of us was a good macadam road, we rode past the Asylum
buildings and were soon out in the country. We stopped at the side
of the road and I set up our grate and cooker for our breakfast.
Hap got some water at a nearby pump and we enjoyed our eggs and
bread, after a rest we rode on,Hap in the lead.

People in cars and wagons stopped to visit with us and they
all wished us good luck. At Eyota we had ice cream sundaes and
then we continued to Dover for lunch of baked beans and bread.
We went to the newspaper office and they took down the "very
important news" about the trip. I went up to a house and tried

## CHAPTER TWO

The Third Day (Cont.) Rochester,Minn. to Winona,Minn.

to sell a card, but no luck. I then tried to sell one to two men sitting in a vacant lot nearby. They said they would buy a picture of us, if we had one, but they didn't want any views of St.Paul. Hap gave the local people an exhibition of speed on his bike before we left.

There was a macadam road beyond this town, at that time a macadam road consisted of broken small stone, placed on the dirt surface. When placed the stone was rolled but under traffic the stones became loose and they were very hard on the tires. They usually used white stone and there was considerable glare from them, and as some of them were ground to powder, the road was very dusty. At least we got away from the mud and water for a while.

We rode through St.Charles and stopped at Utica to get a drink of water at one of the ever present pumps that were every where, particularly in church and school yards.

We sold a few cards at Lewiston and just after leaving we rode down a long, winding road through a thick wooded area. At the bottom was a large stone railroad bridge, Hap climbed up on the base of the bridge and I took his picture. We proceeded over rather hilly country and soon descended into a valley and stopped at Stockton at the very bottom of it.

We met a boy who had a bicycle like ours and he told us that there was a concrete road all the way to Winona, eight miles away. Usually where they had these short stretches of concrete, they were about eight feet wide for one way traffic

CHAPTER TWO

The Third Day (Cont.) Rochester,Minn. to Winona,Minn.

and in some cases about sixteen feet wide for two way traffic.
Where they had the narrow section one vehicle would have to
move over to the shoulder to let the other vehicle pass.

We had to climb out of the valley after leaving Stockton,
it was about a mile and a half to the summit but as the road was
good concrete we didn't mind it much. We had to walk most of the
way up and were rather tired when we reached the top.

From the summit we could see Winona and the valley of the
Mississippi River. It was a beautiful sight and after feasting
our eyes on it for awhile, we started our descent into the river
valley. I had not gone far when my kerosene head light broke off
and I ran over it, nearly throwing me to the pavement. That was
the end of the head light and for the balance of the trip we
did not have a light on the bikes, even though we did a lot of
riding after dark.

We continued down the hill, it was a delightful ride on the
smooth concrete but we had to apply our brakes most of the time
to keep the bikes from getting out of hand. The hill was about a
mile and a half in length and we rapidly approached the city of
Winona.

We were met on the outskirts by two young cyclists who rode
ahead of us, shouting that we were in town. It was about 6 P.M.
when we reached the city so we had time to look around a little.
We rode around in the park on the river front for awhile and we
finally found a store that was open and bought corn meal mush,

CHAPTER TWO

The Third Day (Cont.) Rochester,Minn. to Winona,Minn.

bread and milk for our evening meal. Hap bought a tin pail to carry the milk in as it was in bulk at the store.

We met a young boy who told us he knew of a fine place to camp over near the river. We had to get through a fence to get near the water and discovered it was a regular swamp, full of snakes and high weeds growing all over the place. There were mosquitoes everywhere in the swamp. We looked for a suitable place to pitch our tent but without success. We started across the swamp but it got worse as we went along and soon we were in the dirty water up to our shoe tops. All this time Hap was carrying the pail of milk. We wondered on and on and came to a house with an apple orchard in back of it. We thought we had finally found a place to camp but when we got there we discovered that the ground was wet and soggy. We gave up on this area and went back into town and asked permission to camp in a yard. The people told us to camp on a vacant lot across the street. It was a large corner lot but there were no trees on it and we needed two trees or other supports to hold the tent up. We went next door and asked the neighbor for permission to camp on his lot. He said no but he did lend us two clothes poles to support the tent.

There were several children standing around watching us and one of them ran home and brought us a candle. We then ate our meal by candle light and the kids went home, promising to return in the morning.

We were tired and were soon fast asleep.

## CHAPTER TWO

The Third Day (Cont.) Rochester,Minn. to Winona,Minn.

Winona is in a very beautiful location. It is on a level plain at the base of steep bluffs that rise about six hundred feet above the river. When we were there, the city had many manufacturing plants and no doubt still have.

In the early days the site was an Indian village and fur traders carried on their business there. The first white settlement was established about the middle of the nineteenth century.

RIVER  FRONT

PUBLIC BATHS

## CHAPTER TWO

### SAINT PAUL,MINNESOTA TO CHICAGO,ILLINOIS

July 1st,1915 The Fourth Day    (Thursday)

Winona,Minnesota to La Crosse,Wisconsin.

I woke up about nine, the sun was shining and it looked like we would have a nice day. I dressed but Hap was still in bed,finally,when he didn't get up, I started to take the tent down and he was up in a jiffy. He discovered that he had a wood tick on his foot and gently unscrewed it. I checked to see if I had any unwelcome visitors but all was clear.

After packing our equipment on the bikes we went down to the river and went in swimming. We were very much in need of a bath by now. Afterward we bought some cookies and that consti-tuted our breakfast. We then went to the newspaper office and told them about the trip. An article appeared in the paper later.

We left Winona at noon using our Goodrich road guide for directions. I will quote a little to show how it was set up: "128.0 Winona. Broadway and Main St.,park on left. Keep on Broadway.
121.9 Mankato Ave., one block beyond trolley crossing, turn right across R.Rs. 129.4 and 130.1
130.5 Fork at foot of short grade, bear left.
130.9 Right hand road; bear right around cemetery, leaving river road. Straight off of macadam on direct road across Pleas-ant Valley, running on short stretch of macadam again 134.6. Special caution for long, winding grade with sharp turns."

We bought some food at a store along the way and proceeded

## CHAPTER TWO

The Fourth Day (Cont.) Winona,Minn. to La Crosse,Wisc.

up a grade and stopped to eat our lunch at the side of the road.
I lit my little cooker and Hap made some mush. I went to a house
to get some water but was confronted by a dog who didn't take
kindly to my presence. About that time a lady came out of the
house and talked for some time and finally told me that we were
on a long roundabout road to La Crescent. I walked to the bottom
of the hill to find out where the shorter road was. By now it
was very hot and the glare from the white macadam road hurt my
eyes. I found out which road to take and walked back to the
bikes for our lunch of mush and bread.

We enjoyed the meal and after a rest we went back down the
hill and proceeded on the shorter road. We climbed a long hill
and when about half way up I stopped for Hap to catch up. Before
long he came up the hill, walking and pushing his bike. He had a
puncture and while he was repairing it, we talked about the trip
so far.

We soon reached the top of the hill and rode a long time on
the crest. We passed through Witoka and Ridgeway and continued
to follow the ridge for several miles. We went down a long, winding road into the town of La Crescent which was a very small
collection of houses. We found a store and bought fruit, doughnuts and sardines for our evening meal. The proprietor formerly
lived in St.Paul and was very friendly and bought several cards.
I let him have them at half price so he could sell them at a
profit. I went up to a house in company with the store keeper

## CHAPTER TWO

The Fourth Day (Cont.) Winona,Minn. to La Crosse,Wisc.

to get some milk and the lady gave me about two quarts free. The
store keeper wished us good luck and after thanking him we were
on our way. We stopped near a railroad crossing to eat and then
continued on a level road along the river. The road was wet in
places so part of the way we rode at the edge of the road. We
were riding between two rows of trees and it was cool in the
shade.

We soon came to the bridge across the Mississippi River and
bid goodbye to Minnesota as we crossed into Wisconsin at the
city of La Crosse. We stopped to watch some boys swimming and
they asked us to remember them to Broadway. We each paid five
cents toll on the bridge and I beat Hap into Wisconsin, the
second state on our journey.

We went to the Post Office to get our mail. It was the first
news we had from home and we enjoyed reading the letters. A small
boy wanted me to ride his bike so I rode it around the block to
satisfy him.

The next order of business was to find a place to camp for
the night. A boy we met suggested the Fair Grounds as a good
place. We went over there but it didn't look very promising so
we passed it up. A man who lived across the street from the Fair
Grounds said we could camp close to the road in front of his
house.

We pitched our tent and the man entertained us with stories
of his experiences riding a bike. He provided us with a lamp and

CHAPTER TWO

The Fourth Day (Cont.) Winona,Minn. to La Crosse,Wisc.
a chair so we fared real well our first night in a "foreign"
state. Motorists called to us and waved as they passed our
little brown tent at the side of the road. Bed at 9 P.M.

La Crosse is located on the Mississippi River, at the mouth
of the La Crosse and of the Black rivers. There were a number of
manufacturing plants located there and the city was the site of
a state teachers' college. The city was founded in 1842 when a
settler built a log house and traded with the Indians. Father
Hennepin visited the site in the early days. The city was char-
tered in 1856.

TIRE BLOWOUT  LA CROSSE,WISCONSIN
(The Fair Grounds Across The Street)

CHAPTER TWO

SAINT PAUL,MINNESOTA TO CHICAGO,ILLINOIS

July 2nd,1915  The Fifth Day    (Friday)

La Crosse,Wisconsin to Cashton,Wisconsin.

The boy we had talked to the night before woke us in the morning. We dressed leisurely, took down the tent and put our equipment on the bikes. We then did some riding on the race track at the Inter-State Fair Grounds across the street.

We went back to our camp site and Hap took my tire off so I could take it to town to have it vulcanized. I finally found a small shop and the man said he would have it ready at noon. While I was waiting for the tire I went to a store to buy a cap. The only one I could get was a blue silk one that cost a dollar. I went to the newspaper office and they put a nice article in the paper, it described us as being, "brown as a berry".

I went back for my tire but it was not ready yet so I walked over to the park on the waterfront and tried to sell some cards but with very little success. I watched the activity on the water-front including the loading and departure of a river boat.

I went back and got the tire and on the way back to our campground I bought steak, bread and a cup as well as other groceries for our next meal. Hap put the tire on my bike and after saying goodbye to the people at the camp site we started our journey across the State of Wisconsin. It was late in the afternoon when we got started so we didn't expect to make many miles that day.

CHAPTER TWO

July 2nd,1915  The Fifth Day  (Friday)

La Crosse,Wisconsin to Cashton,Wisconsin.

On the way out of La Crosse we stopped for more food and before long we came to a house with a large yard. We got permission to cook our lunch in the yard so we unpacked our cooking gear, gathered some fire wood and soon had a good fire going. I set up my grill and we roasted the steak and made some toast. This grill which I carried in my knapsack was about 12" x 15" with folding legs and was ideal for setting up over a fire. The steak, which was swimming in butter was delicious and we certainly enjoyed that meal.

We rested awhile in the shade of a large tree. The road was dirt but in fair shape as it had not rained here for a few days. The road rambled up a steep hill and we walked to the top. Once there we were out of the river valley, the first stop was St. Joseph, a small town consisting of a few houses and a small post office. I took a picture of the post office (see page 40). I started out ahead of Hap and reached the town of Middle Ridge ahead of him. I waited and before long he came riding down the hill into town. The town was in a valley at the bottom of a high hill. The road beyond was hilly and being dirt was not in very good condition.

It was growing late when we reached Portland so we continued on without stopping. Hap was in the lead and he was out of sight by the time I reached the church that marked the center of town.

## CHAPTER TWO

The Fifth Day (Cont.) La Crosse,Wisconsin to Cashton,Wisconsin.

POST   OFFICE

ST.JOSEPH,WISCONSIN

CHAPTER TWO

The Fifth Day (Cont.) La Crosse,Wisconsin to Cashton,Wisconsin.

About five hundred feet beyond the town one of my tires blew out as I was coming down a hill. I was in a bad way as Hap was way ahead and out of sight and he had the material to make the repairs. I started to walk but no sign of Hap. As I walked along I could see the tracks his tires made in the soft dirt road. I envied him blissfully riding along. I walked about a mile and a half but still no sign of him. What bothered me most was that I had to walk down the hills as well as up. I knew that it was six miles to the next town and I figured I would probably have to walk the entire distance.

I had just about given up hope of seeing him again that night when he came around the bend in the road. He repaired the puncture but as he didn't bring his knapsack back with him, he didn't have tape to wrap around the cut casing. I tore my hand-kerchief in strips and wrapped it around the tire so we could go on.

It was nearly dark by now but we decided to go to the next town which was about five miles away. We had a couple of narrow escapes from automobiles as we were riding in the dark without lights. We started a system of whistling at intervals so we would not get too far apart.

When we reached the next town, Cashton,we found a garage where we bought some tape for tire repairs. We bought food for our supper and went in search for a place to camp. This was not easy as it was getting late and most of the people were in bed.

Finally we came to a house with some apple trees in the

## CHAPTER TWO

The Fifth Day (Cont.) La Crosse,Wisconsin to Cashton,Wisconsin.

yard, so we asked there. The man said 'no' we couldn't sleep in the yard as he was afraid that we would damage his trees. I kept talking and finally after he looked at the tent and with our promise not to do any damage, he consented. We put the tent up carefully, wrapping cloth around the trees where we tied our ropes.

The reason we always tried to find trees was the fact that we did not carry tent poles and the ideal setup was to put the tent between two trees to tie the tent ropes to, for support. After getting our tent and blankets ready, we ate a cold supper and went to bed.

As a result of the trouble I had today because of the tire blowout, it was decided that in the future we would either ride close together or else I would ride ahead.

Very often in some of the small towns we were escorted by boys on bikes who announced our arrival.

CHAPTER TWO

SAINT PAUL,MINNESOTA TO CHICAGO,ILLINOIS

July 3rd,1915  The Sixth Day  (Saturday)

Cashton,Wisconsin to Reedsburg,Wisconsin.

We were up at eight and I went to the store for rolls and milk for breakfast. Hap busied himself taking down the tent and putting our gear on the bikes. We ate our light breakfast on the sidewalk in front of where we camped.

We were soon on our way and just beyond Cashton we crossed a large valley, it was hilly country and we saw some beautiful scenery from the top of the hills we crossed. The roads were dirt but in fair shape and we made good time although we had to walk up some of the hills. We passed through Ontario and rode down a long winding grade into a large valley covered with trees and shrubbery. The scenery was beautiful and we stopped to admire the surrounding country.

As this was the day before the "Fourth" many of the small towns were already beginning to celebrate the holiday.

We ate our lunch at Kendall and then climbed out of the valley on a long grade. The country was hilly but with the dirt road in fair shape it was not too bad. We didn't waste any time and rode through Elroy and Union Center without stopping and soon reached Wonewoc.

After leaving Wonewoc we struck a very soft sandy road. We found it impossible to ride the bikes and had to walk the next six miles, it was tough going and at times we were in sand up to our shoe tops.

We finally reached La Valle and from there on the road was

CHAPTER TWO

The Sixth Day (Cont.)Cashton,Wisconsin to Reedsburg, Wisconsin.

in fair shape. An auto from Minneapolis passed us and the driver

said,"Hurrah for Saint Paul", this cheered us up a bit to have

some one from Minneapolis say a good word for Saint Paul.

It was getting late so we hurried on toward Reedsburg. I

was in the lead and reached the town about dusk. I crossed a

bridge into town and stopped on the main street to wait for Hap.

A crowd collected around me and I sold several cards. It

was getting late and still no Hap. I was worried about him so I

rode out to find him. I met him a short distance out and he said

he had been delayed because of a tire blowout.

We went back to town and sold some more cards. I sold 26

cards that night at 5¢ each  and this amounted to $1.30, so I

felt pretty flush. In spite of the sandy road and the long walk

we made 55.3 miles that day.

We bought some food for supper and while we were standing on

the corner some boy scouts asked us if we wanted to sleep in

their tree house. We jumped at the chance and they took us over

to see it. It was a very nice house up in a large Elm tree, it

had a good roof and walls, an electric light and two nice bunks

provided with blankets. There was a ladder attached to the tree

for access from the ground. We were well pleased with it, so

after putting our bikes in a garage, we ate our supper in the

little house and turned in for a comfortable sleep.

CHAPTER TWO

SAINT PAUL,MINNESOTA TO CHICAGO,ILLINOIS

July 4th,1915  The Seventh Day.  (Sunday)

Reedsburg to Springfield Corners,Wisconsin

We had a good nights sleep in the tree house and woke up refreshed. It started to rain shortly after we got in bed and we enjoyed listening to the rain on the roof. This was the first night we didn't have to sleep on the ground and we really enjoyed it.

Soon after we got up in the morning the scouts brought over a good hot breakfast of bacon and eggs, toast and coffee. We certainly appreciated it and will always remember how kind they were to us. They certainly did their good deed for that day. After getting our bikes from the garage and bidding goodbye to the boys, we were ready to leave.

When we left Reedsburg the roads were not marked and we got on the wrong road to Baraboo and it was in such bad shape we had to walk most of the way. Because of this we didn't make much progress and it was shortly after noon before we reached Baraboo.The city is located on the Baraboo river and had a number of manufacturing plants. It is built on a number of hills about a thousand feet above sea level. The Ringling Brothers' Circus had their winter quarters there.

While in Baraboo we decided to eat our lunch, this time in a restaurant, and it cost each of us forty cents but it was a good meal. When we left Baraboo the road was worn macadam and while it was better than dirt the loose rock and gravel was hard on the tires.

CHAPTER TWO

The Seventh Day (Cont.) Reedsburg to Springfield Corners,Wisc.

We were soon on dirt roads again and we rode in the automobile ruts where we could. It was almost dark when we reached
Sauk City so we did not stop there. It was soon pitch dark and
as we couldn't see to ride the ruts made by automobiles we had
to walk much of the way. As we did not have lights on the bikes
it was rather dangerous riding at night but fortunately there
were not very many autos on the road.

It was 9:30 P.M. when we reached Springfield Corners(a very
small town) and as the ground was too wet to camp out we got a
room with some people and ate our evening meal of food we had
with us. We didn't lose much time getting to bed as we were
pretty tired.

OAK STREET
BARABOO,WISCONSIN.

CHAPTER TWO

SAINT PAUL,MINNESOTA TO CHICAGO,ILLINOIS

July 5th,1915  The Eighth Day.  (Monday)

Springfield Corners,Wisconsin to Madison,Wisconsin.

After breakfast we started for Madison about 9 A.M. arriving there about 11:30.A.M. In 1904 when I was seven years old
our family lived in Madison at 1205 W. Dayton St. The first thing
I wanted to do was to see the house in which we had lived. We
had a little difficulty finding the place but I was glad to see
it as it looked just the same as when we lived there eleven
years before.

We next called on the Hughes who still lived in the house
next door. Mrs. Hughes didn't know who I was and it took a little
while to get it straightened out but once that was done she was
very friendly. She invited us in for our noon lunch and asked
all about our family in St.Paul. She told us about many people
my folks had known including the Prouds who still lived across
the street. I went over and called on Sarah Proud who wanted to
know all about my older brothers. It was interesting visiting
with people we had known so long ago.

In the afternoon Hap and I went over to Vilas Park where a
big 4th of July celebration was going on.We sold a considerable
number of cards and were interviewed by reporters from the two
Madison newspapers. They wanted pictures of us to accompany the
write-ups but we didn't have any. We also talked to a reporter
from the Twin City Reporter which was a paper back home.

We spent the balance of the afternoon at the park and then
went back to Hughes house where we had a delicious dinner with

The Eighth Day (Cont.) Springfield Corners To Madison,Wisc.

MRS. HUGHES AND FRIEND
(The house in the background
is where we lived in 1904)
MADISON,WISCONSIN

CHAPTER TWO

The Eighth Day (Cont.) Springfield Corners to Madison,Wisc.
all the trimmings. In the evening we went down in back of the
ball park and watched the fireworks display. It was a beautiful
sight and we enjoyed it very much.

Later we went back to Hughes for a light lunch and a friendly visit. We then went to bed in their best bedroom.

Madison is the Capital of Wisconsin. The State House and
the University of Wisconsin are located there. The city is built
on the isthmus between Lake Mendota and Lake Monona and is a
very pretty city. About 1820 a trading post was established on
Lake Mendota on the site of the present city.

CHAPTER TWO

SAINT PAUL,MINNESOTA TO CHICAGO,ILLINOIS

July 6th,1915  The Ninth Day.  (Tuesday)

Madison,Wisconsin to Janesville,Wisconsin.

In the morning we had a good breakfast with the Hughes
and sat around the table for about an hour visiting. I took a
picture of Mrs.Hughes with the house we once lived in showing
in the background. I also took a picture of the Draper Elemen-
tary School that I attended when we lived in Madison.

We thanked the Hughes and said goodbye and went down town
to see the sights of the city. The first thing I did was to write
to my brother John and asked him to send the bicycle guaranties
to me at Chicago. I knew we would need them in order to get the
necessary repairs to the bikes as they were in pretty bad shape
due to the mud and water we had gone through on the way.

We next went to see the Capitol. It was a white granite
building, very beautiful and in general appearance looked much
like the Minnesota State Capitol. We spent some time going
through the building and also visited the Museum. Next we visited
a large machine shop and of course we saw the University buildings.

We left Madison at 1:30 P.M. and rode through Oregon,Verona
and Brooklin, stopping at Evansville for a bite to eat. We did
not tarry long as we were anxious to get to Janesville for the
night. Our Aunt Nell Walker and Cousin Ethel lived there and we
were looking forward to a good bed to sleep in. The road from
Madison to Janesville was dirt but was in fair shape. Shortly
after leaving Evansville it started to rain but we kept on going
and by the time we reached Janesville at 8:30 P.M. it was raining

CHAPTER TWO

The Ninth Day (Cont.) Madison,Wisc. to Janesville,Wisconsin
hard.

We finally found the house where our relatives lived and
were glad to get in out of the rain. They were glad to see us,
they had been advised of our coming but expected us a day or
two earlier. We sat down to a late meal and after a long visit
in the evening we went to bed. How nice it was to have a bed to
sleep in and we slept fine.

Janesville is located on the Rock River about thirteen
miles North of the Illinois State Line. The city is located on
bluffs above the river and much water power is obtained from the
river. There is considerable manufacturing in the city and it is
a trading center. The city was founded in the early 1830s.

MAIN ST. JANESVILLE,WISCONSIN

## CHAPTER TWO

July 7th,1915  The Tenth day   At Janesville,Wisconsin.

We were up early after a good nights sleep and soon sat down to a good breakfast. While at the table Aunt Nell asked us to stay over until the following day. Believe me, it didn't take a great deal of coaxing as we enjoyed the home cooked meals and of course the good bed to sleep in. This would give us a chance to rest up after our strenuous trip so far.

We spent the morning reading our mail from home and answering the letters we received. My Mother said she hoped I hadn't caught my death of cold yet and that we were getting along all right and were able to sell enough cards so we didn't go hungry. She also said that Aunt Cora (Harwood's Mother) was very worried about us.

I wrote my Mother a long letter, telling her about the trip so far and assuring her that all was well and that we were not going hungry. I told her about our visit with the Hughes at Madison and how kind most people had been to us. I figured if I stressed the many good things about the trip she might stop worrying about us.

I answered the short letters I received from my younger sisters, Ruth and Helen and sent my love to Dorothy, the youngest member of the family.

One letter I received suggested that we turn back because of the difficulties we were having. In answering the letter I said; "When we decided to take the trip we knew full well that it would be a most difficult undertaking. As far as we knew no one in this country had ever made a bicycle trip of this

CHAPTER TWO

July 7th,1915 The Tenth Day (Cont.) At Janesville,Wisconsin.

length before. No doubt this was due, in part at least to the
poor condition of the roads, particularly in the Midwest. Knowing this, we expected to have a rough time of it but due to so
much rain and so much tire trouble the trip so far had been
somewhat rougher than we anticipated. Regardless of this and
regardless of what we are faced with on the balance of the trip,
we have no intention of turning back." In the meantime Ethel
went out and bought a supply of food for us to take along so we
were sure of not going hungry the next few days. She also arranged to have a very nice article put in the Janesville newspaper.

After lunch Hap and I went down town to see the sights of
the city. We walked down Main St. which was beautiful with the
large trees on both sides reaching each other overhead forming
an arch over the street. We visited the Parker Pen Co. and a
machine shop and found them very interesting. We then walked
down along the river and as it was getting late we hurried back
to Aunt Nell's for our home cooked dinner. We spent the evening
visiting and went to bed about ten o'clock.

CHAPTER TWO

SAINT PAUL,MINNESOTA TO CHICAGO,ILLINOIS

July 8th,1915  The Eleventh Day (Thursday)

Janesville,Wisconsin to McHenry,Illinois.

After a good breakfast we loaded up our bikes with all the
food Cousin Ethel bought for us which consisted of a loaf of
bread, a can of sardines, veal loaf, peanut butter, canned corn
and some lemons. After thanking Aunt Nell and Ethel we said good-
bye and were on our way.

Our first stop was at Delavan and the road was a fair dry
weather road,we had no trouble on the way. We went to the newspaper office and a write up of the trip was put in the paper. We
sold a few cards in the down town area and the people were very
friendly. We were just 13 miles south of Whitewater where my
Uncle Herman was a teacher in the Normal school. We didn't go up
to see him, not knowing for sure that he was there during the
Summer months.

On the way out we stopped to admire the beauty of Delavan
Lake and then continued on to Lake Geneva. This was a resort
where many of the rich from Chicago and vicinity spent their
time. It was here that we first met with open hostility. They
wouldn't let us sell cards and encouraged us to get out of the
town. It is a very beautiful lake and surrounding area, but
because we were not welcome and as we were short of time, we did
not ride around the lake to see the Yerkes Astronomical Observ-
atory. We were rather discouraged because of our treatment there
but it soon wore off as we continued on our way. We were tired
riding as we were out of practice after loafing at Janesville

## CHAPTER TWO

The Eleventh Day (Cont.) Janesville,Wisc. to McHenry,Illinois
for a day and a half.

After leaving Lake Geneva we were on a macadam road with
short stretches of dirt but they were in fair shape. We went
through Genoa City, the last town in Wisconsin and shortly
thereafter we crossed over into Illinois, the third state on our
journey.

The first town we came to in Illinois was Richmond where we
stopped to eat our lunch. After leaving Richmond we stopped along
the road and picked about a quart of blackberries that were
growing wild along the road. They were delicious and we ate them
in short order.

It was dark long before we reached McHenry so we decided to
spend the night there. I asked a man if we could pitch our tent
in his yard, he said 'no' but at the next place where I asked,
the lady gave us permission to camp. We put up the tent between
two trees and then went to town and each bought two 10¢ ice cream
sundaes, using my last 20¢ for mine. We went back to the tent for
a good nights sleep, once again on the hard ground.

## CHAPTER TWO

### SAINT PAUL, MINNESOTA TO CHICAGO, ILLINOIS

July 9th, 1915  The Twelfth Day (Friday)

McHenry, Illinois to Highland Park, Illinois.

In the morning I cooked a good breakfast, using my cooker. The cooker consisted of a small pan to hold the food and had a support a few inches high allowing room to place a can of so called canned heat under the pan. The fuel was solidified alcohol in a can about $2\frac{1}{2}$ inches in diameter and about 2 inches in depth. The advantage of this was that it didn't take up much room and I carried it in my knapsack.

For breakfast we each ate a pint of corn meal mush, and between us a half dozen rolls, a five cent loaf of bread and a quart of milk. This primitive living has really given us a good appetite but this time we ate too much and we couldn't ride very well.

I had asked my Mother to send us a supply of post cards to Volo, Illinois which was the next town. When we got there I inquired about them and they said that Volo did not have a post office and that we would have to go to Round Lake to get our mail. This meant going eight miles out of our way. We received the cards and while there we sold a few.

We decided not to return to Volo but to continue on to the town of Libertyville. We sold some cards there so now we had a little money again which, of course, we would need when we reached Chicago. Between Libertyville and Half Day we stopped at a farm house to get a drink of water. While visiting with the farmer he said we could have all the cherries on his trees that we wanted,

CHAPTER TWO

The Twelfth Day (Cont.) McHenry,Ill. to Highland Park,Ill.
as they had what they wanted.

The trees were loaded and we ate all we could handle. The
cherries were sweet and we enjoyed our feast. I wanted to send
some home but the lady said they were too ripe to stand the trip
to St.Paul. The road in this area was mostly macadam with some
dirt but in good condition.

After going through Half Day we reached Highland Park about
7 P.M.  Highland Park was a suburb of Chicago, about twenty six
miles from the down town area.

We decided to stay and erected our tent on a vacant corner
lot on Homewood Avenue. While I prepared our evening meal of
eggs, raisin bread and condensed milk, Hap went over to watch
the elevated trains.

While he was gone four little children from half a block
down the street came over to watch me cook our meal. They were
very much interested and I let them go into the tent which they
seemed to enjoy a lot. They ran home and presently returned with
lettuce and a bunch of radishes. On their second trip home they
brought two oranges and four pieces of fruit cake. Later they
brought a big pot of coffee, buttered bread, cream and sugar.
We really had a feast that night and soon went to bed.

The above Reesman children lived on Homewood avenue.

CHAPTER TWO

The Twelfth Day  (Cont.)  At Highland Park,Illinois.

REESMAN CHILDREN

HIGHLAND PARK,ILLINOIS.

CHAPTER TWO

SAINT PAUL,MINNESOTA TO CHICAGO,ILLINOIS

July 10th,1915  The Thirteenth Day  (Saturday)

Highland Park,Illinois to Chicago,Illinois.

We had a good nights sleep and for a change it was not cold sleeping on the ground. The four Reesman children woke us at 7 A.M. and insisted that we come to their house for breakfast. Of course we accepted the invitation and washing up in warm water was a pleasant change. We had a fine meal of cream of wheat with cream, bacon, two eggs each and coffee.

When we left they gave us four hard boiled eggs and a bunch of radishes to take along. We thanked them, they wished us good luck and after taking a picture of the children alongside the tent, we departed.

Note:

This was the John L. Reesman family and they lived at 214 Homewood Avenue,Highland Park,Illinois.

Four years later when I was in the Army during World War One and stationed at Camp Grant,Illinois I spent a weekend with these people. I enjoyed seeing them again, especially the children and it was a very pleasant reunion.

From here our journey into Chicago was over a fine boulevard along the shore of Lake Michigan. The scenery was beautiful as we made our way through the suburbs of the city. At Evanston we visited with a man who was riding a bicycle around town. He invited us to have lunch with him in a restaurant, at his expense. We had a very good meal of ham,potatoes, coffee and pie for dessert.

CHAPTER TWO

The Thirteenth Day (Cont.) Highland Park,Ill. to Chicago,Ill.

He said I resembled Mike Gibbons (a Saint Paul prizefighter)

with the pompadour haircut I got at La Crosse,Wisconsin.

Chicago was some city, the second largest in the United

States. As we rode into the city we were hemmed in on all sides

by autos, wagons and horses and this was a new experience for us.

There were autos, wagons, etc. lined up for blocks waiting

to cross a street at a signal, and there were four traffic police

on each corner. The police were very nice to us, they usually

smiled and let us through.

We went to the post office first to get our mail which in-

cluded our 5 year guarantee on the bikes. Early in the afternoon

we took our bikes to the Mead Cycle Co. located at the Washington

St. Bridge north of the Loop.

We told them about the trip we were taking and also the con-

dition of the bikes because of the mud and water we had been

through. The chains and sprockets were badly worn and so were the

tires. The frame of Hap's bike was bent near the coaster brake

arm. They were much interested in the trip and told us to bring

up the bikes and they would take care of everything and would

make a rush job of it so we could them at 9 A.M. on Monday. They

were real nice about it.

We had to stay over Sunday in Chicago but had enough money

to pay our expenses. We were real glad we had purchased the bikes

at Chicago instead of locally. This way we were able to get the

bikes repaired while on the trip.

## CHAPTER TWO

The Thirteenth Day (Cont.) Highland Park,Ill. to Chicago,Ill.

The bikes had a five year guarantee and the Mead Cycle Co. honored it without question but I bet they were surprised to have to repair the bikes after so short a time.

We paid one dollar a night for a fine clean room with clean sheets and hot and cold water. This was at the Breslin Hotel on Clinton and Madison Sts. across the street from the Northwestern R.R. station and only about five blocks from the Loop.

What with the detours,the heavy rains,the tire trouble and the muddy roads, we had traveled 565 miles since leaving the St.Paul Courthouse.

We walked around the Loop district for a while in the evening but soon went to bed.

BRESLIN HOTEL
WHERE WE STAYED

Highland Park, Ills,
Jan. 18, 1919.

Dear Leon:-

I received your letter and noticed the the address is wrong. We have moved since you visited us our new address is 541 Oakwood Ave. Highland Park, Ill.

I have a good bycycle now, it is a "Perfection" and is very heavy. We live just two doors north of the Lincoln School. There is a fine sckating pond at school and we play hockey most every day after school. There is a hill acaoss the street and it is fine coasting.

How do you like it at camp and what corps are you in. Do you like you officers or are some of them "Upstartes".

I had a very nice Christmas I got three lb. of candy, a sailboat, some handkerchiefs, three books, bubes, and an electric Transformer, a purse, three thrift stamps, and a W.S. stamp and a two and half dollar gold piece ($2.50). Dont you think Santa was purty good to me.

The other day I went to the show to see the play "Americas Answer". Be shure to come if you can.

If you say what train your coming on I'll be at the
station to meet you. As it is getting tword bedtime
I will close good luck and hope you come soon.
<br>With love frome all the
<br>Fambly
<br>Bud.


We would very much enjoy having a
visit from you, the children so often
speak of you and you certin you both
hold a warm place in their affection
Do come we will all be glad to have you
<br>Sincerely
<br>Winnie Reesman

# GUARANTEE

We hereby Bargain and Agree with the purchaser of this bicycle to make good, free of cost to the purchaser, either by repair or replacement, any broken parts or parts caused through defective material or workmanship, on the following conditions:

Where any repairs or renewals are to be made by us, the broken or defective part must first be sent to us and all transportation charges (whether Freight, Express or Parcel Post) must be prepaid by the purchaser. No duplicate or new parts or repairs will be sent free of charge unless the broken parts are first sent to us prepaid as above stated. See instructions for returning parts on the reverse side of this Guarantee.

Tire Guarantee: We use the celebrated Hedgethorn Puncture Resisting Tire as regular equipment on our bicycles, as well as the Samson Red Velvet Cushion Tire, the Record Clincher Tire, the Cactus Rough Rider, Flint Road and Rough Rider Tires as special equipment on some models. These are guaranteed by the manufacturers and we in turn hereby bargain and agree with the purchaser that any of these tires proving defective in material or workmanship may be returned to us to be repaired or replaced free of charge. This guarantee does not cover cuts or natural accidents however, which are not traceable to actual defect either in material or construction. Other makes of tires when used as equipment on customer's orders are guaranteed perfect, fresh and strictly "firsts." Defects that may develop during the use of such tires as are not regular equipment with us must be referred direct to the makers. Name and address of maker branded on tires.

It is often advisable to consult a local repairman before deciding to return parts to us, as he may easily remedy the trouble by making a slight adjustment or furnishing a small part at a low cost, usually less than the expense of sending the shipment to us, thus avoiding the inconvenience of being without the use of your bicycle.

Before returning parts to us for repair or replacement please write to us, as we can in a great many cases save you delay, transportation charges, etc., by a mere suggestion. We will allow no bills for repairs paid by yourself.

Understand in returning broken or defective parts to us, the transportation charges, either Freight, Express or Parcel Post, must be prepaid by you. Your full name and address must be written plainly on the package and your letter must give Order Number and Stock Model Number as shown on back of guarantee.

**RANGER and CRUSADER BICYCLES**

In accordance with above conditions, we hereby guarantee RANGER and CRUSADER Bicycles for FIVE (5) YEARS from date of purchase. Pathfinder Bicycles are guaranteed for TWO YEARS. All our other Bicycles are guaranteed for ONE YEAR.

*Chicago, U.S.A.* *Mead Cycle Company*

## CHAPTER TWO

### SAINT PAUL,MINNESOTA TO CHICAGO,ILLINOIS

July 11th,1915 Fourteenth Day     SUNDAY IN CHICAGO

This day was to be a day for letter writing,sight seeing and relaxation. I wrote a long letter to my Mother telling her all about the trip so far after we left Janesville. I told her I would send an address later so that she could send me some home cooked food as I missed her cooking very much. I also answered other letters to my brothers and sisters.

We walked around the Loop and were much impressed with the tall buildings, so many people and so much traffic for a Sunday morning. We took a ride on the elevated out to Dr.Scott's office (a relative of my Mother)but it was closed so we didn't get to see him.

We went over on Michigan Blvd. and a cop told us to stay off of the boulevard as they didn't allow advertising there. The only advertising we had were the "St.Paul to New York" signs on our backs.

In the afternoon we went out to Lincoln Park to see the Zoological Garden, the Conservatory and the many other interest- ing things. We enjoyed watching the many wild animals.

After returning to the Loop, we ate and took a walk on State St. We stopped at a corner and two detectives grabbed all our cards and looked them over. Evidently they thought we were selling obscene cards but when they found that they were all views of St. Paul they handed them back, evidently satisfied. We soon went back to the hotel and went to bed.

### END OF THE SECOND CHAPTER.

## CHAPTER THREE

### CHICAGO,ILLINOIS TO PHILADELPHIA,PENNSYLVANIA.

July 12th,1915  The Fifteenth Day  (Monday)

Chicago,Illinois to East Gary,Indiana.

We were up early after a good nights sleep in a real bed. We had enjoyed our stay here, what with sightseeing, a good bed and of course the hot water for washing and showers. We took our last shower just before leaving the hotel and went out for break-fast. No telling how long it would be before we again had a good bed and hot water. While on the road we took our baths by swimming in a stream or lake and our bathing suit'underwear' made it convenient to do so.

After eating we walked out to the Mead Cycle Co., arriving at nine o'clock. The bikes were ready for us as promised. They had completely over-hauled them and they were as good as new. They had new tires, new chains,sprockets and all other worn parts replaced. The frame of Hap's bike had been damaged and they re-placed it. There was no charge for the repairs and after they took us for a tour of the plant, we thanked them and were on our way.

It was near noon when we left and headed south out of the city, of course the going was good on the paved city streets but we were slowed up some by the traffic. We went out Michigan Blvd., Garfield Blvd., through Washington Park and then on 'The Midway' past the University Of Chicago Campus and buildings. We contin-ued along the lake and soon crossed over into Indiana, the fourth state on our journey.

We passed through East Chicago and Gary and by the time we

## CHAPTER THREE

The Fifteenth Day    (Cont.)

Chicago,Illinois to East Gary,Indiana.

reached East Gary it was getting late so decided to stay there
for the night. We got permission to camp on a vacant lot. We set
up our tent and while doing so, a neighbor came over for a visit
and insisted that we eat our evening meal at his house, and we
gladly accepted the invitation. The neighbor's name was H. S.
Weisskopl and he lived at 3685 Pennsylvania, East Gary,Indiana.
We went to bed early after a pleasant visit with our neighbors.

Our bed was on the hard ground as usual and we were still
thinking about the Chicago hotel where we had a good bed and hot
and cold water for washing and bathing.

Conditions were not always as good as in the large cities.
Many small town hotels and rooming houses did not have running
water, much less hot water. Many of them had a wash stand in the
room, and on the stand was a large pitcher of cold water. This
pitcher rested in a large bowl for washing and on the floor there
was a bucket to empty the water in. Primitive as it was, it was
still better than when we camped out, which we did most of the
time and washing in a cold stream or at a pump when available.

## CHAPTER THREE

## CHICAGO,ILLINOIS TO PHILADELPHIA,PENNSYLVANIA.

July 13th,1915  The Sixteenth Day  (Tuesday)

East Gary,Indiana to La Porte,Indiana.

We were up early amd soon on our way across Indiana. We planned to go to Valparaiso and from there to Fort Wayne. We went through Hobart with out stopping and reached Valparaiso about 9.30 where we had a late breakfast in a restaurant.

After sending cards home we inquired about the road to Fort Wayne, we were told that the road was practically impassable due to the heavy rains and floods. They told us that the only road open to the East was by way of South Bend.

We decided to look the town over before deciding on our next move. We saw Valparaiso University and Technical Institute. The city is the county seat of Porter County. We did not tarry long as we knew we had no choice in the matter, so after a short time we headed for South Bend. We knew that this would mean going 50 or 75 miles out of our way and the loss of a days time, but nothing else could be done.

Later we were glad we had changed our course because we heard that about the time to have reached Lima on the other road, the flood was much worse, with road bridges washed out and the road impassable.

We were delayed some by rain and a puncture so by the time we reached La Porte it was late in the afternoon. We decided to camp there for the night, so thus ended our second day in Indiana.

La Porte is the county seat of La Porte County. It is an industrial city. Much commerce passed through the city in the early days between southern Indiana and the lake region.

CHAPTER THREE

CHICAGO,ILLINOIS TO PHILADELPHIA,PENNSYLVANIA.

July 14th,1915  The Seventeenth Day  (Wednesday)

La Porte,Indiana to Goshen,Indiana.

We headed for South Bend that morning on a gravel road 26 miles away, and arrived shortly before noon. The downtown area was alive with people and they were very friendly. We had no trouble selling cards, in fact many people not only bought cards, but stopped to visit and inquire about the trip. They were very much interested and it gave us a lift to be so well received by so many people.

The University of Notre Dame is located a few miles from South Bend at Notre Dame,Indiana. This school is a first class educational institution and is well known throughout the country. It was, in later years famous for its football teams, called the "Fighting Irish". This was particulary true when Knute Rockne was coach, in the days of the so called, "Four Horsemen and Seven Mules" of Notre Dame.

There was considerable manufacturing in the city. We saw the Studebaker Plant and also the original County Court House which was very interesting.

In the early days La Salle explored this area as well as territory to the West. The city is located in the south bend of the St.Joseph River from which it got its name.

We left South Bend in the afternoon and four miles beyond we came to Mishawaka, also on the St.Joseph River. There were many manufacturing plants located there but we didn't have time

CHAPTER THREE

The Seventeenth Day  (Cont.)

La Porte,Indiana to Goshen,Indiana.

to visit any of them. Among other things manufactured there were
leather and woolen goods, furniture and sheet metal products.

Mishawaka was an Indian Princess and there had been in the
early days, a village bearing her name on the site of the present
city. On the opposite side of the river there was a settlement
named Indiana City. In 1838 the two settlements were incorporated
as the town of Mishawaka.

We rode through Osceola without stopping and the next city
we came to was Elkhart and while there sold a few cards.

Elkhart is also located on the St.Joseph River at the mouth
of the Elkhart River. There were many manufacturing plants located there, and a great variety of products were produced. The
city was settled in the early 1830s.

After leaving Elkhart we were enjoying our ride through the
countryside when Hap had a puncture in his rear tire. This delayed us some while he made the necessary repairs and we then continued on to Goshen. It was getting late when we reached Goshen
so we decided to spend the night there.

We found a place to camp on a vacant lot, we erected the
tent and then went about the business of cooking our evening meal.
We had a good meal of beans, bread and coffee, and after talking
about the events of the day, we turned in for a good nights sleep.

We made 46 miles that day in spite of our long stay in South
Bend, as we didn't have any rain for a change and the roads were

CHAPTER THREE

The Seventeenth Day  (Cont.)

La Porte,Indiana to Goshen,Indiana.

fairly good.

Goshen is on the Elkhart River at an altitude of about 800 feet. The city is in the fertile St.Joseph River valley and is in a fine agricultural area. It is the county seat of Elkhart County and the County Court House, built in 1868, is in the center of the city. It was a red brick structure with shade trees around it.

Goshen College, a Mennonite school, is located at Goshen. There were many Mennonite and Amish people living in the city and in the surrounding countryside. The city was very pretty with its tree lined residential streets. There were some facto-ries in and about the city but the principal means of livelihood seemed to be agriculture. The town was settled in 1828.

## CHAPTER THREE

CHICAGO,ILLINOIS TO PHILADELPHIA,PENNSYLVANIA.

July 15th,1915  The Eighteenth Day  (Thursday)

Goshen,Indiana to Kendallville,Indiana.

We woke up early but as it was raining we didn't get up until 9 O'clock. By that time the rain had stopped, so we prepared our breakfast on our grill, packed up our gear and were on our way.

There was a long detour between Goshen and Benton, it was a poor road and as it rained most of the time we were on it, our progress was slow. While on this detour we each had a puncture which further delayed us.

We reached Ligonier about noon so we stopped for lunch in a restaurant. We sold a few cards by canvassing the business stores. As was our custom lately, Hap took one side of the business street and I took the other side, calling on all of the stores.

From Ligonier there was a road to Fort Wayne and when we had been unable to make the trip from Valparaiso we thought we might be able to go from Ligonier. We asked about it and were told that there were serious floods to the South with road bridges washed out. Because of this, we gave up the idea of getting back on our planned route and decided to go by way of Toledo as that road was open. This would mean going about 40 or 50 miles out of our way. We would also lose about a days time. By now we were used to the many delays due to detours, rains and tire trouble so it didn't bother us much.

CHAPTER THREE

The Eighteenth Day  (Cont.)

Goshen,Indiana to Kendallville,Indiana.

Throughout our journey in the Mid West we had seen many
horse drawn wagons and buggies, particulary in the small farming communities. The automobile at that time was a long way
from taking the place of horses, wagons and buggies.

We stopped at Kendallville for our nights camping. Due to
the rain and poor roads we only made 37 miles that day.

Kendallville is in the center of a rich farming area. There
were some factories located there, including a refrigerator plant
and the Flint and Walling Plant established in 1865. Of interest
was the old Bundle Tavern which was built in 1833 and still standing. Near the city was an old farm house that I understand was
used as an "Underground Railroad Station" before the Civil War.

The city was founded in the early 1830's. and incorporated
in 1863.

CHAPTER THREE

CHICAGO,ILLINOIS TO PHILADELPHIA,PENNSYLVANIA.

July 16th,1915  The Nineteenth Day  (Friday)

Kendallville,Indiana to Bryan,Ohio.

It rained during the night and was still raining in the
morning. We stayed in the tent and talked over the events of the
trip so far. We had half a loaf of bread and that took care of
our breakfast. Not too good without butter or coffee to go with
it but it served the purpose.

Now that we were about to leave Indiana we decided to re-
count our experiences in crossing the state. We had difficulty
selling cards in the small towns which led me to believe that
times were not too good in the farming communities. This was
offset in the large cities where we sold many cards and didn't
go hungry at any time. With one or two exceptions ( you cant win
them all ) the people were friendly and helpful and we enjoyed
our visit to Indiana very much.

Hap said " How do you think we will fare in Ohio " I said
"I dont know, of course, but we will soon find out because we will
be in Ohio by nightfall."

It stopped raining about 10 O'clock so we got underway. We
rode through Waterloo and stopped at Butler for lunch. While
there we sold a few cards.

It was late in the afternoon when we crossed the state line
into Ohio, the fifth state on our journey. The first town in Ohio
that we came to was Edgerton.

I was ahead of Hap so I stopped on the Main Street to wait

## CHAPTER THREE

The Nineteenth Day  (Cont.)

Kendallville,Indiana to Bryan,Ohio.

for him. I walked up and down the street, visiting with the
people of the town. In a few minutes he arrived and caught up
to me. I asked him if he had trouble on the road, he said no,
but that he was feeling sick and wanted to rest for a few minutes. He stretched out on a bench in front of the Krill Furniture Store. Mr. Krill asked if he could be of any assistance but
Hap said he would be all right in a few minutes. This was the
first time on the trip so far that either of us had felt sick
(in fact this was the only time on the entire trip that either
one of us was sick).

KRILL FURNITURE STORE

EDGERTON,OHIO

CHAPTER THREE

The Nineteenth Day  (Cont.)

Kendallville,Indiana to Bryan,Ohio.

In a few minutes Hap was feeling better and was up and ready
to go. We thanked Mr. Krill for his help and were soon on our
way to Bryan.

We reached Bryan in the early evening and after a bite to
eat we went looking for a place to stay over night. A kindly
Irish lady by the name of Flinn put us up for the night. We spent
a pleasant evening visiting with these people. They were very
much interested in the trip, and asked many questions about our
journey so far.*

Bryan is the county seat of Williams County. It is located
in an agricultural district, the products are poultry, dairy
products, hogs and cattle. There is also some manufacturing in
the city. The town was settled in 1840 and incorporated in 1849.

* About a year later Mrs. Flinn's son was in Saint Paul
and he called on us. We had a nice visit and he said his Mother
was well and wanted to know all about us. He said his Mother
always referred to me as her "other son".

## CHAPTER THREE

### CHICAGO,ILLINOIS TO PHILADELPHIA,PENNSYLVANIA.

July 17th,1915  The Twentieth Day  (Saturday)

Bryan,Ohio to Toledo,Ohio.

We had a good nights sleep in a real bed, our first night in Ohio. We woke up early and lost no time getting washed and dressed. While Mrs.Flinn was preparing an early breakfast, we got out our Goodrich Rubber Company road guide. We had been using their guides on the entire trip and found them very helpful.

We found that the road we would take was not a direct route to Toledo but had been built to take in several small towns along the way. The distance to Toledo was 66 miles, and as we hoped to get there that day, we would have to get started as early as possible.

Right after our delicious breakfast we prepared to leave on our journey across the great state of Ohio. We thanked Mrs. Flinn for her hospitality and as we left she wished us Godspeed on our way. I am sure that the prayers of that kind lady followed us all the days of our long journey.

We rode through Stryker and Archbold, stopping a few minutes to sell cards. The road was not too good but we continued on, stopping at Wauseon for a bite to eat. We continued on through Delta, Swanton, Caragher and Sylvania.

It was dark when we reached Sylvania but we stopped for

## CHAPTER THREE

The Twentieth Day    (Cont.)

Bryan,Ohio to Toledo,Ohio.

something to eat before making the final run into Toledo.

It was long after dark when we reached Toledo, and as we didn't have lights on the bikes it was pretty risky but we made it safely. (my bike light had been broken way back near Winona, Minnesota.)

It was too late to find a place to camp but we came to a park and decided to sleep there. We chained our bikes to a tree, spread out our blankets on the grass, and as we were tired after our long ride that day we soon fell asleep.

OVERLAND AUTOMOBILE WORKS

TOLEDO,OHIO

CHAPTER THREE

CHICAGO,ILLINOIS TO PHILADELPHIA,PENNSYLVANIA.

July 18th,1915  The Twentyfirst Day  (Sunday)

Sunday in Toledo,Ohio.

We decided to spend most of the day in Toledo. After breakfast we walked down to the harbor and watched the large boats,
one of which is shown in the accompanying picture. The city has
a fine harbor and is a port of entry. A great deal of coal was
handled through the port, as well as iron ore and other products.

After spending some time at the harbor we went to the Zoological Garden and enjoyed seeing the animals and other sights there.
Next we went to the business district where we ate lunch in a
restaurant. Of course the factories were closed so we couldn't
visit any of them. Toledo was about the same size as Saint Paul
and reminded me a little of it.

Toledo is located at the mouth of the Maumee River, on
Maumee Bay at the southwestern tip of Lake Erie. The site lies
within a huge tract acquired by the United States from several
Indian tribes in 1795. A stockade fort (Fort Industry) was built

LAKE BOAT

TOLEDO  HARBOR

CHAPTER THREE

The 21st Day    (Cont.)

Toledo,Ohio to Woodville,Ohio.

there in 1800.

The so-called "Toledo War" in the early 1800's was a dispute between Ohio and Michigan over the state boundary. In connection with the dispute, the Governor of Michigan sent troops and in 1835 took possession of Toledo. The dispute was finally settled by the United States Government in favor of Ohio, and Michigan was given the Upper Peninsula.

We had enjoyed our day of sightseeing in Toledo and were glad we stayed to see some of the city.

It was late in the afternoon when we left Toledo and while we were delayed some by the traffic in the city,we were soon out in the open country. We rode the 19 miles to Woodville, arriving there just before dark. We found a place to camp and after erecting our tent, just the food we had with us took care of our evening meal. After talking over the events of the day we went to bed.

Woodville is in a limestone area and is noted for the high quality of the rock.

CHAPTER THREE

CHICAGO,ILLINOIS TO PHILADELPHIA,PENNSYLVANIA.

HAP ON A BABY BIKE

IN A SMALL OHIO TOWN

ON THE WATER WAGON

IN A SMALL OHIO TOWN

CHAPTER THREE

CHICAGO,ILLINOIS TO PHILADELPHIA,PENNSYLVANIA.

July 19th,1915   The 22nd Day       (Monday)

Woodville,Ohio to Norwalk,Ohio.

We were up about seven o'clock and after packing our gear on the bikes, we washed up in the Portage River. We sold a few cards in the business district and after a light breakfast we left for Norwalk.

The road was macadam, very dusty and with many loose rocks. This was hard on the tires and we hadn't gone very far when we each had a puncture. The reflection of the Sun on the white macadam was blinding. Fortunately I had purchased a pair of dark glasses, some time back.

People were very friendly and helpful along the way and many stopped their cars or wagons to ask about the trip. The road we were on was once an Indian trail. For many years it was known as the Western and Maumee Pike and was used by immigrants headed West. For some time in the past it was a stage coach road.

We were selling many cards on our trip across Ohio, and we could have sold many more if we had cards with our picture on them. We reached Hessville before noon and a lady said we could have all the cherries we wanted. The tree was loaded and we took full advantage of it. This reminded us of the similar experience we had in Northern Illinois.

On the way to Fremont we stopped at a park near the town. In the park was a house where Rutherford B. Hayes (19th President of the United States) had lived and nearby his grave. At Fremont we

CHAPTER THREE

The 22nd Day    (Cont.)

Woodville,Ohio to Norwalk,Ohio.

went in swimming in the Sandusky River. This was our way of taking a bath and as it was warm, our bathing suit underwear soon
dried out.

Fremont is on the Sandusky River, the county seat of Sandusky County. The city is in a rich agricultural district. It was
here that Fort Stephenson was built during the war of 1812. In
1813 a large force of English soldiers surrounded the fort and
demanded it surrender. The Commander refused and with a small
force successfully defended it.
He moved his one cannon from
place to place and the English
thinking he was well prepared
to defend the fort,finally
withdrew. The lone cannon he
used is still on display at the
site of the old fort.

We rode through Clyde,
selling cards along the way.
We stopped at Bellevue for a
late lunch and while there Hap
took a picture of me sitting

Drinking Fountain
Bellevue,Ohio

on a drinking fountain in the street. Presume it was a place for
horses to drink. The town had a wide Main St. and there were many
horse drawn buggies and wagons. The town had a railroad terminal,
limestone quarries,flour mills and several small factories.

CHAPTER THREE

The 22nd Day    (Cont.)

Woodville,Ohio to Norwalk,Ohio.

We continued on our journey and a short distance before we reached Norwalk we came to a concrete road a few miles long. It was so seldom that we found a paved road, we took advantage of it and raced each other into Norwalk. I don't remember who won the race but we enjoyed it.

When we reached Norwalk we decided to spend the night, as it was late in the afternoon.We sold a few cards in the business district and went to a restaurant to eat.

A small boy who sold popcorn on the street said he would show us a place to camp. He took us to a large vacant area and said we could camp there if we were not afraid of snakes as there were many in that area.

The Boy Who Showed Us
The Snake Infested
Place To Camp

We decided to think it over and went back to town with him. The people were friendly and a small boy proudly showed us his baby alligator. We decided to camp where the boy showed us, in spite of the snakes. We borrowed a lantern from a neighbor and put up our tent then went to bed.

Norwalk was settled in 1817 by colonists from Norwalk, Connecticut. It is within the "Fire Lands Grant" made in 1792 by the State of Connecticut to the people of 8 Connecticut towns to indemnify them for fire losses during British expeditions in 1779 and in 1781.

CHAPTER THREE

CHICAGO,ILLINOIS TO PHILADELPHIA,PENNSYLVANIA.

July 20th,1915  The 23rd Day  (Tuesday)

Norwalk,Ohio to Medina,Ohio.

We woke up early and were thankful that the snakes didn't bother us during the night. We dressed in a hurry, packed our gear on the bikes and rode down to the business area.

We ate breakfast at a restaurant as we didn't want to cook a meal at our camp site because of the snakes. We met the boy who directed us to the place to camp and I took his picture. I talked to a man who said he once took a hundred mile trip on a bicycle. He said that was enough for him and didn't see how we could make such a long trip with the roads the way they were. After spending some time visiting with the people of the town, we headed out of town.

The road was not too good and by the time I reached Clarksfield I was well ahead of Hap. I crossed the Vermilion River and when I got to Brighton, Hap was no where in sight, so I waited for him to catch up. In due course he came riding into view, he said he was delayed by a puncture.

We continued on to Wellington and stopped there for a short time to sell cards. People in the small towns were very generous and we sold many cards during the day. In all the small towns there were many horses and wagons and of course a few automobiles.

We were highspirited as we rode along because the people were so friendly and generous.

CHAPTER THREE

The 23rd Day    (Cont.)

Norwalk,Ohio to Medina,Ohio.

We reached Medina late in the afternoon and decided to camp there for the night. We first went to a restaurant for our evening meal as we were pretty flush, having sold so many cards during the day.  We had a good meal of meat,potatoes, vegetable, bread, coffee and dessert.

It didn't take long to find a good camp site(this one without snakes) and after putting up the tent we talked about the adventures of the day and went to bed.


Medina is the county seat of Medina County, and is at an altitude of about 1100 feet. It was a farming community and the products were mainly poultry,dairy products and fruit. There was some manufacturing done there and the city was also known for its apiculture.The city was first settled about 1818.

CHAPTER THREE

CHICAGO,ILLINOIS TO PHILADELPHIA,PENNSYLVANIA.

July 21,1915   The 24th Day   (Wednesday)

Medina,Ohio to Akron,Ohio.

It was raining when we woke up, so we took down the tent, packed our gear on the bikes and rode down to the business section for breakfast. We stayed in the restaurant for about an hour and then sought shelter elsewhere.

It stopped raining about noon so we headed out for Akron. We stopped at the Rocky River for a short time and then continued on our way. We had only gone a short distance when Hap had a puncture and about two miles beyond my rear tire went flat. We stopped at Coddingville and Montrose and sold a few cards. With all the delays, it was 5 P.M. when we reached Akron, and we had only made 19 miles during the day.

When we reached Akron we had traveled 1,012 miles since leaving St.Paul, according to the cyclometer on Hap's bike.

We found a place to camp on a vacant lot and then went to the business district to spend the evening. The streets were alive with people and I sold $2.05 worth of cards in a short time. Our price was 5¢ each but I sold three at 25¢ each, as the people were very generous. We went to bed in our tent about 10 P.M. after a good meal in a restaurant.

The friendliness of the people and selling so many cards certainly was encouraging.

CHAPTER THREE

CHICAGO,ILLINOIS TO PHILADELPHIA,PENNSYLVANIA.

July 22,1915  The 25th Day    (Thursday)

Akron,Ohio Today.

We were up early as we had a full day of sightseeing ahead
of us. There was much we wanted to see in Akron, where the large
tire companies had their factories.

Throughout all our journey, the B.F.Goodrich Company had
furnished us with road guides and with much help as to road conditions, etc. This was all done willingly and at no cost to us,
which we appreciated very much. In addition a large percentage
of the road signs along the way had been placed by the Goodrich
people. Aside from their signs the roads were usually poorly
marked and in many cases, not at all.

Naturally, now that we were at the headquarters of that
company, the first order of business was to go out to their factory to thank them for their assistance, and to see their factory.
They were very friendly and took us on a tour of the plant. It
was all very interesting and we found that they made a great
many things of rubber, besides automobile tires. They gave us a
brochure explaining much about the history of the company and
the factory. Following is some of the information shown in the
pamphlet::

The company was established in 1869 by Dr. B.F.Goodrich of
Brooklyn,New York. The first plant, a small brick building 40x
100 feet, two stories high and located at the present factory
site. The ground for the plant cost $1,800. The number of em-

CHAPTER THREE

The 25th Day    (Cont.)

Akron,Ohio Today.

ployees, about 25 and no Branches.

As of 1915 the company was capitalized for $90,000,000. The distance around the plant was two miles and the floor space 75 acres. There were 15,000 employees and 100 Branches and Depots.

The total weight volume of nearly one hundred million pounds of freight was shipped out in a year. This figure was made possible by a daily output of ten thousand automobile tires, fourteen miles of hose, five miles of belting, sixty miles of insulated wire, twenty thousand rubber shoes and similar quantities of material in other forms covering the entire range of everything made in rubber.

All of the above is about 1915, I don't know what the situation is today but presume the volume is much greater. Because of the kindness shown us so long ago by these people, when I buy automobile tires now, I make sure that they are B.F.Goodrich tires.

After our very pleasant experience at the Goodrich factory, we left and decided to go over to the Goodyear Rubber Co. plant. We went to the office and asked if it was possible to go through the factory. The man at the desk took one look at us and in a brusque manner said " We don't allow visitors in the plant ". We thanked him and walked out and as we left, the guard saw the "St.Paul to New York" signs on our backs. He came running and caught up to us and said "perhaps you would like to talk to the

CHAPTER THREE

The 25th Day    (Cont.)

Akron,Ohio Today    Akron,Ohio to Canton,Ohio in the afternoon.

advertising manager". We went back and talked to him, he apolo-
gised for the way we had been treated, asked all about the trip
and said he would put an article about our trip in the magazine
'Motorcycle and Bicycle World'. We did not get to go through
the plant but the article did appear later in the magazine.

We went to see the place where John Brown once lived and
that completed our sightseeing in Akron. We had a very interesting day and by now it was late afternoon so we decided to get
going on our ride to Canton.

The road from Akron to Canton was brick part of the way and
clay the rest of the way.It was in pretty good shape and we
reached Canton just before dark. We found a place to camp,erected
our tent and went to a restaurant for our evening meal. We visited with people who stopped to talk and then we went back to our
tent and went to bed. And that was the end of a very interesting
day.


Akron was a very busy place at that time. More and more
people were discarding their horse drawn vehicles and buying
that newfangled horseless carriage called the automobile. This
led to a greatly increased demand for tires. This kept the rubber companies busy in order to keep up with the demand. The
population of Akron just about tripled between 1910 and 1920.

CHAPTER THREE

The 25th Day    (Cont.)

Akron,Ohio to Canton,Ohio.

The value of the manufactured products increased about seven-
fold during the same period. The number of wage earners increased
about fourfold during this period.

There were other manufacturing plants in Akron producing a
variety of products.

The old Portage Trail, used by the Indians in carrying
their canoes from the Cuyahoga River to the Tuscarawas River
in the journey from Lake Erie to the Ohio River runs through
the city.

TROLLEY CARS IN AKRON

1915

CHAPTER THREE

CHICAGO,ILLINOIS TO PHILADELPHIA,PENNSYLVANIA.

July 23rd,1915  The 26th Day    (Friday)

At Canton,Ohio

In Canton we most wanted to see the McKinley Monument where former President McKinley, his wife and two infant daughters are buried. The building is a beautiful granite structure in the shape of a large cylinder topped by a Roman dome.

It was erected by the people of the nation and is located in a park of 26 acres on Monument Hill. The Memorial was dedicated on September 7th,1907. The dedication was attended by the then President Theodore Roosevelt, as well as Governors and other notables from all over the country.

Part way up the steps leading to the entrance is a bronze, erect figure of McKinley, with one hand in his pocket and a number of papers in the other hand.

In front of the building is a lagoon built in sections, each one a little higher than the one before with walks and trees on each side.

We entered the building and while there we talked to some men working on the Monument. One of them took us through the building and to the top of the Monument where visitors are not allowed. From the top we had a beautiful view of the city. We spent some time up there, taking pictures and enjoying the sight. When we came down we thanked the man for his kindness and he told us a great deal about the Monument. We then left as we wanted to see the other sights of the city.

CHAPTER THREE

The 26th Day  (Cont.)   At Canton,Ohio

McKINLEY NATIONAL MEMORIAL   CANTON

VIEW OF CANTON FROM THE TOP OF THE MEMORIAL.

## CHAPTER THREE

The 26th Day    (Cont.)    At Canton, Ohio

---

### DEDICATION McKINLEY NATIONAL MEMORIAL

## PROGRAM FOR THE DAY
### CANTON, OHIO, SEPTEMBER 30, 1907

The President will be met at his train at 10:15 a. m., and escorted to the congregation of school children at the High School, thence to the reviewing stand on the Public Square, not leaving his carriage until he reaches the stand.

Parade starts past reviewing stand at 10:45.

At 12:30 o'clock the President will be escorted to the Auditorium for luncheon.

At 1 p. m., President *Theodore* Roosevelt will be escorted to the speakers' stand at the Memorial where the exercises will begin at 1:45 and conclude in time to escort the President to his train. leaving Canton at 4.05 p. m.

---

## MILITARY AND CIVIC PARADE OFFICIALS

MAJOR GENERAL CHARLES DICK, Commanding Division O. N. G.,
CHIEF MARSHAL.

AIDES-DE-CAMP.

Captain Ira I. Morrison, O. N. G.
Lieut. John L. Pond, 19th U. S. Infantry.
Lieut. Leo. B. Dannemiller, 11th U. S. Infantry.
Lieut. John C. Moore, 7th U. S. Infantry.

Colonel George M. Wright, Chief of Staff, Div. O. N. G., Chief of Staff.
Colonel Worthington Kautzman A. A. G., Adjutant General
Lieutenant-Colonel C. Barton Adams, Inspector General.
Lieutenant-Colonel Frederick C. Bryan, Judge Advocate.
Lieutenant-Colonel Oliver H. Hughes, Chief Quartermaster.
Lieutenant-Colonel Frank M. Ritezel, Chief Commissary.
Lieutenant-Colonel Edmund C. Brush, Chief Surgeon.
Lieutenant-Colonel George G. King, Chief Ordinance Officer.
Major Charles B. Winder, Inspector Small Arms Practice.

4

## CHAPTER THREE

The 26th Day  (Cont.)

Canton, Ohio to Columbiana, Ohio.

Canton was the home of
President McKinley after
1867 when he opened a law
office there.

The city of Canton was
laid out in 1805 and became
the county seat in 1808.
There were many factories
in the city and the population increased considerably
between 1910 and 1920. The
park system consisted of
several hundred acres. The

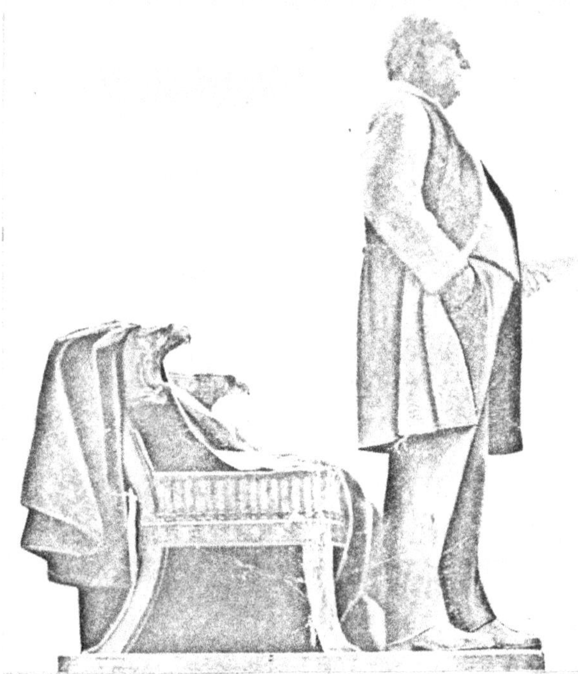

STATUE OF McKINLEY
ON THE STEPS OF THE MEMORIAL

city is located in a rich agricultural area.

We spent some time visiting other parts of the city, ate our
noon lunch and were on our way in the early afternoon. We took
the road to Alliance where we stopped to sell cards. Alliance was
a small city with a population of 15 or 20,000. There were a number of factories in the city producing a variety of products.

We continued on through Sebring, Beloit, Westville and
Damascus without stopping, it was all beautiful farming country
but we were anxious to be on our way. When we reached Salem we
decided to stop and rest awhile. We canvassed the business area
and had no trouble selling cards.

CHAPTER THREE

The 26th Day    (Cont.)

Canton,Ohio to Columbiana,Ohio.

Salem is in a fertile agricultural region and there were numerous factories in the city. The town was settled by "Friends" a religious organization, a branch of the Quakers, in 1806. The settlement became a city in 1887. It was a station on the so-called "Underground Railroad" about the time of the Civil War between the States.

Just out of Salem we came to our first big hill in this area and we had to walk and push the bikes to the top. We were now getting into the foothills of the Allegheny Mountains. We will be faced with these hills and mountains until we get about two-thirds of the way across Pennsylvania.

We decided to camp at Columbiana for the night, our last night in Ohio as we were only eleven miles from the Pennsylvania line.

Columbiana was a small town at an elevation of about 2,500 feet which was 1,500 feet higher than Canton. Harvey S. Firestone of the Firestone Tire and Rubber Company was born here.

CHAPTER THREE

CHICAGO,ILLINOIS TO PHILADELPHIA,PENNSYLVANIA.

July 24th,1915   The 27th Day   (Saturday)

Columbiana,Ohio to Pittsburgh,Pennsylvania.

We were up early as we hoped to reach Pittsburgh by night-fall, sixty miles away. The going was slow because of the long walks up the hills. It was nearly noon when we crossed over into Pennsylvania, the sixth state on our journey.

Now that we had completed our trip across Ohio, it was time to pause and reflect on our experiences in that great state. The people accepted us and treated us more like their own, rather than as strangers from far off. They were hospitable, kind, helpful and very generous. I will always remember the fine treatment we received there. We were learning more and more about the wonderful people who lived in this great country of ours.

Shortly after crossing the state line I had a puncture which delayed us some. We reached Beaver Falls about three P.M. and rested there for a short time. Progress was slow due to the hills, tire trouble and some rain.

Beaver Falls had a population of about 10,000 in 1915. It is located on the west bank of Beaver River, at the falls of the river and a short distance from the confluence of Beaver River with the Ohio River. There were stone and coal mines in the vicinity.

After leaving Beaver Falls we rode down the valley of Beaver River to Rochester which is at the confluence of the

CHAPTER THREE

The 27th Day    (Cont.)

Columbiana,Ohio to Pittsburgh,Pennsylvania.

Ohio River. We were further delayed by tire trouble and some rain.
With all the delays we were still 15 or 20 miles from Pittsburgh
when it was pitch dark. We had to ride the balance of the way in
the dark, without lights and of course bikes did not have reflec-
tors in those days.

When I think of the many times we rode at night, always without lights, and at times in or near large cities, I realize how
fortunate we were not to have a single accident on the entire
trip involving an automobile, horse or wagon.

As we approached Pittsburgh we passed several steel mills.
The black smoke was pouring out of the tall chimneys and the glow
of the furnaces lit up the sky. It was an interesting sight as we
rode along in the darkness.

We reached the downtown area of Pittsburgh at 11 P.M. tired,
hungry and with very little money. A policeman asked us if we had
a place to sleep and when we said no, he suggested we go to the
city jail and see if they would put us up for the night. We did
as he suggested and the officer at the desk said they would be
glad to have us as guests for the night.

After putting our bikes in the police garage, an officer
took us up to the third floor and locked us in a cell. By now it
was after midnight. While the accommodations were not exactly
first class, we certainly appreciated the kindness of the police

CHAPTER THREE

The 27th Day     (Cont.)

Columbiana,Ohio to Pittsburgh,Pennsylvania.

for providing us with a place to spend the night.

The cell was seven or eight feet square with steel walls
on three sides and the front, including the door, was made up of
heavy steel bars extending from the floor to the ceiling.

In the cell were two steel plates each about $2\frac{1}{2}$ feet by 7
feet, one above the other. These plates were attached to the
rear wall and when not in use folded up against the wall. To use
as bunks they could be let down to a horizontal position and
were held in that position by chains at the ends of the bunks.

We each spread out our one blanket on these hard steel
plates, one thickness of blanket under us and one over us. It
was not very comfortable to say the least. At 1:15 A.M. we were
awakened by a commotion in the room outside our cell. We looked
out through the bars and saw about twenty prisoners they had just
brought in. They put the prisoners in cells all around us but we
felt pretty safe (if not comfortable) in our position behind the
steel bars of our cage.

In a short time the noise died down and when all was quiet
we went to sleep.


Pittsburgh was a city of about 550,000 population. It is
located on the Allegheny, Monongahela and Ohio Rivers. The city
is hilly, the difference in elevation between the low and the high

CHAPTER THREE

The 27th Day    (Cont.)

Columbiana,Ohio to Pittsburgh,Pennsylvania.

points is about six hundred feet. There are a number of steel
mills in and about the city. The main business area called the
"Golden Triangle" covers about one and a half square miles. The
triangle is formed by the confluence of the Alleghany and Monongahela Rivers which forms the beginning of the Ohio River. The
hills, the three rivers with narrow valleys from which rise steep
hills or bluffs make a beautiful setting for the city.

There are several schools in Pittsburgh including the University of Pittsburgh and the Carnegie Institute of Technology.

CHAPTER THREE

CHICAGO,ILLINOIS TO PHILADELPHIA,PENNSYLVANIA.

July 25th,1915   The 28th Day     (Sunday)

Sunday In Pittsburgh,Pennsylvania.

In the morning the police woke us at 5 A.M. We didn't have much sleep during the night but were glad to get out from behind the bars. At the same time they got all the prisoners up and we went out into the large room with the others. They ordered all of us down to the first floor.

At first when we got down there, the officers thought we had been arrested with the prisoners. After we got that straightened out they let us go. We appreciated the place to sleep,it was very interesting and we learned a lot about jails in large cities. However one experience like that is enough.

We got our bikes out of the garage and went looking for a restaurant for breakfast. We found a small place to eat and for breakfast we each had a large bowl of oatmeal with sugar and real cream. We also had coffee and they brought a whole loaf of sliced french bread and put it on a plate in front of us. We had a real good meal and believe it or not, it only cost us 15¢ each.

I received a letter from my Mother in which she suggested we have our picture taken with the bikes and our equipment. We thought that would be a good idea and as we had money enough to do so, we went out looking for a photo studio. We finally found one that was open that Sunday morning and made arrangements for the picture. We carried our bikes and equipment up to the second

CHAPTER THREE

The 28th Day     (Cont.)

Sunday In Pittsburgh,Pennsylvania.

floor studio. We had the picture taken (it appears at the beginning of this story) but as the prints would not be ready until
the following morning we decided to spend the day in Pittsburgh.

    We went out sightseeing and sold a number of cards giving
us money enough for our meals and a place to spend the night. We
spent some time looking around the "Golden Triangle" and then
went up on Mt. Washington where we had a beautiful view of the
city.

    We wanted to go through a steel mill but being Sunday this
could not be done. We had our evening meal, found a reasonably
priced place to spend the night and went to bed.

PITTSBURGH,PENNSYLVANIA.

CHAPTER THREE

CHICAGO,ILLINOIS TO PHILADELPHIA,PENNSYLVANIA.

July 26th,1915   The 29th Day   (Monday)

Pittsburgh to Greensburg,Pennsylvania.

We slept late and after breakfast went to the photo studio
to get our pictures. They were ready at 9 A.M. as promised. We
next went to the Post Office to send some of them home. The St.
Paul newspapers wanted our picture to use in connection with
the articles they were putting in the paper about the progress
of our trip.

It was about 10 A.M. when we left Pittsburgh. There were many
hills and we had to walk up some of them. Progress was slow and
the rain we had in the morning didn't help and neither did the
puncture I had, in the rear tire.

When we reached Irwin we stopped to rest awhile. We went to
the office of the local newspaper, "Republican Standard" by name
and they put an article in the paper about the trip.

We moved on and reached Greensburg in mid afternoon. We rode
out to Jeannette as we wanted to see the factory of the Pennsylvania Rubber Co. We found it very interesting and learned some
more about tire making. By the time we got back to Greensburg it
was time for our evening meal.

Greensburg is in the heart of the bituminous coal fields of
western Pennsylvania. It is the county seat of Westmoreland
county and is at an elevation of about 1100 feet. In addition to
the coal there were a number of manufacturing plants in the city.
The place was settled about 1770 and became the county seat about
fifteen years later. It was near Greensburg that the battle of

CHAPTER THREE

The 29th Day      (Cont.)

Pittsburgh to Greensburg,Pennsylvania.

Bushy Run was fought in 1763 when Colonel Bouquet won a decisive
victory over the Indians.

After eating we decided not to stay in Greensburg for the
night so we left there about five in the afternoon. We hadn't
gone very far when it started to rain. Thinking it might just
be a shower we rode some distance in the rain. Before long it
was raining hard so we sought shelter in an old, vacant cabin
near the road. We waited hoping to continue on but the rain did
not stop so we decided to spend the night there. It was a spooky
place but we had no choice so we decided to make the most of it.

We were soon rolled up in our blankets on the hard floor.
We listened to the rain for a long time while we talked about
the events of the last few days. Our night in the Pittsburgh
Jail was still fresh in our minds but now that it was behind us,
we were glad that we had that experience.

All went well until about three in the morning when we were
awakened by a noise in the cabin. We were a little startled but
soon found out it was a couple of small animals running around in
the cabin.We were quite willing to share the cabin with our visitors but it was some time before we got back to sleep. No more
excitement during the night and we had a good sleep.

The 29th Day    (Cont.)

Pittsburgh to Greensburg, Pennsylvania.

PENNSYLVANIA RUBBER CO.
AT JEANNETTE, PENNSYLVANIA

A U.S. MINE RESCUE TRUCK
IN THE COAL FIELDS OF WESTERN PENNSYLVANIA

CHAPTER THREE

CHICAGO,ILLINOIS TO PHILADELPHIA,PENNSYLVANIA.

July 27th,1915   The 30th Day    (Tuesday)

East of Greensburg to Laughlintown,Pennsylvania.

When we woke up in the morning it was still raining but we
decided to be on our way anyway. We were anxious to leave our
not too pleasant surroundings during the night.

Since leaving Pittsburgh and until we got to Philadelphia
we were on the Pennsylvania Turnpike almost all the way. This was
one of the better roads so far but as much of it was surfaced
with loose rock macadam, it was hard on our tires, and we had
many punctures and tire blowouts. Even so, it was nice to get away
from the mud and water for a change.

It soon stopped rain-
ing and on the way we visited a small coal mine near
the road. This was a "one
man" operation, the owner
took us into the adit and
showed us the coal forma-
tion and explained much
about coal mining. Hap took

STRIP MINING
IN THE COAL FIELDS

a picture of the mine entrance with the miner,his assistant and
me in front of the adit.

The road was fairly level for the next few miles and we saw
several strip mines and gas wells along the way. The road was
mostly loose macadam and was pretty rough on our tires. The rest

## CHAPTER THREE

The 30th Day    (Cont.)

East of Greensburg to Laughlintown,Pennsylvania.

of the way to Ligonier the road followed the Loyalhanna Creek so
it was fairly level with no hills that we couldn't negotiate. It
was about nine miles to Ligonier and we made good time.

Ligonier was a mining and farming community and was named
for an early fort located
there. In the city park
was a small monument with
the history of the fort. I
took a picture of it and
after selling a few cards
in the business district
we were on our way.

Three miles beyond
this town was Laughlintown
a small farming community
at the base of Laurel Hill
mountain. Ahead of us now
were the Allegheny Moun-
tains. Hap had a tire puncture as we entered the town
and while he was repairing

We visit a coal mine

it, the rain started falling so we decided to camp there for the
night. We found a good place to camp and then went out to eat.
While at the restaurant other customers bought several cards and
this paid for the meal. The rain continued so we went to bed.

The 30th Day    (Cont.)

East of Greensburg to Laughlintown, Pennsylvania.

FORT LIGONIER MONUMENT

COURT HOUSE GREENSBURG, PENNSYLVANIA

## CHAPTER THREE

### CHICAGO,ILLINOIS TO PHILADELPHIA,PENNSYLVANIA.

THE  PHILADELPHIA  AND  PITTSBURGH  TURNPIKE
THIS WAS THE ROAD WE USED
ACROSS PENNSYLVANIA

CHAPTER THREE

CHICAGO,ILLINOIS TO PHILADELPHIA,PENNSYLVANIA.

July 28th,1915   The 31st Day   (Wednesday)

Laughlintown to Kantner,Pennsylvania.

When we got up it was still raining so we dressed and went out for breakfast. had a good hot meal of oatmeal, toast and coffee. We visited with several people while we waited out the rain.

It cleared up late in the morning so we packed up and started our journey across the Allegheny Mountains. The elevation at Laughlintown was about 1,300 feet and the summit of the first ridge was at an elevation of 2,681 feet. This was called Laurel Hill Mountain. It was uphill all the way and we had to walk and push our bikes the five or six miles to the top. The road was surfaced with loose rock and this coupled with the single speed bikes made it out of the question to ride up the slope.

The view from the top was beautiful, overlooking the valleys both sides of the ridge. We rested for awhile after our long uphill walk while we enjoyed the scenery. From the summit it was downhill all the way to Jennerstown, about $3\frac{1}{2}$ miles. Because of the steep grade we had to use our coaster brakes nearly all the time. Every mile or so we had to pull off the road and stop and let the brakes cool off.

From Jennerstown to Stoystown the road was fairly level and we made good time. There were wildcats and some bears in this county but so far we hadn't encountered any.

It was getting late so we decided to call it off for the day.

CHAPTER THREE

The 31st Day     (Cont.)

Laughlintown to Kantner,Pennsylvania.

In looking for a place to camp, some mountain people living in the neighboring town of Kantner gave us permission to camp in their yard. We set up our tent and went out for a bite to eat.

In the evening after a pleasant visit with these friendly people we went to bed.

CHILDREN
WHERE WE SPENT THE NIGHT
KANTNER,PENNSYLVANIA

CHAPTER THREE

CHICAGO,ILLINOIS TO PHILADELPHIA,PENNSYLVANIA

July 29th,1915    The 32nd Day    (Thursday)

Kantner to the Top of a Mountain in Pennsylvania.

In the morning we were invited in for breakfast. We gladly accepted and had a very good meal of bacon and eggs, toast and coffee. It started to rain, so after our meal we sat out on the porch and discussed our plans for the day.

Hap said, if it stops raining lets make it to the next ridge and camp there. We decided it would be an interesting experience to sleep on top of a mountain. So, when the rain stopped and it looked like it was going to be a nice day, we decided to do just that.

We thanked the people and I took a picture of their five children. The first order of business was to get food to take along to last us for the balance of the day and for breakfast the following morning.

We got started about 11 A.M. It was all uphill to the summit of this ridge of the Allegheny Mountains. We had to walk and push the bikes most of the 10 or 11 miles to the summit and we were pretty tired when we got there.

We were near a lookout called "Grand View" and it was indeed a grand view. We could see for vast distances of the country below us. After a good rest we pitched our tent and cooked our evening meal.

We spent the evening enjoying the beautiful surroundings. When it was time to go to bed, we chained our bikes to a tree, put our lunches on top of the saddles, and were soon fast asleep,

CHAPTER THREE

The 32nd Day      (Cont.)

Kantner to the Top of a Mountain in Pennsylvania.

aided by the cool, fresh mountain air.

About 3 A.M. we were awakened by a commotion outside the
tent. We looked out just in time to see a large animal,probably
a bear or a wildcat, departing with our breakfast. It was dark
so we couldn't tell what it was, but of course not being armed,
except for a small hand axe, we didnt want to tangle with whatever it was. We went back to bed and felt lucky that the encoun-
ter turned out no worse than it did. It was a long time before we
went back to sleep.

"GRAND VIEW"
ALLEGHENY MOUNTAINS

CHAPTER THREE

CHICAGO,ILLINOIS TO PHILADELPHIA,PENNSYLVANIA.

July 30th,1915     The 33rd Day     (Friday)

Mountain Top to Everett,Pennsylvania.

We were up at daybreak as it was rather cold on the mountain. We wanted to get out of there before we had another visitor.

It was about 6 miles down the east side of the ridge and I let the bike go full speed where it was safe to do so. We reached the base near Schellsburg, where we stopped for our postponed breakfast. After selling a few cards we were on our way. Shortly after leaving this town we each had a tire blowout and two more before reaching Bedford, resulting in considerable delay. We spent some time in Bedford and saw some places of historical interest, including Washington's headquarters when, in 1794 he was here in connection with the Whiskey Insurrection.

Bedford was a small town on the Raystown branch of the Juniata River. It is situated in a beautiful valley at an elevation of about 1,000 feet, in the heart of the Allegheny Mountains. Washington's headquarters as well as other early buildings were still standing.

We sold a few cards, visited with the local people and were soon on our way. The road was fairly  level except for one hill but we were able to ride over it without any trouble. We had not gone very far when we each had another tire blowout, making six in all for the day. Our tires were in terrible shape and the

## CHAPTER THREE

The 33rd Day    (Cont.)

Mountain Top to Everett,Pennsylvania.

casings were taped in many places. We did not have the money to buy new tires and were wondering just how far we would get with the tires.

It started to rain just before reaching Everett so we decided to camp there for the night.

Everett was on the Juniata River with mountains each side. There were many coal mines and quarries in the vicinity.

IN THE MOUNTAINS OF SOUTHERN PENNSYLVANIA

CHAPTER THREE

CHICAGO,ILLINOIS TO PHILADELPHIA,PENNSYLVANIA

July 31st,1915   The 34th Day   (Saturday)

Everett to McConnellsburg,Pennsylvania.

We took the tent down and packed our gear on the bikes and went looking for a place to eat. We didn't find a restaurant open so early in the day so decided to eat later at some town on the way.

Beyond Everett the road continued to follow the Raystown Branch of the Juniata River. The road was fairly level in the valley of the river and we enjoyed the scenery along the way. About six miles east of Everett we crossed the river at Juniata Crossing.

From there the road swung north away from the river and was ascending on a fairly steep grade to the summit of Rays Hill, a distance of about three miles. We had to walk all the way to the top and I had a tire blowout about that time.

From there the road continued up about three miles to the summit of Sideling Hill. This part of the road was not too steep and we rode part of the way to the top. On the way up we passed Bald Knob on the right and with mountains all around us the scenery was beautiful.

It was down hill from the summit to Harrisonville and on the way we passed through timber country for part of the way. At Harrisonville we stopped for our late breakfast which we combined with our noon day lunch.

We sold a few cards in the business district and as it was

## CHAPTER THREE

The 34th Day      (Cont.)

Everett to McConnellsburg, Pennsylvania.

beginning to rain, we hurried on our way. From Harrisonville
the road was on a steep ascending grade and we had to walk the
2½ miles to the summit of Scrub Ridge. From there it was fairly
level to the next ridge, called Little Scrub Ridge.

About the time we crossed the above ridge the rain increased
but we kept going as we wanted to get to McConnellsburg for the
night, as it was not very far to the town.

We arrived in McConnellsburg about 6 P.M. in the rain. We
sought shelter and when the rain stopped about 7 P.M. we put up
our tent and went out to eat, after which we went to bed as we
were tired after our long uphill walks.

McConnellsburg was a small town, founded in the 1700's and
never grew very much. It is located in a valley west of Tuscarora
Mountain of the Appalachian Mountains.

A BEAUTIFUL STREAM
IN SOUTHERN PENNSYLVANIA

CHAPTER THREE

CHICAGO,ILLINOIS TO PHILADELPHIA,PENNSYLVANIA

August 1st,1915   The 35th Day   (Sunday)

McConnellsburg to Chambersburg,Pennsylvania.

We left McConnellsburg about 9 A.M. after cooking our breakfast at the camp site. From there the road was a steep grade up,
with many curves, to the summit of Tuscarora Mountain. We walked
and pushed the bikes the 3½ miles to the top.

The summit was in the Tuscarora State Forest and the view
from there of the timber, the valleys to the west and McConnellsburg way below was a sight to behold.

The road swung north from there to the crossing of Cove
Mountain at Cape Horn. There was a slight down grade on this
section of the road so riding was no problem.

From there the road descended on a steep grade and we had
to make a stop on the way to cool off our coaster brakes. At
the bottom of the grade we came to the town of Fort Loudon where
we stopped to rest.

Fort Loudon was a farming community in the valley below
Tuscarora Mountain. To the north was Kittatinny Mountain and to
the south was fairly level country. The town is located on the
West Branch of Conococheague Creek.

From there the road ran southeast to clear Broad and Front
Mountains, the road being fairly level, the riding was easy.
However, the loose rock road was hard on our tires and we each
had two tire blowouts during the day causing considerable delay.

CHAPTER THREE

The 35th Day    (Cont.)

McConnellsburg to Chambersburg, Pennsylvania.

Shortly after leaving Fort Loudon it started to rain but as it was a light rain we kept going. We soon passed the village of Saint Thomas and from there to Chambersburg the road was fairly level and we made good time, except when we stopped to repair the tires.

It stopped raining on the way and we reached Chambersburg late in the afternoon and decided to spend the night there. We knew that we had to do something about our tires and this would give Hap a chance to work on them. The rear tires were in the worst condition as they bore the brunt of the riding. Hap decided that the thing to do was to put the front tires on the rear and the rear tires on the front. After finding a camp site he reversed the tires, we cooked our evening meal, walked around the town and sold a few cards, then went to bed.

Chambersburg was somewhat larger then the towns we had been in recently. It is located in the peach and apple district of the Cumberland Valley. There was some industrial activity in the town. John Brown had his headquarters here many years before.

### CHAPTER THREE

CHICAGO,ILLINOIS TO PHILADELPHIA, PENNSYLVANIA

August 2nd,1915   The 36th Day    (Monday)

Chambersburg to Gettysburg,Pennsylvania.

When we got up in the morning it looked like rain so we packed up in a hurry and went out for breakfast. We had high hopes that our reversed tires would stand up for awhile.

Gettysburg was one of the "must see" places on the trip so we left as soon as possible as we were anxious to get there.

The road was on a slight upgrade but we were able to ride without difficulty. We soon passed Stoufferstown and then the town of Fayetteville.

Beyond this town we went through a pass in South Mountain, following the Conococheague Creek bed. We followed the creek, which had mountains on both sides, to Caledonia Park. At this point we left the creek bed and headed for the main pass through South Mountain. It was only about a mile to the summit but we had to walk part of the way.

From this point it was down grade, we were following various stream or creek beds. We passed various hills and mountains both sides of the road and reached Cashtown after going to the south of Rock Top, a hill alongside the road.

Cashtown was an agricultural village. A man told us a story about how the town got the name Cashtown. It seems there was a tavern keeper there in the early days who always insisted that the patron pay cash, so the town came to be known as Cashtown.

## CHAPTER THREE

The 36th Day    (Cont.)

Chambersburg to Gettysburg, Pennsylvania.

The road continued on a slight down grade as we passed through McKnightstown and Seven Stars. We reached Gettysburg late in the afternoon in a shower that didnt last long.

The Allegheny and Appalachian Mountains were now behind us and we looked forward to a little easier time from here to Philadelphia.

We found a place to camp and as we planned to spend the next day at the battle field, we would be here two nights.


Between Chambersburg and Gettysburg we rode over the same road used by Confederate General Lee's forces prior to the battle of Gettysburg. After the battle Lee retreated with part of his army on this road as far as Greenwood where he turned South. In doing so he left his rear guard defending the passes of South Mountain to hinder pursuit of the Union Army.

CHAPTER THREE

CHICAGO,ILLINOIS TO PHILADELPHIA,PENNSYLVANIA

August 3rd,1915   The 37th Day   (Tuesday)

At The Gettysburg National Military Park.

We had an early breakfast as we were very anxious to see the Battlefield of Gettysburg. I had been looking forward to this for sometime so we lost no time and rode our bikes out there.

We were very much impressed with the National Military Park. There were monuments, statues and markers everywhere, including many Civil War cannons. All the points of interest in connection with the battle were well marked and an excellent picture of what happened could be gained from the inscriptions on them. We had our picture taken in front of the equestrian statue of Major General John F.Reynolds of the Union Army who was killed during the battle.

MAJOR GENERAL
JOHN F. REYNOLDS

We stood at the place where Pickett's charge was turned back. The failure of Pickett here and his retreat has been called "The High Water Mark" of the rebellion. Had he succeeded the whole course of the war might have been changed.

Pickett's division lost over three fourths of the men, 3,393 officers and men out of 4,800 were

CHAPTER THREE

The 37th Day     (Cont.)

At The Gettysburg National Military Park.

left on the field. Two of his three brigadiers were killed and
one wounded and of fifteen regimental commanders, ten were killed
and five wounded. One regiment lost ninety per cent of it's men.
The failure of the charge virtually ended the three day battle.

We visited the National Cemetary where 3,654 Union soldiers
are buried. We stood at the spot where President Abraham Lincoln
delivered his famous Gettysburg Address in November, 1863. We
were very proud and happy to actually be where his speech was
made. We remembered the speech well, from school, with its beginning with "Four score and seven years ago" etc.

It is one thing to read about these things in school and
another thing, far more interesting to actually visit the places.

We visited the Cyclorama building adjacent to the cemetary
to see the painting "The Battle of Gettysburg".The building interior was circular and around the entire circumference of the
interior was this great painting in an elevated position on the
wall. When standing in the center of the room, one could follow
the progress of the battle and it was a very wonderful experience.
The painting was considered the largest and finest war painting
in the world.

We visited Devil's Den opposite Little Round Top. The Union
Army first held it but later it came into possession of the Confederates.

## CHAPTER THREE

The 37th Day      (Cont.)

At The Gettysburg National Military Park.

Numerous comet shaped marks still showed on the rocks, indicating
where bullets struck.

We stopped to see the statue of General Buford and the monument of Hall's second Maine Battery as well as many other monuments and markers. The cannon in front of General Buford's
statue fired the first shot of the battle.

We had done a lot of walking around the battlefield and as
it was getting late we went back to Gettysburg and set up camp
for the night. After going to bed we talked about the events of
the day for a long time.

THE SOLDIERS' NATIONAL CEMETARY
N.M.P.*.GETTYSBURG,PENNSYLVANIA

CHAPTER THREE

The 37th Day     (Cont.)

At The Gettysburg National Military Park

THE HIGH WATER MARK

A PORTION OF CYCLORAMA
"THE BATTLE OF GETTYSBURG"

## CHAPTER THREE

The 37th Day    (Cont.)        ___

At The Gettysburg National Military Park.


### THE BATTLE OF GETTYSBURG

The battle lasted three days       July 1st, 2nd and 3rd, 1863


30,000 Confederate forces killed, wounded or missing

23,000 Union forces killed, wounded or missing


75,000 Confederate and 82,000 Union forces in the battle


After the battle the Confederates under General Robert E. Lee retreated to Virginia thus ending their invasion of Pennsylvania.

CHAPTER THREE

CHICAGO,ILLINOIS TO PHILADELPHIA,PENNSYLVANIA

August 4th,1915   The 38th Day    (Wednesday)

Gettysburg to Lancaster,Pennsylvania.

We were up early and after packing our gear on the bikes, we went to a restaurant for a good breakfast. We went out to the battlefield for one last look and then headed out for Lancaster.

We hadn't gone very far when my rear tire blew out and a short time later the same happened to Hap's rear tire. Hap repaired and we were again on our way.

We stopped at New Oxford and sold a few cards and then continued on to Abbottstown. Just before reaching the town it started to rain so we decided to stop there for lunch while we were waiting out the rain.

It soon cleared up so we were once more on our way.Since leaving McConnellsburg we have been riding through the country overrun by Lee's army when they invaded Pennsylvania, prior to the battle of Gettysburg. According to the accounts of the invasion, the Confederates plundered the surrounding country of foodstuff, cattle, horses and anything else the army could use.

General Lee insisted that the people be reimbursed for what was taken by force. The record states that this was not always done and in many cases was paid for with Confederate currency which was more or less worthless. Some of the men paid with so-called "shin plasters" issued by the city of Richmond and they were absolutely of no value.

CHAPTER THREE

The 38th Day     (Cont.)

Gettysburg to Lancaster,Pennsylvania.

Hap had another tire blowout and I had the same trouble just before we reached West York. Our tires were just about "shot" and as we didn't have the money to buy new ones we were in serious trouble.

When we got to York it started to rain again so we waited there. We went to the Harley Davidson dealer's store and told the man of our troubles. He said he would trust each of us for a tire and we could pay for them when we reached home. I said to him, "dont you want to know our names and where we lived". He said "no, I will trust you for them".

Once again, like so many times before, we were saved from a serious situation by the kindness of people along the way and we were very thankful for the help he had so gladly given. I am not sure but I think his name was J.P.Wolf and his place of bus-iness was at 411 South Market Street.

It soon stopped raining and after Hap put on the new tires' we went on our way, feeling greatly relieved now that we had good tires on the rear.


YORK,PENNSYLVANIA

York was a fairly large city, it was laid out in the middle of the 18th century. There was a large Farmers' Market on the corner of Market and Penn Streets. There were many wagons and a few cars bringing in and taking out market products.

CHAPTER THREE

The 38th Day     (Cont.)

Gettysburg to Lancaster,Pennsylvania.

The city is located in a rich agricultural area and had
some manufacturing plants located there. York was the National
Capital from 1777 to the middle of 1778. Franklin did his print-
ing of Continental money in York about the time of the revolution. The headquarter's building used by General Anthony Wayne
while recruiting his force for the march on Yorktown, still
stood in the heart of the city.

Many of the downtown streets had names like King, Queen,
Duke, Princess, etc.

Farmers' Market, Corner Market and
Penn Streets, York, Pa.

FARMERS' MARKET
YORK, PENNSYLVANIA

CHAPTER THREE

The 38th Day     (Cont.)

Gettysburg to Lancaster,Pennsylvania.

We were in high spirits as we rode fast toward Lancaster, the going was easy after our long trip across the mountains. We stopped at Wrightsville and sold a few cards. At Columbia we crossed the Susquehanna River on a toll bridge. The river was very wide at this point and the scenery was beautiful.

The Susquehanna River was about as far east as General Lee got when he invaded Pennsylvania during the Civil War.

We sold a few cards at Columbia and were soon on our way again. We reached Lancaster in the afternoon and decided to spend the night there.

In talking to a man we met on the street, he offered to let us sleep in a large livery stable and of course we accepted the opportunity to get in out of the weather. We put our bikes and

PENNSYLVANIA R.R. STATION
LANCASTER,PENNSYLVANIA

CHAPTER THREE

The 38th Day     (Cont.)

Gettysburg to Lancaster,Pennsylvania.

gear in the stable and went out to eat.

After our meal we walked down North Queen Street which was
one of the main business streets. There were many horses and
wagons and a few autos on the street. In walking around the city
we came to an outdoor dog and pony show. We stopped to watch it
as it was very interesting. One of the acts consisted of a high
platform 30 or 40 feet high with a large container of water
below. A man started a small dog up the steps leading to the platform. The dog didn't seem very anxious to go up but with a little
prodding, he made it.

The dog was supposed to jump into the tub of water but it
had other ideas. The dog just stood on the platform instead of
jumping, in spite of a lot of coaxing. Finally after a long time
he made the jump much to the amusement of the crowd.

While we were standing there, one of the actors in the show
came up to us and in a loud voice so all could hear, told us
that if anything went wrong, we should wire him collect and he
would send us all the money we needed. He lived in New York City,
gave us his address there, and said if we would look him up when
we got to New York he would take us for a ride to see the city.

We went back to the stable after an enjoyable evening. We
slept on a raised platform at one end of the stable. It was not
very comfortable but we were glad to be in, out of the weather
as it looked like it was due for another rainstorm. There must
have been 40 or 50 horses in the stable but in spite of the

CHAPTER THREE

The 38th Day    (Cont.)

Gettysburg to Lancaster, Pennsylvania.

strong odor of the horses and the constant swishing of their
tails, we soon fell asleep.

LANCASTER AND THIS PART OF PENNSYLVANIA

From York east we were in the so-called "Pennsylvania
Dutch" country. The farms were well maintained and they usually
had fine large barns, painted red as a rule and many had
painted decorations of horses, stars or lilies, etc.

The area east of York and around Lancaster was settled
largely by Quakers, Mennonites, Dunkards and Amish. For the
most part they still used their horse drawn wagons and buggies.

There were many of these people on the streets with their
black beards and large black broad brimmed hats. The women wore
bonnets and long, full skirts.

Lancaster is located in a rich farming area and there were
some manufacturing plants in the city.

The "Pennsylvania Dutch" country is bounded by Philadelphia
on the east, York on the west and Bethlehem on the north. The
colony was founded by Wm. Penn as an asylum for persecuted
people from all lands.

CHAPTER THREE

CHICAGO,ILLINOIS TO PHILADELPHIA,PENNSYLVANIA

August 5th,1915   The 39th Day   (Thursday)

Lancaster to Philadelphia,Pennsylvania.

We were up at the crack of dawn and were soon ready to leave without breakfast. We were glad to get out of the stable as the odor was terrific, but nevertheless we appreciated the accommodations as it rained during the night. It was drizzling in the morning but we started out anyway.

We hoped to reach Philadelphia by nightfall some seventy miles away. We rode through several towns, Bridgeport, Peradise, Coatesville and Paoli. We stopped a short time at some of them and had breakfast along the way. We came to a long detour where they were surfacing the road with 2" crushed rock. We decided not to take the long, roundabout detour, but to get through on the closed road. Of course we couldn't ride on the loose rock surface so we rode at the side of the road in the grass where we could and where we couldn't we walked. Valley Forge was only a few miles off our course so we decided to go over there.

We wanted to see the place where George Washington and his men spent that bitter cold winter during the Revolutionary War. It was well worth seeing but we didn't tarry long as we were still some distance from Philadelphia.

We rode through Wayne and then passed Villanova College and beyond we passed Bryn Mawr College, and at Haverford we saw Haverford College. We next went through Ardmore and reached downtown Philadelphia at 6 P.M. tired and hungry. We had made

CHAPTER THREE

The 39th Day    (Cont.)

Lancaster to Philadelphia,Pennsylvania.

better than 70 miles during the day, the roads were good except
for the detour and the country was fairly level.

We put our bikes in a garage and obtained a room at the
Keystone Hotel at 75¢ a night. The first order of business was
to take a shower with good hot water. We felt a lot better afterwards so we went down to the coffee shop in the hotel for our
evening meal. In the evening we walked around the downtown area
and had no trouble selling cards. The people were very friendly

KEYSTONE HOTEL

M. BOYLE       RESTAURANT AND CAFE ATTACHED        A. SWEENEY

European Plan                    Rates, 75c. to $1.50 per Day

KEYSTONE HOTEL
1524-42 MARKET STREET

PHILADELPHIA, PA.

Situated in the heart of the Business and Shopping District
Opposite Broad St. Station and three Squares from Reading Terminal
(Over)

and were very much interested in the trip.

We went back to the hotel and I wrote a long letter to my
Mother telling her about our experiences crossing the state. I
mentioned that it had rained all or part of every day while in
Pennsylvania.

When we reached Philadelphia we had traveled 1,485 miles
since leaving Saint Paul,Minnesota.

## CHAPTER THREE

### CHICAGO,ILLINOIS TO PHILADELPHIA,PENNSYLVANIA.

August 6th,1915   The 40th Day   (Friday)

At Philadelphia,Pennsylvania.

We were up early as this was to be a full day of sightseeing. We each took a hot shower and as we had a good nights sleep
in our warm, comfortable bed, we were ready for our days adventure.

We went to Cox's restaurant where we had a good, hot breakfast. Our meal consisted of a large bowl of oatmeal with cream,
toast and coffee. All this cost us 15¢ each and was well worth it.

We were soon on our way and the first stop was Independence
Hall. This was a colonial type building constructed of red brick.
It was originally the State House of Pennsylvania and was built

during the 1730's. It was here that the Constitution of the
United States was framed, also the Declaration of Independence
was adopted and the Articles of Confederation were ratified
here. Washington received command of the Continental Army in this
building. The building has a tower and beautiful interior wood-
work.

CHAPTER THREE

The 40th Day     (Cont.)

At Philadelphia,Pennsylvania.

Also in the building were many important historical documents, other relics including portraits of statesmen and other
patriots. This building housed the Liberty Bell and that was
what we most wanted to see. The cracked bell was mounted on a
wooden support and was just like we pictured it from reading
about it in school.

After our very interesting and rewarding visit to Independence Hall we stopped at the old city hall for a short visit.
While there we looked at many relics in this old building which
was built in 1791. We visited Carpenter's Hall where we saw many

historical exhibits. We
then continued on our way
to the Betsy Ross House
where Betsy Ross designed
the American Flag as now
used.

While visiting this
place, they told us that if
we sold ten memberships in
the Betsy Ross Memorial
Association at 25¢ each
they would send each one of
us a certificate with the
picture of "THE BIRTH OF
OUR NATION'S FLAG" ON IT.

Liberty Bell, Philadelphia, Pa.

THE LIBERTY BELL

CHAPTER THREE

The 40th Day      (Cont.)

At Philadelphia,Pennsylvania.

They said that if I did this they would send me a large
picture of the above. When I got home I took care of it and the
large picture they sent, about 22" x 26" is now hanging on our
living room wall.

It was past noon by now so we walked down Market Street to
the City Hall. This was the tallest  building in Philadelphia

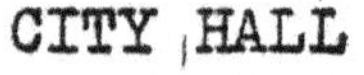

CITY HALL

MARKET STREET

STATUE OF WM. PENN
TOP OF CITY HALL

and at the top of the tower was a statue of Wm. Penn and in the
tower were clocks facing four ways. It was a beautiful building
and was located in Penn Square with plenty of open space around
it. We visited the Pennsylvania R.R. Broad st station and as it
was getting late in the afternoon we went back to the hotel to
rest up before eating our evening meal.

After eating a good 20¢ dinner we went down to the main business district to try to sell some cards. A crowd collected and
the cards went like hot cakes. People lined up to buy them and
as usual they were very friendly in the "City of Brotherly Love"
The crowd got larger and larger, in fact before long half the
street was blocked by the huge crowd. We kept on selling cards and

CHAPTER THREE

The 40th Day  (Cont.)   At Philadelphia,Pennsylvania.

about this time a policeman came up and asked us in a very polite

manner if we would move on, as the crowd was interfering with

the traffic on the street.

We decided to go back to the hotel and take advantage of

our hotel rooms, no telling how long it would be before we again

had such a nice place to sleep. We counted our money and found

that we each had $3.50, this was more money than we had at any

one time on the entire trip so far. We figured we had enough

money to see us through the four days we planned to stay in

New York City. We then went to bed, very well pleased with the

kind treatment we had received in Philadelphia.

THE BIRTH OF OUR NATION'S FLAG.

END OF CHAPTER THREE

CHAPTER FOUR

PHILADELPHIA TO NEW YORK CITY AND BOSTON,MASSACHUSETTS.

August 7th,1915   The 41st day   (Saturday)

Philadelphia to Langhorne,Pennsylvania.

After a good nights sleep, a hot shower and a good fifteen cent breakfast we were ready for the activities of the day.

Hap was very much interested in the making of motion pictures so we rode our bikes out to the Studio of the Lubin Motion Picture Company. They invited us in and said that we could watch them film an interior scene they were taking for a movie. We were in the room with the camera and could see all that was going on. The setting for the picture they were taking was a living room and the actor, Jack Standing, had just told his wife, actress Mary Charleson that he was leaving her.

BEN. FRANKLIN'S GRAVE

She was supposed to start to cry, so they "rolled it" but she was unable to make the tears come so they stopped. In a few minutes they tried again but still no tears. The director said we'll take a break for awhile.

Mary Charleson did came over to where we were standing, she was very friendly and asked all about our trip. Needless to say we were thrilled to get to talk to a real live motion picture star.

MARY CHARLESON

A man then took us around the studio and showed us many things used in connection with taking movies.

CHAPTER FOUR

The 41st Day     (Cont.)

Philadelphia to Langhorne, Pennsylvania.

After our interesting visit at the studio we went back to
the hotel for lunch, then went out to do some more looking
around the business district. We visited with a
number of friendly people and sold a few cards.

It was late in the afternoon when we left
Philadelphia. There were two roads to Trenton,
New Jersey, the longer one was by way of Camden.
The shorter road was by way of the old York road
so we took the shorter one.

BROAD STREET
P.R.R.STATION

We passed the toll gate about seven miles
out. I do not remember how much the toll was but I am sure that
it wasn't much for a bicycle. We did not stop at Ogantz and
just before reaching Fox Chase we passed the other toll gate. So
far the roads this close to Philadelphia were in good shape
(oiled macadam) but as usual one lane in each direction and
without center markings. We did not stop at Fox Chase but continued on to Bustleton where we stopped for a rest and to sell
some cards.

We went through Janney Station and it was rather late when
we reached Langhorne so decided to camp there for the night.

After getting something to eat at a restaurant we asked at
a house if we could camp in the yard; the man of the house,
Harry McHale said we could. That part of the yard where we put
up the tent was low which would have been fine except for the

## CHAPTER FOUR

The 41st Day    (Cont.)

Philadelphia to Langhorne, Pennsylvania.

fact that about ten o'clock it started to rain hard. A regular stream of water was running through the tent and the blankets got soaking wet. Mr.McHale came out and when he saw what was happening invited us to sleep on his front porch. We welcomed the opportunity and had a good nights sleep protected from the rain. However the wet blankets were not too comfortable.

A GOOD ROAD
BETWEEN PHILADELPHIA AND LANGHORNE, Penn.

THE HARRY McHALE FAMILY
LANGHORNE, PENNSYLVANIA

CHAPTER FOUR

PHILADELPHIA TO NEW YORK CITY AND BOSTON,MASSACHUSETTS.

August 8th,1915    The 42nd Day    (Sunday)

Langhorne,Penn. to Franklin Park,New Jersey.

The McHales woke us early and invited us for breakfast.
After washing up with all the comforts of home, we sat down to
a hearty meal. We enjoyed the meal immensely, we really appreciated a home cooked meal for a change. After our meal we had
a nice visit with these people.

I took a picture of Mr. and Mrs. McHale and their three
children. They were sitting on the porch where we had spent
the night protected from the rain. We packed up our wet gear
and after thanking these people for their kindness, we said
good-by and were on our way.

We rode through Glen Lake Station, Oxford Valley and soon
reached the Delaware River which was only about ten miles from
Langhorne. We crossed the river on the Calhoun Street bridge to
Trenton. We had now entered New Jersey, the seventh state on
our journey.

Where we crossed the river was only about eight miles
south of the place where General Washington cressed it on
Christmas night in 1776 prior to the battle of Trenton. This
was interesting as I had seen the famous painting entitled,
"Washington Crossing the Delaware."

We rode past the New Jersey State Capitol but didn't
stop, it being Sunday and the building was not open to the
public.

CHAPTER FOUR

The 42nd Day      (Cont.)

Langhorne,Penn. to Franklin Park,New Jersey.

While in the main part of the city we visited the Battle Monument which is a 155 foot shaft with a statue of George Washington on top. At the base of the shaft are three bronze bas-
reliefs picturing, "The Crossing of the Delaware' "The beginning of the Fight", "The Surrender of the Hessians".

This monument commemorates the Battles of
Trenton and Princeton. Washington, by a series
of bold maneuvers, including the crossing of
the Delaware River, surprised the Hessian
Troops at Trenton. As a result nearly a thous-
and Hessians surrendered. When a large force
of British Troops arrived, Washington

BATTLE MONUMENT

secretly moved his army back to Princeton at night, overcame
the resistance there, and moved his army to Morristown, where
he was in an advantageous position.

Trenton is the Capital of New Jersey and at the time we
were there had a population of about 100,000. There were many
other things of interest to see in Trenton but we did not tarry
long because we were excited about being so close to New York
City and soon left the city.

Beyond Trenton were two roads leading to New Brunswick,
both roads were macadam, so we took the shorter one by way of
Princeton. The loose rock was hard on the tires and we each had

CHAPTER FOUR

The 42nd Day      (Cont.)

Langhorne,Penn. to Franklin Park,New Jersey.

a puncture along the way. We stopped at Princeton to see
Princeton University with it's beautiful Campus. One of the
interesting sights there was Nassau Hall but of course we only
saw it from the outside. We were anxious to be on our way so
did not stop there very long.

It was early evening when we reached Franklin Park, what
with the delays due to the punctures and some rain. We decided
to spend the night there and found a private home where we
rented a room for the night. We had our evening meal and went
back to our room and got ready for bed. We made about 33 miles
during the day.

We were too excited to go to sleep for a long time. We
expected to reach New York City the following day as it was
only about 40 miles away.

CHAPTER FOUR

PHILADELPHIA TO NEW YORK CITY AND BOSTON,MASSACHUSETTS.

August 9th,1915   The 43rd Day   (Monday)

Franklin Park, New Jersey to New York City,New York.

I woke up early but Hap was still asleep so I woke him at once. I said, let's get started as we were only 40 miles from the city so many people said we would never reach.

We hurried with our preparations to leave as we were very excited about the prospect of reaching New York City that day. Our first stop was New Brunswick where we had a good breakfast at the Home Lunch, 54 Albany Street. Later we sold a few cards in the business district.

We rode through Metuchen and stopped at Rahway where we sold a few cards and visited with people we met on the street. We didn't spend much time there as we were anxious to be on our way. We reached Elizabeth about noon so had our lunch and had no trouble selling cards during the noon hour.

Elizabeth was a large city of about 100,000 population, the county seat of Union county. The city is located on Newark Bay opposite Staten Island. There was much manufacturing there in- cluding the Singer Sewing Machine Company as well as ship build- ing yards.

Our next stop was Newark which we reached about 1:30 P.M. We were now only about ten or twelve miles from the big city so we stopped to rest a short time before proceeding.

Newark was a city of about 350,000 population,the county

## CHAPTER FOUR

The 43rd Day     (Cont.)

Franklin Park, New Jersey to New York City.

seat of Essex county. It is located on Newark bay and the Passaic
river. Some of the down town streets were very wide, unusual in
an older city. In the business area was a Military park which
was used in colonial days as a drill ground. The park was surrounded by a number of buildings. The city
is a manufacturing center.

We crossed the Passaic river and rode
through Harrison. West of Jersey City we
crossed a bridge with a sign, as follows;
"Drive your Horses not Faster Than a Walk,
Under penalty of the
Law".We rode through
Jersey City Heights
and then to Weehawken.
We took the Ferry to
42nd Street in New
York City. We had now
entered New York,the
eighth state on our

OUR FIRST VIEW
OF THE CITY

BRIDGE WEST OF JERSEY CITY

journey. Since leaving Saint Paul we had traveled 1,587 miles.

We reached the city about 3 P.M. and rode our bikes right
down Broadway in the down town area. People turned to look at
an unusual sight, two bicyclists on Broadway. The Police let us
go without interference and some waved us through.

The 43rd Day     (Cont.)

Franklin Park, New Jersey to New York City

---

**TUESDAY. AUGUST 10. 1915.**                    **ST. PAUL DISPATCH**

## ITOR MAY STOP
## HIPMENTS OF ORE

**Making  His  Decision
s Will Confer With Attor-
ney General Smith.**

**GIVES HIM DISCRETION**

**of Hibbing Tries to Hurry
te Officials Into Announce-
ment of Policy.**

e making a decision as to
r e will prevent mining compa-
om shipping ore from the Hib-
ines until $750,000 in back taxes
d. J. A. O. Preus, state auditor,
fer with Attorney General Lyn-
Smith.

is a big proposition," said Mr.
today. "I want to go carefully
deciding what action may be

r Victor Power, of Hibbing,
Mr. Preus asking if he would
decision today. Mr. Preus tele-
Mr. Power that he must first
with the attorney general.

**tutes Give Auditor Power.**

statutes leave in the hands of
t auditor the question of pre-
removals of structures, stand-
ber or minerals from lands on
a lien for taxes has attached.
n' 2184 of the general statutes
reads in part:

the state auditor has reason to beat any such structure, timber or
will be removed from such trust be-
h taxes have been paid, he may di-
county attorney to bring suit in
the state to enjoin any and all per-
m removing such structure, timber or
therefrom, until such taxes are paid."

**ction Is Not Mandatory.**

r the law it will be for Mr.
o decide whether the state's in-
will be best guarded by enjoin-
removal of ore. It is not man-
th t he proceed in this manner.
ney General Smith is expected
rn from a trip to the western
the state tomorrow. The mat-
be placed in his hands on his
As yet no application for an
ferent from the state's legal depart-
as been asked by Mr. Preus.

## SEED CONTEST GROWS

**Clubs Are Organized to Com-
Cash Prizes Offered by**

L E O N
SCHROE-
DER, 1010 Fair-
mount avenue,
at left, and
Harwood Tem-
ple, 758 Lincoln
avenue, who ar-
rived in New
York yesterday
on a bicycle
trip from St.
Paul.

## TEMPO
## PARK

**Nash Giv
That Th
Service**

Efforts w
ment of par
buildings to
civil service

This assu
ice Examin
Nash head
who issued
nus Norma
porary emp
until the me
civil service
instated.

**Inter**

Mr. Norm
civil service
that of Joh
perintenden
ferent from
by the civil
poration A
man insist
employes i
days, shift
other, and
under the
have been
men.

---

THE WORLD
NEW YORK CITY NEWSPAPER
AUGUST 10,1915

### BOY CYCLISTS RIDE
### HERE FROM ST. PAUL.

**Message to Mayor of City Deliv-
ered Here by Pair After
Long Endeavor.**

Two tired boys came into the office of
The World last night and said that they
had come by bicycle all the way from
St. Paul, Minn. The boys, whose names
are Leon Schrader, eighteen, and Harwood Temple, seventeen, brought with
them a letter from Mayor Winn Powers
of St. Paul, certifying their good
character and the date of departure.

Both are high school students. They
made their way by selling picture postcards, and have supported themselves
in this way altogether, even to the ex-
tent of replacing five tires which were
worn out on the trip.

The journey was made by way of
Madison, Chicago, Pittsburgh and Philadelphia.

The boys claimed to be able to
diagnose the condition of money affairs
in the States through which they passed
by the number of postcards they were
able to dispose of, and by that method
decided that times were very hard in
Indiana.

## ST. PAUL BOYS REACH
## GOTHAM ON YCLES

**Harwood  Temple  and  Leon
Schroeder Ride 1,575 Miles
in Thirty-three Days.**

**PLAN RETURN ON WHEELS**

**Postcards Views of St. Paul Are Sold
to Help Pay Way—Camp Out
Many Nights.**

A telegram received by the Dispatch
today announced the arrival in New
York yesterday afternoon of Harwood
Temple, 758 Lincoln avenue, and Leon
Schroeder, 1010 Fairmont avenue, St.
Paul high school boys, who, starting
here, covered the entire distance on
their bicycles. The telegram reads:
"Arrived in New York 5 P. M. Actual
riding 33 days. Delayed by rains and
tire trouble. Feeling fine. Will return
via Boston and Buffalo." They plan
to journey homeward on their wheels.

**Left St. Paul on June 28.**

Temple and Schroeder left the Court
House at 6 A. M. June 28. They have
covered 1,575 miles in thirty-three days,
averaging fifty miles a day. This is a
good record, considering the time the
boys have taken to visit the big cities.
They rode through La Crosse, Madison,
Janesville, Chicago, Valparaiso, Akron,
Pittsburgh and Philadelphia.

Before leaving St. Paul the boys pro-
cured from Mayor Powers a letter of
introduction "To Whom it May Concern." This "passport" always was
duly acknowledged.

**Camp on Road Many Nights.**

Temple and Schroeder carried their
baggage and equipment on their
wheels, including a tent in which they
camped on the road many nights. Each
carried a knapsack, and on the bars of
each wheel a blanket and raincoat.
With a full outfit of tools they were
able to make repairs.

Pinned to each knapsack was a pen-
ant with the words "St. Paul to New
York." The boys took with them a
supply of 1,000 postcard views of St.
Paul. These they sold at all points on
the way from here to New York at 5
cents each. The proceeds gave the
only money they had except a small
cities along the way newspapers gave
larger towns they lodged at hotels. In
amount they started with. Only in the
them considerable publicity.

CHAPTER FOUR

The 43rd Day     (Cont.)

Franklin Park,New Jersey to New York City

     Our first concern was to find a place to store our bikes
during our stay. There were many things we wanted to see in
New York so we planned to stay in the city four days. We found
Frenchy's bicycle store and arranged to leave the bikes for
$1.00 a day rental.

     The next order of bus-
iness was to find a place
to stay. We were told about
the Mills Hotel on 7th Ave.
and 36th St. We went and secured rooms at 30¢ each per
night. The Mills ho-
tel was similar to
the Y.M.C.A. Hotels
but was privately
owned. The rooms were
small but clean and
comfortable.

     By the time we
got squared away it was time for our first meal in the city. After
eating we went down to see the sights, we visited Times Square,
the heart of the theatrical area as well as Broadway with the
hundreds of flashing signs, marquees and great crowds of people

GUNSMITH and GENERAL MECHANIC — SUNDRIES and REPAIRING

FRENCHY'S BICYCLE STORE

BICYCLES

Agency for Iver-Johnson Bicycles and Motorcycles

308 WEST 39th STREET
NEAR EIGHTH AVENUE        NEW YORK
O. BESAN, Prop.

J  11973
THE MILLS HOTEL
7th Ave. and 36th St., New York
Room No. 1055  EAST.
One Night, 30 Cents
Date, Aug 10 1915  for 2
THIS TICKET MUST BE SHOWN WHEN ASKED FOR
(OVER)

CHAPTER FOUR

The 43rd Day     (Cont.)

Franklin Park,New Jersey to New York City.

hurrying along, not to mention the tall buildings everywhere.

This part of Broadway is known as "The Great White Way".

It was quite a thrill for us to see the lights, the crowds, the many theatres and the tall buildings. While on the street we met a reporter from the New York World newspaper. He asked about the trip and said he would put an article about us in the paper. He said he would put our picture along with the article but unfortunately we did not have one with us. Well anyway we got a write-up in the New York newspaper.

TIMES SQUARE

After our exciting evening we went back to the hotel for a good nights sleep.

It might be of interest to show the cost of a newspaper in 1915. The New York World cost 1¢ in greater New York and Jersey City and 2¢ elsewhere. The subscription rates for a month as follows: Evening and Sunday 75¢, Daily only 30¢.

CHAPTER FOUR

PHILADELPHIA TO NEW YORK CITY AND BOSTON,MASSACHUSETTS.

August 10th,1915    The 44th Day     (Tuesday)

New York City

We were looking forward to a full day of sight-seeing but
first we had some business to attend to. After
breakfast we went to the Mayor's office in the
Municipal Building. It was a beautiful structure
of 34 stories, 580 feet high, including a 30 foot
statue of Miss.Civic Pride on top, the largest
building of its kind in the world.

We presented our letter from the Mayor of
St.Paul and asked if they would give us a letter
stating that we had called on the Mayor. They agreed to do so
and presented us with
a nice letter complete
with gold seal and red
ribbons.

We went to the top
of the building where
we could get a beauti-
ful view of the city with its many tall
buildings. While there I took a picture of
the Brooklin Bridge far below.

MUNICIPAL
BUILDING

BROOKLYN BRIDGE
FROM TOP OF MUNICIPAL BUILDING

We then walked down to the Grand Central Terminal Station. This terminal cov-
ered 69.8 acres, the largest and most costly railroad station

GRAND CENTRAL
R. R. STATION

CHAPTER FOUR

The 44th Day    (Cont.)

New York City

in the world. It had 31 miles of tracks under cover, with a
capacity for handling 200 trains and 70,000 passengers each
hour.

While at the station we each sent a telegram home, advising our relatives and the St.Paul newspaper of our arrival
in New York City. We told them that we were behind schedule
due to so much rain, so much tire trouble, and so many poor
roads.

My Mother wanted us to call on her cousin, the Reverend
Charles H. Parkhurst,minister of the Madison Square Presbyte-
rian Church. He was well known as he was a reformer, who in-
spired a successful campaign against Tammany Hall in New York
City. We walked down to the large church where he was pastor
and after looking the situation over, we decided that he probably wouldn't be too thrilled to have a couple of not too well
dressed bicycle riders call on him, so we continued on our way
without making the call.

In the afternoon we bought a copy of the New York World
newspaper and saw the article about us in it.

In the evening we went to Coney Island to see the sights.
While there several people came up to us, said they had seen
the article in the paper and asked to buy cards and we sold
several to them. People were very friendly and we were enjoying our visit to this famous place.

## CHAPTER FOUR

The 44th Day      (Cont.)

New York City

   As we proceeded down the street, two mounted police cor-
ralled us and acted like we had just robbed a bank. They said,
"you cant sell cards here unless you have a permit". Of course
we didnt have a permit so we told them we had come to see the
sights and not to sell cards. They didn't bother us again and
we didn't sell any more cards.

   We spent the evening taking in the sights, took a few
rides and enjoyed our visit very much. Then back to the Mills
Hotel for our second night in New York City.

CONEY ISLAND

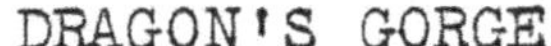

DRAGON'S GORGE                    STEEPLECHASE

   Coney Island is a popular seashore resort and has many
fine beaches in addition to the amusement center that we visited.

## CHAPTER FOUR

The 44th Day        (Cont.)

New York City.

The Mayor's Letter

CITY OF NEW YORK

Office of the Mayor

August 10th,1915

TO WHOM IT MAY CONCERN:

This is to certify that Leon Schroeder and Harwood Temple called at this office today, bearing a letter of introduction from the Mayor of St.Paul,Minnesota and stated that they had made the trip from St.Paul to New York on bicycles, arriving at City Hall about ten o'clock.

B. Chlr. Cruger
Executive  Secretary

CHAPTER FOUR

PHILADELPHIA TO NEW YORK CITY AND BOSTON,MASSACHUSETTS.

August 11th,1915    The 45th Day    (Wednesday)

New York City

Our first stop today was the Woolworth Building. We took
the elevator to the observa-
tion platform near the top of
the building. From there we
had a fine view of the city
and harbor with the great
ocean liners coming and going. I took a picture of an
ocean liner from my vantage
point. In the distance can
be seen the Statue of Liberty.

WOOLWORTH BUILDING

At that time the Wool-
worth Building was the tallest building in the world,
57 stories, 792 feet high.
It was the second tallest
man made structure in the
world, exceeded only by the
Eiffel Tower in Paris, France.

NEW YORK HARBOR
AND STATUE OF LIBERTY

We enjoyed the beautiful
view from there so we spent
considerable time taking in the sights.

CHAPTER FOUR

The 45th Day      (Cont.)

New York City

At last we had to leave so went to the post office to see if any more mail had come for us. We had several letters from back home so went to the hotel to read them. It was getting close to noon so we took time

POST OFFICE

out to eat. While on our way there was a fire and we were very much interested in the motor driven fire engines. I took a picture of one of them.

In the afternoon we took a trip on the Staten Island Ferry, a very pleasant ride on the harbor. We enjoyed watching the big ocean liners coming and going, and wondered where they all came from. Took a pic-ture of the city from the boat on the way.

NEW YORK FIRE ENGINE

From the boat we had a beautiful view of the Statue of Liberty on Bedloe's Island.

THE CITY FROM STATEN ISLAND FERRY

CHAPTER FOUR

The 45th Day     (Cont.)

New York City.

It lights the harbor with an electric torch held 306 feet
above the water, the highest beacon in the world. The statue
is one of the first things incoming people see as a symbol
of our great country. It was presented to the United States
by France.

The inscription on the pedestal is in part
as follows:

"Give me your tired, your poor, Your huddled
masses yearning to breathe free,The wretched ref-
use of your teeming shore, Send these, the home-
less, tempest-tossed, to me: I lift my lamp be-
side the golden door.

STATUE
OF LIBERTY

The statistics of the Statue and pedestal as follows:
Total height of the statue and pedestal 305 feet, the statue
alone is 151 feet, the right arm holding the light is 42 feet
long and the hand is 16 feet, the head 17 feet by 10 feet.
The weight of the statue is 450,000 pounds. There is room in
the head for 40 persons and 12 in the torch.


"The Great White Way" with its thousands of lights and
crowds of people fascinated us so we spent the evening there
before going to bed.

CHAPTER FOUR

PHILADELPHIA TO NEW YORK CITY AND BOSTON,MASSACHUSETTS.

August 12th,1915    The 46th Day       (Thursday)

New York City

In the morning we walked to Broadway and 5th Avenue to see
the Flat Iron Building so-called because it is built in the
shape of a flatiron. It is 300 feet high
and has 120,000 square feet of floor
space above ground and 33,000 square
feet below sidewalk level. It is the
first steel frame skyscraper built in
the world. I took a picture of the
building before continuing on our way.

We walked down 5th Avenue where
many of the best shops were located
but of course we didn't have the money
to buy anything.

Back at the hotel we checked on
our finances and found that we had very
little left. We were going to stay in
the city one more day, as planned, and

FLAT IRON BUILDING

we were not about to change our plans, come what may.We knew
we didn't have enough money to carry us over but what to do.

About this time we happened to think about the actor we
met in Lancaster,Pennsylvania and his generous offer to help
us if needed. He lived on West 56th Street so we decided to

CHAPTER FOUR

The 46th Day      (Cont.)

New York City

walk out to his place. It was a long walk but we finally got there. He lived in one of those typical New York houses with the front porch some distance above the street with a flight of steps leading up to it. We asked for him and the lady said, "wait outside and I'll call him" We waited on the sidewalk and pretty soon he came out and sat on the steps. We told him we would like to borrow two or three dollars and would pay him back when we got home.

He told us a hard luck story, which didn't sound much like the generous offer he made to us at Lancaster, where all could hear. He finally said he would lend us 50¢ (which we paid back when we got home). We learned a lesson about big talk and no action that day.

We were only about three blocks from Central Park so before heading back to the hotel we went there for awhile. It was interesting to see that part of Manhattan so all was not wasted effort.

On our long walk back to the hotel we sold a few cards and met a woman passing out pamphlets so we took one. This was from the Woman Suffrage Party and a copy of the pamphlet is shown on the following page. It may be of interest to see what the voting situation for women was in 1915.

We walked around a little in the evening and then went to bed. We were tired after our long walk that day.

CHAPTER FOUR

The 46th Day      (Cont.)

New York City

---

*1915*
*NEW YORK STATE*

# THE NEXT PRESIDENT

THE women of twelve States can vote for the next President.

THESE States are Wyoming, Colorado, Utah, Idaho, Washington, California, Oregon, Arizona, Kansas, Illinois, Nevada and Montana.  They also vote in Alaska.

THE number of women who can vote is nearly four million.

THE women of this State will be able to vote for the next President if the men of this State are as generous and just as are the men of the West.

THE men will vote this year upon a Constitutional Amendment to give women the vote in this State.

THE women of this State are as intelligent, sane, law-abiding, public-spirited, patriotic as the women of the West.  Why not give the same political rights to them?

THE women of this State could remove to the West, and in any of those States vote for President in 1916.  Why should they not have the same privilege in their home State? Are political rights to be a question of geography?

---

## VOTE FOR WOMAN SUFFRAGE,
### GIVE THIS TO A FRIEND AND ASK HIM TO VOTE FOR IT

---

**WOMAN SUFFRAGE PARTY**
Headquarters: 48 East 34th Street, New York
N. W. S. Publishing Co., Inc.

---

WOMAN SUFFRAGE PARTY PAMPHLET
1915

## CHAPTER FOUR

PHILADELPHIA TO NEW YORK CITY AND BOSTON,MASSACHUSETTS.

August 13th,1915    The 47th Day     (Friday)

New York City

This was to be our last day in New York City and we wanted to see a number of things before leaving the city.

NEW YORK SKYSCRAPERS.

We walked down to Greenwich Village south of 14th St. a long way from our hotel. There were many artists around and many so-called Bohemians who lived in an unconventional manner. The quaint old buildings, the narrow winding streets presented an interesting picture.

WALL ST.

From there we went to Wall Street, the financial center of the city,with its many banks and other financial institutions. Wall Street is like a narrow canyon with the tall buildings on each side.It was nice to see all these things that we had heard so much about.

BROOKLYN BRIDGE

We next walked over to see the Brooklyn Bridge which just about took care of our sight seeing for the day. We took the long walk back to the part of the city where we had been staying.

## CHAPTER FOUR

The 47th Day        (Cont.)

New York City

We each had just 5¢ and there we were in the great city of
New York, 1500 miles from home almost penniless. We didn't have

money for food or lodging, not
to mention the money we needed
to pay for the storage of our
bikes.

We wanted to leave the
city the next morning so we
were in real trouble and faced
with disaster for the first
time on the trip. We didn't
know what to do about it.

N.Y. ELEVATED TRACKS

Then we happened to think about a letter a friend of Hap's
had given him. This letter was a letter of introduction to the
friend's relatives who lived in Brooklyn. This looked like our
only chance so we decided to spend our last nickels for carfare
and go over and call on them.

It was nearly dinner time when we reached their house. We
rang the bell and and a man came to the door and Hap presented
the letter. The man took the letter, said nothing, and went in
and closed the door leaving us on the porch. Hap said,"Well
Leon, what do we do now". I said "We will just have to sit here
on the porch floor and hope that door opens again".

CHAPTER FOUR

The 47th Day      (Cont.)

New York City

Finally, after what seemed like an eternity, the door opened and the man invited us into the house. It was dinner time and the people were entertaining a number of guests for dinner. We sat down with them and enjoyed a delicious meal. The people were very much interested in the trip and bought over six dollars worth of cards, paying up to 25¢ each for them.

Their kindness saved us from disaster as we now had enough money to get back to New York, get a room at the Mills Hotel and get our bikes so we could leave the next morning. I have always been thankful to them for the much needed help. Always on the trip, when we were in trouble financially there always were kind people to help us over the hump.

CHAPTER FOUR

PHILADELPHIA TO NEW YORK CITY AND BOSTON,MASSACHUSETTS.

August 14th,1915    The 48th Day    (Saturday)

New York City to Norwalk,Connecticut.

We were up early and went down to get our bikes. It cost
us $5.00 for the five nights, which was much more than we paid
for our hotel rooms. However we were thankful that we had the
money to get them.

While in the city I made new signs for our knapsacks,"St.
Paul to New York and Boston".
These replaced the signs, "St.
Paul to New York" that we had
been using so far.

We were soon on our way. We
went out Broadway to Central Park,
rode the length of the park on
8th Avenue, then turned right on
110th St., then on 7th Avenue to
153rd St. We then crossed the Central Bridge into Jerome Avenue,
following the double trolley to Fordham Road at 189th St. We
continued to follow the trolley into Pelham Parkway,thence on
Shore Road to New Rochelle.

At New Rochelle we visited the Thomas Paine Monument. He
lived in New Rochelle for a few years and was originally buried
close to where the Monument now stands.

The studio of the Thanhouse Film Corporation was located
at New Rochelle. We visited the plant and were escorted through

CHAPTER FOUR

The 48th Day      (Cont.)

New York City to Norwalk,Connecticut.

the studio. They were not
taking any movies at the
time so didn't get to see
any actors or actresses as
we did at the Lubin Studio
in Philadelphia.

When we left New Ro-
chelle we were on the old
Boston Post Road and will be on it practically
all the way to Boston.

New Rochelle was a residential suburb
of New York City and had many beautiful
homes, some were old Colonial type houses.

NEW ROCHELLE

MAIN STREET

We continued on through Larchmont and
next Mamaronect where J.Fenimore Cooper
once lived. These cities were more or less
residential suburbs of New York City.

HIGH SCHOOL

Next we came to Rye where we stopped
for lunch and to sell a few cards. So far
we only had one puncture that day. Rye was
also a residential community for people who worked in the city.
An old tide-mill built before the revolution was still standing
so we visited it before leaving.

CHAPTER FOUR

The 48th Day    (Cont.)

New York City to Norwalk,Connecticut.

The next stop was at Port Chester at the mouth of the
Byram River which is the boundary between New York and Connecticut. This city was mainly residential but there were some
manufacturing plants there. We were 27 miles from New York City.

We crossed the river and entered Connecticut, the ninth
state on our journey. The first city we came to was Greenwich.
It was the home of many wealthy New York business men, artists
and writers. They had beautiful estates and as the city extends
from sea level to an elevation of 5 or 600 feet, it affords a
beautiful view of the surrounding hills, valleys,rivers and
lakes as well as of Long Island Sound. There were many bridle
paths and places to swim for the liesure time of the wealthy.

We rode through Mianus and soon came to Stamford. From
there I sent a card home with the following
message, "The trip is a success". I guess I
thought having made it safely in and out of
New York City all would be fine from now on.

STAMFORD

TOWN HALL

Stamford was a residential community
but also was an important manufacturing
center. Atlantic Square in the business
district was once the site of the whipping-
post, stocks and pillory. Of course all
that was in the early days but when we visited it, it was an attractive place with

ATLANTIC SQUARE

The 48th Day      (Cont.)

New York City to Norwalk,Connecticut.

many trees. The town hall was a beautiful building and for transportation they had trolley cars. The city is located on Long
Island Sound.

We continued on our way through Noroton and Darien and
arrived at Norwalk late in the afternoon after a 43 mile run
from New York City. This was not bad considering the fact that
we had some rain and two punctures during the day. We decided
to camp out at Norwalk for the night.

Trolley Party to Shore, Norwalk, Conn.

TROLLEY PARTY TO SHORE, NORWALK, CONN.

CHAPTER FOUR

PHILADELPHIA TO NEW YORK CITY AND BOSTON,MASSACHUSETTS.

August 15,1915    The 49th Day    (Sunday)

Norwalk,Connecticut to New Haven,Connecticut.

We packed up our gear, stopped at a restaurant for a good
breakfast of cereal, toast and coffee and
were soon on our way.

This was the second Norwalk we had visited, the other one was in Ohio. During the

BELLE ISLAND
NORWALK

Revolutionary War the British burned the
Norwalk in Connecticut. The State offered
free lands, called "Fire Grant Lands" in what is now Ohio to com-
pensate the people for losses. A number of Norwalk families took
advantage of the offer and in establishing a new community, they
called it Norwalk after their former home.

Norwalk was an industrial city. It is located on Long Island
Sound at the mouth of the Norwalk River, which forms a harbor.
There were many oyster beds in the vicinity and these were an
added source of income for the people.

The road beyond Norwalk continued along the coast and we
stopped at Westport and Southport. We sold a few cards there
and continued on, reaching Bridgeport about noon. It being
Sunday we had a good chicken dinner at a restaurant.

Bridgeport is at the mouth of the Pequonnock River. It
was a large manufacturing ciy and the down-town area is crowded
but there are beautiful residential areas in the outskirts.

## CHAPTER FOUR

The 49th Day        (Cont.)

Norwalk,Connecticut to New Haven,Connecticut.

One of the large plants was that of the Locomobile Co.
manufacturers of automobiles. The Tom Thumb
house, is where, according to the story, Tom
Thumb, the midget with Barnum and Bailey Circus, lived with his midget wife.

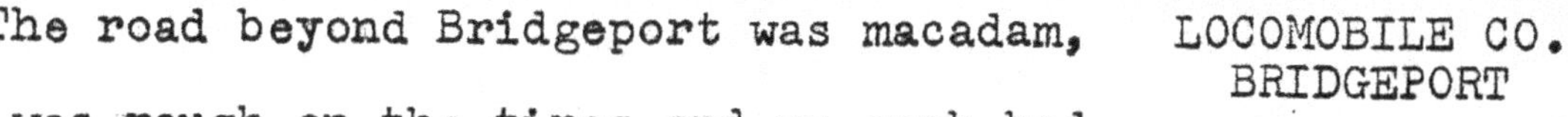

LOCOMOBILE CO.
BRIDGEPORT

The road beyond Bridgeport was macadam,
which was rough on the tires and we each had
a tire blow-out during the day. We rode through Stratford without stopping and continued on to Milford where we stopped to
sell some cards.

The local people told us that the bridge over the river
there was the first bridge built over a river in America. We
went to see it, this bridge called Memorial Bridge replaced
an earlier bridge. It may have been the earlier bridge that the
people were talking about. I have never been
able to verify the story. Milford Green, a
park about one half mile long was very pretty.

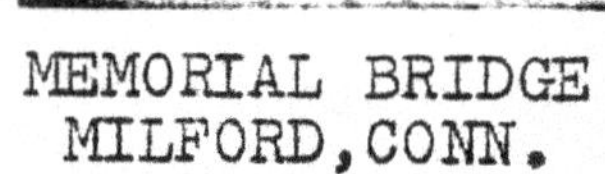

We continued on and reached New Haven
late in the afternoon so we decided to spend
MEMORIAL BRIDGE
MILFORD,CONN.

the night there. We found a suitable place
on a vacant lot and set up our tent. (400 block of Orange St.)

In the evening we walked through the business section,
there was considerable activity with many people on the streets.

CHAPTER FOUR

The 49th Day     (Cont.)

Norwalk,Connecticut to New Haven,Connecticut.

People were friendly and were much interested in our trip.They
were also generous and we sold a great many cards.

I started to talk to a Yale student and come to find out,
he lived on the same street I did in Saint Paul and in the
next block. I had a very pleasant visit with him. He said he
would get word to Saint Paul and tell them that we were well
and getting along fine.

After a very pleasant and rewarding evening we went to bed
in our little tent.


In 1915 there were many electric automobiles in use in
the New England states. Electric Charging Stations had been
established in cities and towns along the way. In the cities
of Connecticut we had visited so far there were charging stations at Greenwich, Stamford, South Norwalk, Bridgeport and
New Haven.

CHAPTER FOUR

PHILADELPHIA TO NEW YORK CITY AND BOSTON,MASSACHUSETTS.

August 16th,1915   The 50th Day    (Monday)

New Haven,Connecticut to Mystic,Connecticut.

When we were taking the tent down the lady next door came over and invited us for breakfast and we gladly accepted the invitation. After a good meal we sat at the table and visited awhile. The lady was very much interested in the trip and asked a lot of questions. At first she thought we were from nearby and when we told her we were from Minnesota she was very much surprised. She said, "Weren't you boys afraid to ride your bikes alone through that Indian Country?"

NEW  HAVEN

NOAH WEBSTER
HOUSE

The only Indians we saw in Minnesota were statues of Indians in front of tobacco stores. In those days an Indian statue was a symbol of a tobacco dealer just as a striped pole was a symbol of a barber shop. It goes to show how little some people in the East knew about conditions in the Mid-West.

SHOT  TOWER
WINCHESTER ARMS CO.

We soon left the lady's house as we wanted to do a little sight-seeing before leaving New Haven. First we went over to see the Yale University Campus and Buildings. We saw the Noah Webster house. He compiled the first Webster Dictionary and also

LIGHTHOUSE POINT

CHAPTER FOUR

The 50th Day     (Cont.)

New Haven,Connecticut to Mystic,Connecticut.

the first revised and enlarged edition.

New Haven is located on Long Island Sound at the confluence of the Mill, West and Quinnipiac Rivers. In the downtown area was a beautiful "Green" which is the name for a park in this area. Facing the Green were churches and public and commercial buildings. The plant of the Winchester Repeating Arms Company, as well as a number of other manufacturing plants were located in the city. We visited Lighthouse Point with its old cannons and found it very interesting.

We soon left the city and while the road was dirt or macadam, it was in good shape and as it was level country we made good time. We rode through East Haven, Branford, Guilford, East River, Madison, Clinton and Westbrook. We stopped at Old Saybrook for a rest and lunch. Old Saybrook at the mouth of the Connecticut River is one of the oldest towns in the State and was a quiet, peaceful place. I had been impressed by the New England cities and towns, with the houses and yards well kept and the streets clean.

TOLL BRIDGE CONNECTICUT RIVER

CHAPTER FOUR

The 50th Day      (Cont.)

New Haven,Connecticut to Mystic,Connecticut.

We crossed the Connecticut River on a toll bridge to the
village of Old Lyme. At Lyme we bought a card that showed a
typical gasoline filling station at that time. It was a small
residence with one small gasoline tank on the porch, from which
the gasoline was pumped into the automobiles by hand. There were

GASOLINE STATION  LYME,CONNECTICUT.

three or four, five gallon cans of oil on the porch.

We rode on through Laysville, East Lyme and Flanders. We
stopped at New London to eat and to sell some cards.

New London is located at the mouth of the Thames River and
has a fine harbor. It is a very pretty city. There were military
and Coast Guard Units stationed there.

CHAPTER FOUR

The 50th Day       (Cont.)

New Haven,Connecticut to Mystic,Connecticut.

It was here on the Thames River that the annual Yale Harvard
boat races were held every June. We continued our journey in
the evening and camped out for the night at the village of
Mystic.

It didn't rain during the day, so in spite of the dirt
and macadam road we made 63 miles that day.

Mystic was a quiet, peaceful little
village and we enjoyed spending the night
there.

MYSTIC, CONN.

Below is shown a typical electric automobile of 1915.
During our ride that day we noticed electric charging stations
at Madison and at
New London.

ELECTRIC
AUTOMOBILE

CHAPTER FOUR

PHILADELPHIA TO NEW YORK CITY AND BOSTON,MASSACHUSETTS.

August 17th,1915    The 51st Day   (Tuesday)

Mystic,Connecticut to Providence,Rhode Island.

Mystic was a small village at the outlet of the Mystic
River where it empties into Long Island Sound. Like most New
England villages it was a clean, quiet place with its many
trees, well kept lawns and houses. In the early days there was
considerable shipbuilding here, particularly during the California gold rush and later. At that time there was a great demand
for ships for people headed for the gold fields.

We packed up and left Mystic without breakfast, intending
to eat later in a larger town. We rode through Stonington and
Wequetequock and shortly after crossed the Pawcatuck River into
Rhode Island at Westerly. Rhode Island was the tenth state on
our travels and of course the smallest one.

We were hungry by now so the first order
of business was breakfast at a restaurant.
It was raining so we spent some time there
and sent cards home.

R.R. STATION
WESTERLY, R.I.

Westerly was a typical New England
town with some of the old homes still standing. The town has a
number of manufacturing plants with most of the mills around
the falls of the Pawcatuck River. There was a beautiful new
Post Office and the railroad station was an attractive building and well landscaped. There were a number of summer resorts

CHAPTER FOUR

The 51st Day        (Cont.)

Mystic, Connecticut to Providence, Rhode Island.

in the vicinity. There were several horse drawn vehicles at the
railroad station and one or two automobiles. West Broad Street
was a typical small town main street with a
few one and two story buildings. A trolley
car ran down the street and there were a few
horse drawn vehicles and one or two automobiles.

W.BROAD ST.
WESTERLY

After looking the town over we were on our way, as it had
stopped raining. After leaving Westerly we went up Quarry Hill
and after about seventeen miles we came to Wakefield but did
not stop there. We rode on through Delacarlia Corners and continued on to Narragansett Pier. We stopped there and had lunch
at a restaurant and sold a few cards.

Narragansett Pier was located in the town of Narragansett.
It was still called by that name although the Pier had long
since been destroyed. The town is located on the west shore of
Narragansett Bay. It is a famous summer resort with one of the
finest beaches on the coast. The beach was lined with hotels
and many beautiful summer homes. The town was named after the
Narragansett Indian Tribe that lived there in the early days.
Noticed  an electric charging station in this town also.

We continued on our way passing through the town of Saun-
derstown, a ferry ran from this town to Newport across the bay.

CHAPTER FOUR

The 51st Day        (Cont.)

Mystic, Connecticut to Providence, Rhode Island.

We rode through Hamilton and Wickford and stopped at East

Greenwich to rest and sell some cards. This village was on

the side of a hill facing the bay. There were still many early

American homes located there.

Continuing on we rode through Apponaug, Hills Grove, past

Roger Williams Park and reached Providence about 6.

P.M. after our 65 mile ride that day.

After a meal in a restaurant we walked around

the business district. The people were very friend-

ly and we sold lots of cards. While on the street a

man stopped to talk and asked if we would like to stay over

night in a hotel. We told him we would like to but didn't have

money enough for that purpose. He said we could stay there free

if we wanted to and of course we did.

He took us to a first class hotel (Hotel Duseln) and we

were taken to a nice clean room. It was very comfortable, a

good bed and a welcome shower. We certainly appreciated the

kindness of so many people in Providence.

CHAPTER FOUR

PHILADELPHIA TO NEW YORK CITY AND BOSTON,MASSACHUSETTS.

August 18th,1915    The 52nd Day    (Wednesday)

Providence,Rhode Island to Boston,Massachusetts.

Providence, the Capital of Rhode Island was a very nice
city, but what we liked most about it was the friendliness of
the people. It is located at the mouth of the Providence River
and is a Port of Entry. It is bounded on the
East by the Seekonk and Providence Rivers.
The main business section was along the West
bank of the Providence River. There were a
number of factories on the banks of the

WEYBOSSET ST.

Woonasquatucket and the
Moshassuck. The old section
had street names such as
Friendship, Hope, Benefit,
Benevolent, Peace, Pound,
Shilling, Dollar and Dou-
bloon, which shows the religious spirit of the early
city, and its commercial background.

STATE HOUSE(CAPITOL) OF R.I.

Brown University is located in Providence and there are
many landmarks of historical interest in and about the city.
There were many old red brick colonial houses, many with white
marble 'trim.

We first visited the State Capitol which is situated
to the west of the business section. It is built of Georgia

CHAPTER FOUR

The 52nd Day          (Cont.)

Providence,Rhode Island to Boston,Massachusetts.

marble and white granite with a marble dome 235 feet high.

The interior of the Capitol(or State House as it was called)
was beautiful. There was a full length portrait of George Washington by Gilbert Stuart and many other paintings of historical
interest in the building. The original charter of the Colony
is kept there and is well protected in its frame. We visited
a number of places of historical interest and then were on our
way to Boston, now only 45 miles away.

On the way out we passed the Brown University buildings
and soon came to Pawtucket. This city had a population of about
60,000. There were many manufacturing plants, textiles being
the leading product. The old mill of Samuel Slater, built in
1790 was still there. The name of the city is an Indian word
meaning "fall of the waters". This city as well as Providence
had auto electric charging stations.

About two miles beyond Pawtucket we
crossed the State Line into Massachusetts,
the eleventh State on our journey.

MANUFACTURERS BLDG.
- NO.ATTLEBORO

The first city we came to in Massachusetts was North Attleboro, a fairly
large town. The principal business there was the manufacture
of jewelry.

We sold a few cards and then continued on our way.

## CHAPTER FOUR

The 52nd Day        (Cont.)

Providence,Rhode Island to Boston,Massachusetts.

The road was macadam and in fairly good shape so we made very

good time. We rode through Plainville and stopped at Walpole

for a bite to eat.

It started to rain while we were eating so

we delayed our departure for about an hour till

it cleared up. A mile out of town I had a puncture

which delayed us further.

A few miles beyond Walpole we came to Nor-

wood, a city of about five or six thousand.

Norwood was a residential suburb but with some

manufacturing plants.

MONUMENT
NO. ATTLEBORO

We reached Dedham about 4

in the afternoon. This was a

city of about 10,000. The city

was mostly residential with

some manufacturing. It is lo-

cated on the Charles River.

We reached Boston about 6

P.M. and some people let us

sleep in a shed on the rear of

CHILDREN: WHERE WE
SLEPT IN THE SHED

the lot as it had started to rain again.

The people where we stayed invited us in for a snack and

we then went to bed as it was still raining.

## CHAPTER FOUR

The 52nd Day     (Cont.)

Providence, Rhode Island to Boston, Massachusetts.

It was some time before we fell asleep that night. We enjoyed listening to the rain and talked about our trip so far.

We had now reached the farthest point on our trip, so after spending some time in Boston we will start the long trip home. Since leaving Saint Paul we had traveled 1858 miles. As we were actually traveling on the road for 37½ days this figures out to about 50 miles a day.

PLYMOUTH ROCK

END OF CHAPTER FOUR

## CHAPTER FIVE

### BOSTON,MASSACHUSETTS TO BUFFALO,NEW YORK.

August 19th,1915    The 53rd Day      (Thursday)

At Boston

We were up early and were invited in for a good breakfast. After a short visit I took a picture of their three children. We thanked the people for our meal and for a place were on our way to the downtown area of Boston. We found a place in a garage to keep our bikes and were ready for a full day of sightseeing.

FANEUIL HALL

We first went to Faneuil Hall which is called, "The Cradle of American Liberty". It was built in 1742, was destroyed by fire in 1762 and was re-built in accordance with the original plan. It is called Cradle of American Liberty be-cause so many of the early meetings leading to the rebellion were held here. We spent some time in the building viewing the paintings and the other things of histor-ical interest.

PUBLIC GARDENS
WASHINGTON STATUE

We visited the site of the "Boston Massacre", walked around Boston Common, visited the old State House and also the new State House with its golden dome. There were many things of interest in the buildings that we visited.

OLD
SOUTH CHURCH

It was now about noon and being in Boston, we just had to try Boston baked beans and they were very good.

CHAPTER FIVE

The 53rd Day      (Cont.)

At Boston

After lunch we made arrangements for our nights lodging
at Hotel Two Bits and as the name implies it cost
us twenty five cents each.

We then went to the site of the battle of
Bunker Hill. While the first shooting of the rebellion was at Lexington, the first real battle of the
war was at Bunker Hill. The British finally won
the battle when the Americans ran out of ammuni-
tion. It was a costly victory for the British as they lost more
than twice as many men as did the Americans. It gave the Americans confidence as they now knew that they could hold their
own against the regular troops of Great Britain. The Bunker Hill
Monument which marks the location, is 220 feet high and 30 feet
square at the base. It is shaped like the Washington Monument
in Washington, D.C.

BUNKER HILL
MONUMENT

When we got back to our hotel it was time to eat our evening meal, so naturally, we had a New England boiled dinner.

After eating we went down to the place where the so-called
"Boston Tea Party" took place when the colonists dumped a ship-
load of English tea in the bay as a protest against the tax on
tea.The old part of Boston has many narrow, crooked streets and
we had trouble finding our way around. There was so much to see
in Boston and would have liked to stay several days but we were
behind schedule, so decided to leave the next day after first
visiting old North Church.

## CHAPTER FIVE

### BOSTON,MASSACHUSETTS TO BUFFALO,NEW YORK.

August 20th,1915    The 54th Day    (Friday)

Boston to Shrewsbury,Massachusetts.

We lost no time getting up and having breakfast as we wanted to visit Old North Church before leaving at noon on our long trip home.

We finally found the church which was in the old part of the city with the narrow, crooked streets. We climbed the old wooden stairs to the belfry arch. It was a long climb to the top but well worth the effort. It was here that the two signal lanterns were hung advising Paul Revere on the opposite shore of the Charles River that the British were coming by sea.

The following excerpts from Longfellow's poem,"Paul Rever's Ride" explains this: "Listen my children and you shall hear of the midnight ride of Paul Revere"---- "He said to his friend, If the British march by land or sea from the town tonight, hang a lantern aloft in the belfry arch of the North Church tower as a signal light,- one if by land, and two if by sea; and I on the opposite shore will be, ready to ride and spread the alarm through every Middlesex village and farm!"

OLD NORTH CHURCH

As we stood in the belfry arch and looked out across the water to the opposite shore we could visualize Paul Revere waiting there for the signal from the belfry arch where we stood. It was a wonderful experience to actually be where this historical event

CHAPTER FIVE

The 54th Day      (Cont.)

Boston to Shrewsbury,Massachusetts.

took place.

We have seen so many places of historical interest, have met
so many kind and helpful people, we could not but be proud and
thankful to be a part of this great country in which we live.
It all brought home to us the
courage and foresight the colonists had to endure the
bloodshed and hardships of

BOSTON AND ALBANY R.R.

the rebellion to establish this nation.

We went back to the business district
where we had a lunch of Boston baked beans.
After lunch we went to get our bikes, the
man at the garage wanted a dollar for keeping them overnight. We only had 45¢ between
us and he finally settled for that, taking

our last penny. We changed the signs on our knapsacks as follows,
"St.Paul to New York and Return". We were now ready to begin our
nearly 1,800 mile ride back home.

We had trouble getting through the crooked streets of the
old part of the city but to the west in the newer section the
streets were wide and very pretty. We had relatives at Shrewsbury
and wanted to get there by dinner time so we hurried on our way.

We went west on Boyleston St., Massachusetts Ave., and then
on Commonwealth Ave. to Beacon Blvd. and then back on Commonwealth Ave. to Auburndale. The trolley we had been following

CHAPTER FIVE

The 54th Day        (Cont.)

Boston to Shrewsbury,Massachusetts.

ended at Auburndale. The road was macadam and in fairly good shape.

At Weston we were back on the old Boston Post Road, and went through Wayland and South Sudbury, selling a few cards. Just beyond South Sudbury and a short distance north of our road was the Wayside Inn. This was the site of Longfellow's poems, "Tales of a Wayside Inn". We went to see it and while we didn't go inside, we did get a drink of water at the well in the yard. The Inn was not open that day. We saw many fruit stands along the way.

The next place we came to was Marlboro, a fairly large city. We stopped there to sell some cards and look the city over. There was considerable manufacturing in the city.

We arrived at Shrewsbury at 5 P.M. and soon found the Shaw's house. (Our Uncle Horace, Aunt Queenie,  and Cousins Irene and Kenneth).

MAIN ST.          WILLIAMS TAVERN    PATOEL'S CORNER
                  MARLBORO, MASS.

They were glad to see us as we were to see them and we sat down to a good home cooked meal. After a long visit in the evening and after reading our mail from home, we went to bed in a real bed for a change.

## CHAPTER FIVE

### BOSTON,MASSACHUSETTS TO BUFFALO,NEW YORK.

August 21st,1915        The 55th Day     (Saturday)

At Shrewsbury,Mass.

We were up at 7;A.M. Hap formerly lived in Shrewsbury and one of the reasons he wanted to make the trip was so he could visit some of his boyhood friends as well as the relatives. Our other relative who lived in Shrewsbury, the Drinkwines,(our Uncle Irwin, Aunt Goldie and Cousin Olive) were on vacation at Lake Lashaway and as the lake was on our way home we would stop and see them there.

The Shaws were going to visit them at the lake over the week-end so after breakfast they left, turning the house over to us. Our Mothers spent much of their early years in and around Shrewsbury so it was nice to see where they had lived.

THE SHAWS
AUNT QUEENIE*IRENE*KENNETH

We decided to go to Worcester and on the way we stopped at Lake Quinsigamond for a refreshing morning swim. We visited the huge Worcester Market and this being Saturday it was the big day. The farmers brought their produce and it was all on display outdoors in the open. It was an interesting sight and we walked around the area watching the large crowds buying their supply of

## CHAPTER FIVE

The 55th Day      (Cont.)

At Shrewsbury, Mass.

food and other products. While there we bought meat and butter
for our evening meal at Shaws.

We had lunch in a restaurant in Worcester afterwards we
visited the City Hall and other places of interest. We headed
back to Shrewsbury and on the way stopped at Lakeview so Hap
could look up a friend. He stayed there and I continued on to
Shaws. Hap arrived about 5:30 P.M. and we cut the grass and
then I prepared our evening meal.

After eating we went out for a bike ride around town. We
met two girls and as Hap knew one of them we stopped to talk.
While we were standing there, an old boyhood friend of Hap, R.
McKenzie, happened to come along. Hap stayed with him while I
walked the two girls a mile or so home. We then returned to
Shaws and went to bed.

THE COMMON              MINUTE-MEN TABLET
SHREWSBURY, MASS.

## CHAPTER FIVE

### BOSTON,MASSACHUSETTS TO BUFFALO,NEW YORK.

August 22nd,1915    The 56th Day     (Sunday)

At Shrewsbury,Mass.

We were up at 8:30 A.M. and I prepared breakfast, after our meal I washed the dishes before leaving for the day. It was nice having the house all to ourselves. We walked down to the Common. It was a very pretty grassy open space with many trees, a tall monument and a old church facing the Common. Hap took a picture of me in front of the Shrewsbury Post Office.

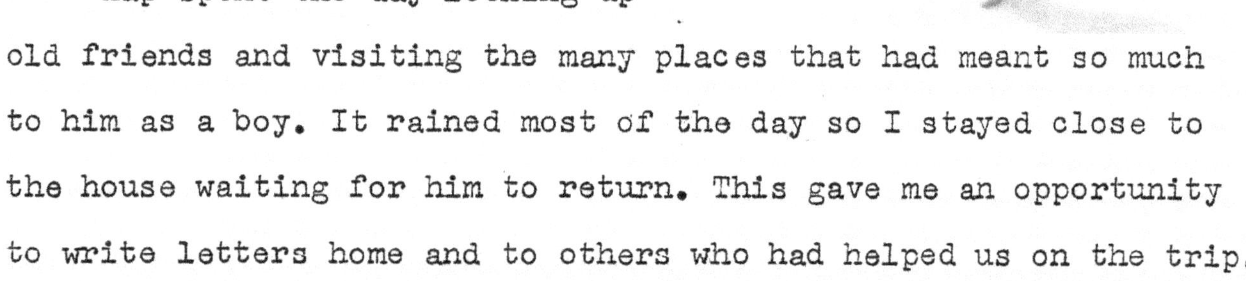


We saw a brass plate set in a large rock with information about the men from Shrewsbury who responded to the Lexington alarm of April 19th,1775.(Paul Revere's ride) According to this tablet 128 Minute-Men from Shrewsbury responded.

Hap spent the day looking up old friends and visiting the many places that had meant so much to him as a boy. It rained most of the day so I stayed close to the house waiting for him to return. This gave me an opportunity to write letters home and to others who had helped us on the trip.

The Shaws returned from Lake Lashaway about seven P.M. and after a long visit with them in the evening we went to bed.

CHAPTER FIVE

BOSTON,MASSACHUSETTS TO BUFFALO,NEW YORK.

August 23rd,1915    The 57th Day    (Monday)

At Shrewsbury,Mass.

In the morning Hap rode his bike over to Westboro, about
six miles away, to see an old friend of his. While he was gone
I packed up all my souvenirs,etc. to send home so as to lighten
the load I was carrying. The package weighed 16 pounds and the
postage was $1.29.

I walked around the town for awhile in order to get a better idea of the place. I spent most of my time visiting with
the Shaws. Hap returned in the afternoon and his friend R.Mc
Kenzie came over and printed some of our pictures. We rode a-
round town in the evening and went to bed about nine o'clock.

Shrewsbury was a very nice small town, mostly residential,
and is located only about five or six miles from Worcester, a
large city.

Worcester was a large manufacturing center, including wire
products, machine tools and shoes. There are several educational
institutions in the city. A number of famous Americans lived
there for a time including Eli Whitney, General Putnum and Edward
E.Hale as well as others. The city is located on the Blackstone
River which furnished water power for the factories. The building of the railroads and the opening of the Blackstone Canal
from Worcester to Providence in the early 19th century helped
make it a manufacturing center.

## CHAPTER FIVE

### BOSTON,MASSACHUSETTS TO BUFFALO,NEW YORK.

August 24th,1915    The 58th Day    Tuesday)
Shrewsbury to Lake Lashaway,Massachusetts.

Up at 7:30 A.M. Hap took some pictures of various places he was interested in, and called on some of his boyhood friends. I got a much needed haircut.

We went back to Shaws for lunch and visited with them afterwards. We left for Saint Paul at 3 P.M. after thanking them for all they had done for us.

About a mile out I had a tire blowout. As Hap had gone ahead I was stuck with no repair parts to fix it. Two small boys went back the mile to get tire cement and a patch for me. By the time I had made necessary repairs it was 5:30 P.M.

A MASSACHUSETTS FARM

I hurried on my way and as the road was good macadam I made good time. I went through Cherry Valley, Leicester, Spencer and East Brookfield without a stop, I enjoyed the trip through this

CHAPTER FIVE

The 58th Day        (Cont.)

Shrewsbury to Lake Lashaway,Massachusetts.

pretty country and reached Lake Lashaway at 7:35 P.M. after a
21 mile run in two hours and five minutes. It was dark and it
was some time before I located the Drinkwine's cabin.

The relatives were glad to see me but Hap had not arrived
yet. I had not seen these relatives for many years so was glad to
get to visit with them. Aunt Goldie prepared a meal for me and
while I was eating, Hap arrived. He said he was delayed account
visiting with friends.

The
land was
rocky so in
clearing the
ground they
built the
fences out
of the
rocks.

NOTE THE ROCK FENCES

In the evening Uncle Irwin took us out fishing but after
about an hour on the lake without even a nibble, he called it off.
We visited for awhile after we got back and then went to bed on
the porch floor.

CHAPTER FIVE

BOSTON,MASSACHUSETTS TO BUFFALO,NEW YORK.

August 25th,1915    The 59th Day    (Wednesday)

At Lake Lashaway

Uncle Irwin was going to work so we said goodby to him. Hap and I went fishing in the morning but no luck. We went swimming and after lunch we went fishing again but no batter luck. We gave up on the fishing and in rowing around the lake came to the mouth of Five Mile River.

We decided to explore the river and continued upstream about two miles. We had fun going up the rapids and occasionally

DRINKWINE'S CABIN

getting grounded where the water was shallow. In several places the branches of the trees came to the top of the water and we had to work our way under them. The river wound in and out and we had a great time working our way upstream using our oars as paddles. At last we reached a place where the water was too shallow so we turned back. It was fun shooting the rapids but it seemed ages before we got back to the lake.

When we got back to the cabin they all came down to the beach to see what luck we had fishing. We only had two small perch to show them. There was a little girl about eight,Beatrice Woodburn, visiting the Drinkwines with her Mother and friends. I gave the girl a boat ride before dinner. In the evening all of us played games and then Hap and I went to bed on the porch floor. It was cold but Aunt Goldie furnished us with extra blankets so we had no trouble sleeping.

## CHAPTER FIVE

### BOSTON, MASSACHUSETTS TO BUFFALO, NEW YORK.

August 26th, 1915     The 60th Day     (Thursday)

Lake Lashaway to West Springfield, Massachusetts.

We were up at 8 A.M. and went in swimming. I took a picture of the group after breakfast and they took a picture of us. Aunt Goldie gave each of us a picture of the cabin.

We were ready to leave so after thanking them we were on our way. We wont see any more relatives until we get to Iowa. The road was macadam all the way to Springfield.

THE DRINKWINES & GUESTS

Our first stop was Brookfield and while there a reporter talked to us and took the information on the trip for the local newspaper. We went through W. Brookfield and next came to Warren. We were selling lots of cards in the towns we were passing through. Warren was a pretty town with a "Square" with a large Soldier's Monument. We continued on through West Warren, Palmer and North Wilbraham. We stopped at North Wilbraham to take a picture of the railroad station. From there we followed the trolly into Springfield. We went through the Indian Motor Cycle Plant in Springfield and found it very interesting.

THE SQUARE
WARREN, MASS.

KNOX
AUTO PLANT

CHAPTER FIVE

The 60th Day        (Cont.)

Lake Lashaway to West Springfield,Massachusetts.

Note:    **
      From Brookfield to
Palmer the road followed
the Quaboag River valley,
wandering back and forth
between the high hills on
both sides. From North Wilbraham the road followed
the Chicopee River for
about two miles. **

      In leaving Springfield
I took the wrong road and
went about a mile and had
to come back and start over
again. We stopped at West
Springfield to get some
food at a store. The woman
proprietor gave each of us
a cup of coffee and a sandwich. We asked permission
to sleep in a barn nearby
and the women said we could

      In the evening we sat
on the porch and visited
with these people. They were very interested in our trip.

INDIAN MOTORCYCLE FACTORY

TROLLEY            SUMNIT HOUSE
      MT.TOM HOLYOKE,MASS.

CHAPTER FIVE

The 60th Day        (Cont.)

Lake Lashaway to West Springfield,Massachusetts.

After talking to them for awhile, the lady said it was a shame we had to sleep in a barn. We assured her that we were used to sleeping under all kinds of conditions and were glad to get in out of the weather.

A little girl made us cocoa and we had apples and pears to eat. We visited all evening and enjoyed our visit with such nice people. They were real New Englanders and their dropping of the 'Rs' seemed odd to us. We were soon bedded down in the hay loft for a comfortable, warm sleep.

Springfield was a fairly large city, it is situated on the east bank cf the Connecticut River. Facing the Public Park was the municipal group which was new, having been dedicated in 1913. The city has many fine parks including a zoological section. There were two or three museums and a U.S. arsenal. Hundreds of thousands of the famous Springfield muskets were made during the Civil War. There was much manufacturing of rifles, revolvers, in addition to electrical and other products. The publishers of the Merriam dictionary had their headquarters there. We visited the U.S.Armory Museum. There were many exhibits of guns and other weaponry.

A MASSACHUSETTS COUNTRY ROAD

## CHAPTER FIVE

### BOSTON,MASSACHUSETTS TO BUFFALO,NEW YORK.

August 27th,1915     The 61st Day      (Friday)

West Springfield to Huntington,Massachusetts.

We were up at 7:30 A.M. The lady of the house prepared a warm breakfast for us, which was appreciated very much. We visited with the people for a long time, and the lady asked us to send a card when we reached home. I took a picture of the little girl who made cocoa the night before.

WHERE WE STAYED
WEST SPRINGFIELD

Hap sharpened his hatchet and we ate several pears and apples from the trees growing in the yard. It was a rewarding experience to meet so many fine people on the trip.

It was 11 A.M. when we said goodby and started our trip across the Berkshire Hills of western Massachusetts. These hills, or low mountains, are part of the Appalachian Mountains and are very beautiful. They consist of a num-

FACTORY
ON THE RIVER

ber of ridges with deep valleys between and the area is considered one of the most beautiful regions in the United States.

The region was covered with trees with the Westfield River running through the area. Shortly after leaving West Springfield the road followed the river for many miles and as the road was

CHAPTER FIVE

The 61st Day      (Cont.)

West Springfield to Huntington, Massachusetts.

macadam and in good shape and we really enjoyed our ride that day.
We stopped at Westfield for lunch, sold some cards and walked
around town awhile. The Columbia bicycle was made in Westfield
but we didn't have time to visit the
plant. Beyond Westfield the road continued in the valley of the Westfield
River through Russel and Huntington.

CHURCH

GENERAL
SHEPHARD ELM

About 2 miles beyond this town we
passed two girls walking along the
road. We hadn't gone very far when
I had tire trouble and the girls
caught up to us. We visited with
them awhile, I took their picture,

TOBACCO
FIELD

PARK SQUARE

WESTFIELD, MASS.

then walked them back to the place where
they were staying. They were from Pittsfield and were spending their vacation near
Huntington.

We rode ahead about a mile and found a
good camp site along the river. We cooked
our evening meal and after a swim in the
river we went to bed.

PITTSFIELD GIRLS

* The place where we stayed in West
Springfield was at 496 Riverdale St. and
the ladies name was Mrs. Taylor R. Parsons.

CHAPTER FIVE

BOSTON,MASSACHUSETTS TO BUFFALO,NEW YORK.

August 28th,1915     The 62nd Day     (Saturday)

Huntington to Pittsfield,Massachusetts.

We slept late, getting up about 10 A.M. and after washing
in the river were on our way. The road was macadam and followed
the Westfield River as far as Chester. We stopped there for
breakfast and sold a few cards.

The principal industry there was
the production of maple sugar and
also some mining.

At this point the road left
the river and ascended on what
was called Jacob's Ladder. It was
an easy grade and we were able to
ride the six miles to the summit.

There was a roadside stand at
the summit and we indulged in sodas
and bought some cards to send home.
The lady who ran the stand turned
us loose in a blueberry patch and

OBSERVATION TOWER

we made the most of it. Hap took a picture of the observation
tower from which there was a beautiful view of the surrounding
country side.

There was a sort of triangular monument about 10 or 12
feet high. This was made up of all shapes and sizes of stones,
boulders, granite blocks and other things. Each had the name

CHAPTER FIVE

The 62nd Day        (Cont.)

Huntington to Pittsfield,Massachusetts.

and address of some visitor or visitors on it. From the looks of

it I would say the material was brought in by the visitors.

There were addresses in Maine, New York, Massachusetts and one

from Frog's
Landing, wher-
ever that was.
Some of the
blocks looked
like grave
head stones.

AN OLD TAVERN BACK EAST

SUMMIT OF JACOB'S LADDER

CHAPTER FIVE

The 62nd Day        (Cont.)

Huntington to Pittsfield, Massachusetts.

From the summit of Jacob's Ladder it was nearly all downhill to East Lee. Between East Lee and Lee the road followed
the Housatonic River and alongside the road was a trolley which
we followed into Lee. The road ran through
the fertile fields alongside. There were
marble quarries in the vicinity and we were
told that much of the marble for the U.S.
Capitol came from here. There were paper
mills and the first India paper was made here.

HOUSATONIC RIVER

At Lenox we saw the beautiful summer
home of Mr. Proctor of ivory soap fame. Near
the Lenox station was a large stone painted
to look like a frog and it really looked

12 TON
STONE 'FROG'

like one. Nathaniel Hawthorne once
lived on the outskirts of Lenox for
awhile and wrote, 'The House of Seven
Gables' at that time. Lenox is a
beautiful summer resort and Tangle-
wood, a 200 acre estate is one of
the show places as well as other
large estates owned by wealthy
people.

OXEN
IN THE BERKSHIRES

Just beyond Lenox we climbed a hill and after about five
miles we reached Pittsfield, arriving there about five thirty P.M.

CHAPTER FIVE

The 62nd Day        (Cont.)

Huntington to Pittsfield,Massachusetts

I sold a number of cards on a downtown corner with the aid of
a fellow who was a little the worse for too much to drink. He
shouted our wares to the public.

While in the business district a boy about fourteen approached us, said he was riding his bike to Syracuse, New York.
We didn't want anything to do with him thinking he might be a
runaway but try as we did, we could not shake him. We ate supper of Boston baked beans, brown bread and pie. The boy didn't
have any money so we bought him something to eat out of our
meager cash on hand. We met a man who had been with the Barnum
and Bailey Circus two years before and he told us about his experiences with the circus.

We left Pittsfield about 7 P.M., went out West Housatonic
St. About a mile out we asked to sleep in a barn but were turned
down. We continued on and came to an auto with two women in it.
The car was stalled but we could not help so were on our way.

At the next house, a girl about 16 who was baby sitting
her younger brother and sister said we could sleep in the barn.
She asked us if we wanted to come in and visit, we were glad to
do so, we prepared our beds in the barn for all three of us.
Hap and I then went to the house and I was catching up on my
diary in a comfortable chair and a good light. Before long the
parents came home, the father was very angry and told us we

CHAPTER FIVE

The 62nd Day      (Cont.)

Huntington to Pittsfield,Massachusetts.

couldn't sleep in the barn. We went out to the barn, woke the
boy up, packed up and left.

At the next house we were again turned down, and we were
worried as it was getting late and turning cold. At the next
place we had better luck, the man not only said we could sleep
in the barn but brought out a pot of coffee, bread and butter.
I told him about the boy and that we didn't want him along but
he kept riding along with us. We made arrangements for him to
sleep in the barn also. We appreciated this mans kindness
after our unpleasant experiences that evening.

Pittsfield was a fairly large city. The city park was
an oval shaped "green" at the intersection of four streets,
named North, South, East and West. There was considerable
manufacturing including the General Electric Co. South Mountain is the highest point in the city. There were a number of
historical buildings still standing.

CHAPTER FIVE

BOSTON,MASSACHUSETTS TO BUFFALO,NEW YORK.

August 29th,1915    The 63rd Day    (Sunday)

Pittsfield,Massachusetts to Nassau,New York.

Sunday morning, I was up at 8 A.M. but Hap and Frank, our not wanted guest, were still in bed. The man of the house brought us coffee, bread and butter for breakfast.

We thanked the man and left at 10:30 A.M. We did not stop at West Pittsfield and soon came to Shaker Village. The Shakers, a religious sect were the sole occupants of the town. We saw a number of Shaker women, mostly old, who were dressed in long dark blue garments reaching almost to the ground. They wore large yellow sunbonnets and over them a blue veil. Around their necks were large ruffles and they had a very pious expression on their faces.

We stopped at a store of theirs and bought some candy and a pincushion to send home. The store, a one room affair was filled with home made articles, mostly things that would appeal to a woman. There were knit shoes for a baby, pincushions, doilies and many other things. A very old woman waited on us and as they probably sold mostly to tourists, their prices were high.

The buildings in the village were well maintained and the surrounding farms were neat and orderly. Everything about the place was in shipshape condition.

We were about to enter New York State and as we didn't want to take Frank across the state line we ordered him to remain behind in a barn until we crossed into New York.

## CHAPTER FIVE

The 63rd Day      (Cont.)

Pittsfield,Massachusetts to Nassau,New York.

We rode up Lebanon Mountain without dismounting. From the top we could see an immense valley below in New York State. Far below us was a small village surrounded by green fields. In the center of the town was a small white church with its steeple reaching up above the trees. It was a beautiful sight and we waited there for several minutes to enjoy the scenery.

We rode down the mountain full speed, not using our brakes at all and with our arms folded in front of us. It was great sport going down at 30 or 40 miles per hour, shooting around the curves with the bike guiding itself as if it was alive. It was 3 miles to the bottom and we were soon in the village of New Lebanon, the one we had seen from the top of the mountain. We were now in New York State with Massachusetts and New England behind us. Many people, dressed in their Sunday finery were coming from church in this small town.

We continued on our way, the road was macadam and ran through the valley of Wyomanock Creek. About the time we reached West Lebanon it started to sprinkle so we hurried along and when we reached Nassau it was raining hard. We sought shelter in a livery stable to wait out the rain. We ate our lunch on the covered bandstand and while there Frank showed up so we were still not able to shake him. At 3:20 it was still raining and we were in the livery stable, we washed up and felt a little better. In order to kill time I described Frank for

NASSAU,N.Y.

## CHAPTER FIVE

The 63rd Day        (Cont.)

Pittsfield,Massachusetts to Nassau,New York.

my diary. He was 14 rather small for his age, light hair, freck-
les galore. He had a light yellow hat, a dirty  ragged gray
sweater, short brown pants, not buckled at the knees and covered
with dirt. He had black shoes, several sizes too large and out at
the toes and no socks. He was not a very acceptable person.

We told the stable man about the boy and he said he would
handle it. We were still in the stable at 6 P.M. and it was still
raining when the stable man told Frank he would turn him over to
the police unless he headed back home. The last we saw of him,
he was riding back in the direction from which he came.

Later we were standing on a street corner when a man came
up to us(Oscar G. Winters) and after visiting for awhile said we
could sleep in his barn, if we cared to. We jumped at the chance
and went with him to the Fairview House,a hotel that he owned.
We washed up and they gave us our evening meal.
After eating we sat on the back porch and
visited awhile. How very kind most people
were. We slept in the hay loft with a comfortable bed. There was an electric light

FAIRVIEW HOUSE

right above us. Mr Winters brought us blankets so we were warm.
Hap dozed off but soon woke up and told me how he got the nick-
name "Happy". I don't remember the story but I always called him
"Hap" for short. We were now only 13 miles from Albany.

CHAPTER FIVE

BOSTON,MASSACHUSETTS TO BUFFALO,NEW YORK.

August 30th,1915     The 64th Day      (Monday)

Nassau,New York to Schenectady,New York.

9:30 A.M. and still raining. I slept fine last night down in a hollow with piles of hay on all sides. It was the best bed we had for some time. It was fun watching the crickets leap from place to place and watch the spiders descend from the roof over our heads or now and then pick a bug off our necks. In spite of all the activity we slept fine and were well rested.

We bought some cakes and potatoe chips for breakfast and a butcher gave us some meat to go with it. After eating we started for Albany at 11:23 A.M. The road was macadam and in fair shape. We rode through E.Greenbush and at 1 P.M. we were in Rensselaer across the river from Albany. We could see the Capitol from where we were. We paid 2¢ toll on the bridge across the Hudson River and entered the somewhat dirty streets of the city.

We went to the Capitol, not very impressive from the outside and Hap thought it was the Post Office because of lack of beauty. I bought some cards to send home. We wanted to see the socalled "Million Dollar Staircase" in the building. A million dollars in those days was worth many times its value today.

We saw some girls with their Mothers and two or three children who were sightseeing in the Capitol. I was very much interested in one very pretty girl with blond hair. I wanted to get acquainted with her, so when she was looking at an exhibit I went over and tried to engage her in conversation. She would listen politely to what I had to say but then she would walk

CHAPTER FIVE

The 64th Day       (Cont.)

Nassau, New York to Schenectady, New York.

away without saying anything, but she smiled as she left.

We saw these people several times in various places in the building. I tried twice more to talk to her but always with the same result. If we passed each other she would always smile but that was all. She seemed to be trying to tell me that while she didn't want to hurt my feelings, this was not the way it should be done. I guess she felt she  needed a formal introduction before talking to a stranger. I finally gave up on her but I sure wanted to meet her as she was pretty and so nice about brushing me off. We soon lost sight of her, I figured I would not see her again.

Before leaving the Capitol we took a look at the staircase, which was beautiful of all carved work of dull red stone. The interior of the building was beautiful, the Senate Chamber was very lovely as well as the resting room for the Senators. I did not think it equalled the Minnesota Capitol for real beauty.

We left the Capitol and went across the street to the New York State Educational Building. It was a magnificent structure dedicated in 1912. There were thirty six Corinthian Columns extending across the entire front. The exterior of the building was constructed of white stone and was more beautiful than the exterior of the Capitol.

Inside the building near the entrance was a broad staircase leading to the Rotunda. In the Rotunda were many murals pertaining to education. The Building houses the State Library, the State Museum, Chancellor's Hall and the offices of the

## CHAPTER FIVE

The 64th Day        (Cont.)

Nassau,New York to Schenectady,New York.

State Education Department.

GENERAL VIEW

CAPITOL

STAIRCASE

After we
looked around
downstairs we
went up to the

EDUCATIONAL BLDG.

D.& H.BLDG.
ALBANY,NEW YORK

Museum on the fourth floor. It certainly was interesting with
the many exhibits of skeletons of large extinct animals and fish.
There were also relief maps of New York State and many old
Indian relics. After our visit to the Museum we went back to the
Rotunda to take a good look of the three story chandelier hang-
ing from the ceiling.

I said to Hap, I'd sure like to see that girl again. I
turned around and there,just coming into the building, was that
same group with the girl with the golden hair. The girl's
Mother looked displeased when she saw me but the girl didn't see
me. Later the girl did see me and she smiled as she passed by.

We were soon in the Zoological section where many high cab-
inets contained exhibits. The girl would smile every time she saw
me and finally we were both looking at the same exhibit.

## CHAPTER FIVE

The 64th Day      (Cont.)

Nassau,New York to Schenectady,New York.

She walked around one side of the cabinet and I the other
and there we met. She asked if I was following them and I told
her that we got there first. That broke the ice and we started
a conversation. Now that she had accepted me as a friend, the
fact that I was rather the worse for appearance having camped
out or slept in barns for eight weeks seemed to make no difference to her. There she was in her Sunday best and me in my
soiled and worn clothing. We visited for about an hour and each
promised to write. I will refer to her as Miss'A' and she lived
on Long Island,New York.

She and her relatives were on a vacation at a lake near
Albany. I had a very enjoyable visit and had a great time looking at the many exhibits with her.

After about an hour her younger brother came over and said
they were ready to leave and after another promise to write I
said goodby to her. No story of a boy's adventure would be complete unless there was a girl somewhere in the picture. When I
left her that day I felt that I had finally met the girl of my
story.

We corresponded for a year and the following Summer I was
invited to visit them. I didn't have the money to go to New
York so of course I couldn't accept the invatation. I hoped that
some day we might meet again but it has not come to pass.

During the school year when we corresponded, I attended
a public high school in St.Paul and she attended an exclusive

## CHAPTER FIVE

The 64th Day          (Cont.)

Nassau,New York to Schenectady,New York.

private school on Long Island,New York.

We left Albany about 6 P.M. after sending cards home and looking around a little. I got a road guide from the Goodrich Co. which will serve until we reach Ohio or beyond. The road was macadam most of the way to Schenectady and we made good time. It was soon dark but we kept going. When we reached the outskirts of Schenectady it

NEW YORK CENTRAL R.R.

started to rain so we stopped and got permission to sleep in a barn. We found a bed in the old hay loft which was comfortable.

We found a store about 9 P.M. and the store keeper gave us a free meal of Boston baked beans and milk. It was a good meal and after answering the many questions of the people in the store, the store keeper took the information for the newspaper.

At 10:30 P.M. I was sitting on our bed in the barn bringing my diary up to date. There was an electric light overhead near the bed. Hap was asleep so I decided to turn in. Didn't see any-thing of Frank, our temporary companion today.

A ROAD SIGN

CHAPTER FIVE

BOSTON,MASSACHUSETTS TO BUFFALO,NEW YORK.

August 31st,1915    The 65th Day     (Tuesday)

Schenectady,New York to Nelliston,New York.

Had a good sleep and got up at 8:30. We started out at 9 A.M.
and it was cold riding. There were street cars running alongside

the road
and we
descended
a long

STATE ST.

GEN'L ELECTRIC CO.

UNION COLLEGE

SCHENECTADY,NEW YORK.

hill into

the business area of Schenectady. The road was paved into the
city which was about two miles from where we slept.

We sold a few cards and had a breakfast of scrambled eggs
at a lunch wagon on Clinton St. We rode out to the General Electric Plant but were ordered out as no visitors allowed. The
plant was a huge layout of red brick and concrete buildings
about 3/4 of a mile overall. The city is situated on the Mohawk
River, in one section of the city there were streets from Colonial times with Elm trees and white clapboard houses.

In leaving the city we rode on in the valley of the Mohawk

River. The road was loose rock macadam with
dirt road part of the way. The N.Y.Central
R.R. ran near the road and the trains were
really going fast. We stopped at Amsterdam

N.Y.C.R.R.STATION
AMSTERDAM, N.Y.

but only sold one card there.This city was not as lively as
Schenectady.I met a man who had walked from Chicago and we had
a nice visit telling about our experiences.

## CHAPTER FIVE

The 65th Day        (Cont.)

Schenectady, New York to Nelliston, New York.

Many of the people in Amsterdam came from Holland which no doubt accounts for the name. There was considerable manufacturing in the city, mostly knitting and carpet concerns.

1:35 P.M. Hap just had a tire blowout and went back to change his rear tire. I waited for him on the outskirts of the city. When I started out I tried to ride the car rail because the pavement was torn up. I didn't go far when I took a bad spill but fortunately I didn't break any bones. About this time my rear tire had a blowout which delayed us while Hap repaired it.

We sold a few cards at Fonda and at Palatine Bridge we could see the plant of the Beech-Nut Co, but as it was getting late we did't visit it. We rode on to Nelliston and it was dark when we got there. We met a Boy Scout leader from Boston and thinking we were scouts he stopped to talk and was much interested in our trip.

Five cents worth of sugar rolls constituted my evening meal. Our new acquaintance told us of a place where we might find a place to sleep. The farmer told us we could sleep in a pit in the barn which had some straw in the bottom. He brought a long ladder and we descended into what we called our dungeon. Our bed in the straw was very comfortable and it was nice and warm in the pit.

We had covered forty seven miles that day, mostly in the P.M. so we were tired and soon went to sleep.

CHAPTER FIVE

BOSTON,MASSACHUSETTS TO BUFFALO,NEW YORK.

September 1st,1915     The 66th Day     (Wednesday)

Nelliston,New York to Chittenango,New York.

It was cold when I woke up in the morning. I hated to get up,I was tired but I made it at 6 A.M. I finally got Hap up at 6:20. We enjoyed ourselves for a while jumping into the pit from the ladder.

We were off and running at 6:40. It was very cold riding. I had to cover my ears now and then and also rode with my hands in my pockets to keep them warm. We were riding in the valley of the Mohawk River and the railroad trains ran near the road.

FINKS BRIDGE

We ate breakfast at St.Johnsville and at Little Falls we sold a few cards and I bought a film for my camera.

Little Falls is on the Mohawk River about 20 miles east of Utica. The city got its name from the cascade rapids of the Mohawk near by. This rapid water furnished plenty of water power for manufacturing. Bicycles and many other things were made there. There was much dairying in the surrounding area and the country side was beautiful.

Leaving Little Falls I took a picture of a sign along the road which showed we were halfway between New York City and Buffalo. It also showed that we were 74.9 miles from Albany and 222.6 miles from Buffalo. We continued on and stopped at Herkimer for a short time to sell a few cards. We rode through Ilion

## CHAPTER FIVE

The 66th Day        (Cont.)

Nelliston,New York to Chittenango,New York.

where the Remington typewriter was made but didn't visit there.

We reached Utica about 1:25 P.M. and had lunch at the
Belmont Restaurant. We had fried halibut with tomato sauce for
15¢ each. I also had a piece of blueberry pie and it was a very

MAIN ST.
HERKIMER N.Y.

GENESEE ST.
UTICA N.Y.

COURT HOUSE
UTICA N.Y.

good meal. Hap bought a new tire and tube and we sold a few
cards.

In the early days there was a stage coach running from Utica
to Albany. It took a long full day to make the trip. The canal
packets made the trip in about the same length of time. We had
been riding on loose rock macadam roads and some dirt roads and
they were in pretty good shape. It didn't rain that day and we
were making good time. We saw the statue of Baron Von Steuben
which was erected and given to the city just a year before.
There were many electric street cars in the city.

Utica was a large city with much manufacturing. Knit goods
and cotton cloth were the principal products but many other
things were also made there. Understand it was the location for
the first Woolworth 5¢ and 10¢ store but it didn't make it.

We left Utica about 2:30 P.M. and sent cards home from New
Hartford. The road departed from the Mohawk Valley a short way

CHAPTER FIVE

The 66th Day      (Cont.)

Nelliston,New York to Chittenango,New York.

west of Utica. After leaving New Hartford Hap got way ahead of
me and I caught up to him at Kirkland. We traded a boy two post
cards for two sandwiches which was a good bargain for us. After
leaving Kirkland one of my tires blew out and while Hap was repairing it I brought my diary up to date. We did not have any
gas to repair it,I hailed a passing Ford car, the driver was
very nice about giving us some out of his tank. I got under the
car, turned on the gas, and much of it ran down my arm getting it.

We were trying to make a record run and at this point we
had gone 49 miles and the Sun was sinking fast. When we started
again we did not stop and it was soon dark. We descended into a
valley riding as fast as we could. We continued long after dark
and of course without lights. We came to a stretch of freshly
oiled road and then a fine road and kept going. By 8:15 P.M. we
had traveled 73.2 miles which about equalled our previous high
between Lancaster,Pennsylvania and Philadelphia.

We asked at a farm house near Chittenango and they were very
nice about letting us sleep in the barn. We have been in the
habit of sleeping in barns lately as it is usually too cold at
night to sleep out with only one blanket each.

We have only gone to bed hungry two or three nights on the
entire trip and this was one of the times. Hap and I didn't have
a penny between us.

CHAPTER FIVE

BOSTON,MASSACHUSETTS TO BUFFALO,NEW YORK.

September 2nd,1915    The 67th Day    (Thursday)

Chittenango,New York to Elbridge,New York.

Up at 8:45 A.M. The Sun was shining and it looked like it
would be a nice day. The farmer gave each of us 8 fine red apples,
which were more than welcome as we were pretty hungry. We sold
enough cards in Chittenango so we could have breakfast.

After leaving the town I got way ahead of Hap so I waited
for him in the shade of a tree at the side of the road. We were
now 7½ miles east of Syracuse, the road was good and the weather
warm so I rode all the way without a cap. We were on Gennesee St.
which was supposed to be the longest street in the world, extending from Albany to Buffalo, according to natives. The road at
this point was oiled macadam and in fine shape. Hap arrived soon
and repaired a puncture in one of his tires.

We were soon in East Syracuse and we entered Syracuse on a

SYRACUSE, NEW YORK

UTICA, NEW YORK

CHAPTER FIVE

The 67th Day       (Cont.)

Chittenango,New York to Elbridge,New York.

well paved street. A man stopped me in front of the Post Office
and asked if I knew several people in St.Paul but I didn't know
any of them. I sold a few cards including five to a man I met
riding a motorcycle.

We had lunch
of hamburgers and
I took a picture
on the main street
in front of the
Woolworth 5 and 10
cent store. There
were several women
in the picture who
had long skirts on
almost reaching to
the ground. Of
course that was

CITY HALL
SYRACUSE,NEW YORK.

SO. SALINA ST.

CLINTON SQUARE

S.U. STADIUM

the way women dressed at that time. One thing that interested
me was the fact that steam trains ran through the city on one
of the business streets. We rode out to see Syracuse University
with its large stadium for sporting events. I took a picture of
the city hall which reminded me of the Post Office in St.Paul.

Syracuse was an important manufacturing and commercial city.
It is located near Onondago Lake and is surrounded by a rich

CHAPTER FIVE

The 67th Day       (Cont.)

Chittenango,New York to Elbridge,New York.

agriculture region. It had wide streets and of course electric
trolley cars.

We left Syracuse about 5 P.M. and rode 16 miles to Elbridge
where we had our evening meal. A farmer gave us permission to
sleep in an old wagon in his yard. We put our belongings in the
wagon and went to the business district where they were having
a flower show. They had a fine collection of flowers and plants
on display which was well worth seeing. We were the honored
guests at the show and visited with mostly prominent people in
this town of about 600 people. They presented us with purple
asters which we pinned on. We were very well received and had
an enjoyable evening.

Between Syracuse and Elbridge we rode through Camillus, a
small town which is one of the claimants as the birthplace of the
present Republican Party. There are other claimants including
Ripon,Wisconsin where my Grandfather attended the meeting in
connection with the founding of the party.

After giving a reporter the information on the trip for the
local newspaper we went back to the wagon. We got to bed about
11:15 P.M., putting the tent and blankets over us we were quite
comfortable.

We didn't make many miles today having spent so much time
in Syracuse.

CHAPTER FIVE

BOSTON,MASSACHUSETTS TO BUFFALO,NEW YORK.

September 3rd,1915     The 68th Day     (Friday)

Elbridge,New York to Canandaigua,New York.

We were ready to start our days run at 7 A.M. About 7:45
Hap was way behind so I waited for him. We had covered 6½ miles
and were 3½ miles from Auburn where we stopped for breakfast.
We had a breakfast of coffee and sweet rolls. We each ate a
whole pie of four pieces. I sold a few cards and bought two

Syracuse papers which had an
article in it about our trip.
When leaving the town we stopped at the Harley-Davidson
agency for free oil and graph-
ite.

HILL WEST OF AUBURN,N.Y.
(SWAMP BEYOND THE HILL)

Eight miles west of Auburn
the road was closed and we were
supposed to take a detour on a
sandy road. We decided to go
through the closed road but
with some loss of time. We
stopped at a farmhouse and
were given several delicious
pears and apples.

11:30 A.M. We were on a
high hill overlooking the famous Montezuma Swamp. The view was
beautiful so we stopped to rest and admire the scenery.

After our rest we descended to the swamp. I took a picture

CHAPTER FIVE

The 68th Day      (Cont.)

Elbridge,New York to Canandaigua,New York.

of a pile driver driving piles for a bridge. The road across the
swamp was macadam so there was no trouble getting across. We
passed a barge canal and soon reached Seneca Falls. The water-
fall at this location gave the city its name as well as water
power resulting in considerable industrial activity.

A Mrs.Bloomer who lived in Seneca Falls was one of the
first to advocate equality for women including suffrage. The
outfit that was worn by the women members of the organization
was called "bloomers" after her. Susan B.Anthony worked with
her for many years. The Gould Pump Works was the principal
industry in the city.

We sold some cards in
town and continued on our
way. We stopped at Water-
loo to repair a cut tire.

SOLDIER' SAILOR'          GOULD
MONUMENT              PUMP WORKS
SENECA FALLS,N.Y.

The road was very poor between Waterloo and Geneva so progress
was slow and hard to come by. We stopped to rest at a very nice
park in Geneva and then continued on to Canandaigua arriving
there about 6:30 P.M. This place seemed like a lively town so
decided to spend the night there.

We sold a few cards and went to look for a place to sleep.
We tried five places and they all turned us down. We then tried
to get permission to pitch our tent but once again we were refused. This was the hardest time finding a place on the entire
trip and we were pretty discouraged. Then we asked at another

CHAPTER FIVE

The 68th Day      (Cont.)

Elbridge,New York to Canandaigua,New York.

place and the man said "sure you can sleep in the barn". In a

few minutes he came out and asked us to sleep in the house.

That was the way it had always been, once in a while we were not

welcome, but always some kind person saved the day for us.

We sold a few cards in the business district and then went

to the Temple Theater and saw the movie, "Marrying Money". It

was a good show and we enjoyed it. We then went to bed in the

house about 10:15.

I do not have the name of the man who was so kind to us, he

lived on West Gibson at Pearl Street.

Canandaigua was a city of 5 or 6,000 people, and is in an

agricultural region. There were many attractive streets with

old homes and with lawns well kept. The City Hall was a two

story brick building, very old but still a nice looking struc-

ture. The Ontario County Court House, a two story gray brick

building on Main Street was erected about 1860. It was here that

Susan B. Anthony and associates were tried for voting in a

national election.

CHAPTER FIVE

BOSTON,MASSACHUSETTS TO BUFFALO,NEW YORK.

September 4th,1915      The 69th Day      (Saturday)

Canandaigua,New York to E.Pembroke,New York.

After a good nights sleep we sat down to a delicious breakfast at the people's house. After visiting with them for awhile
and thanking them for their kindness, we were on our way. The
next town Holcomb where I got a shave for 10¢. At Avon I sold
85¢ worth of cards which was better than usual in a small town.

The baker gave us some doughnuts to take along after our
lunch of milk,rolls and doughnuts.

Three miles west of Avon one of my tires blew out. Hap repaired it in short order, by now he had a lot of experience re-

COURT HOUSE

HIGH SCHOOL

R.R.  STATION

pairing tires. We rode        BATAVIA,NEW YORK
through Caledonia, Le Roy and Stafford. We stopped at Batavia
for our next meal and sold a few cards. Batavia was the trade
center for a farming region and there was considerable manufacturing there.

It was dark when we left there at 7:25 P.M. Going out of
town we were stopped by a policeman for riding without lights.
After telling him about our trip he let us go with a warning to
be careful. It was pitch dark on the road but an occasional
automobile lit it up some. It was perfectly level country and

## CHAPTER FIVE

The 69th Day        (Cont.)

Canandaigua,New York to E.Pembroke,New York.

we could see the lights of approaching autos for miles.

We rode 6½ miles to East Pembroke and as it was dangerous riding in the dark we decided to spend the night there, as it was about 9:20 P.M.

There was a two story band stand in the town and as this looked like a good place to spend the night we decided to sleep there. We borrowed a broom to clean the second floor and then by means of a borrowed rope we hoisted the bikes up to the second floor. We then closed the trap door in the floor and I made my bed on it to prevent visitors from coming up the stairs.

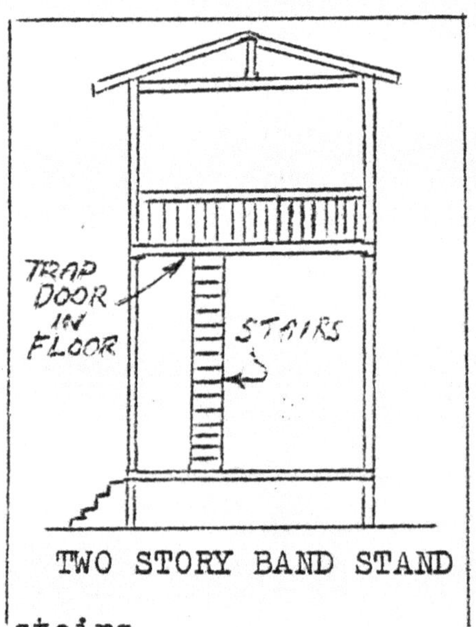


TWO STORY BAND STAND

A number of boys were across the street and we were afraid we might have visitors during the night so we locked the two bikes together just to be on the safe side. We had borrowed a lantern and I brought my diary up to date, the light soon went out so we turned in for the night.

We rode 55 miles that day and were only 33 miles from Buffalo.

CHAPTER FIVE

BOSTON,MASSACHUSETTS TO BUFFALO,NEW YORK.

September 5th,1915    The 70th Day    (Sunday)

E.Pembroke,New York to Buffalo,New York.

Up at 7:30, we were not bothered by visitors and had a good nights sleep. We let our bikes down by means of the rope, packed our gear and played a few games of horse shoe. We had breakfast and left about 9:15 and as there was a good concrete road the last 23 miles to Buffalo we made good time. People in autos waved at us and wished us good luck. When 19 miles from the city Hap had a puncture and then we came to a closed road with a long detour. We decided to go through the closed road and had it all to ourselves as the autos, motorcyles and wagons had to take the long detour.

The weather was warm, the roads were good and we enjoyed the ride as we sped along, minus our caps. I was ahead of Hap and some people eating lunch at the side of the road flagged me down. I went back to where they were eating. They asked about the trip and gave me a bottle of beer, an egg and a sandwich. One of the men was Mr.Koch, owner of the Koch brewery of Dunkirk,New York.

When we were eight miles from the city it started to rain but we kept going. We soon reached the city and parked our bikes in the newspaper company garage.

We took the train to Niagara Falls, round trip fare 60¢ each. We reached the falls in a short time and on the way saw the Carborundum plant and also the Shredded Wheat factory. The

## CHAPTER FIVE

The 70th Day        (Cont.)

E.Pembroke,New York to Buffalo,New York.

city was almost like Coney Island with many souvenir stands. We

first saw the falls from the brink of the American

Falls at Pros-

pect Point. It

was a most

magnificent

sight with the

GENERAL VIEW
NIAGARA FALLS, NEW YORK

ELEC.POWER PLANTS

CAVE OF WINDS
IN WINTER

great mass of water tumbling over the brink and

making a never ending roar.

The Horseshoe Falls were won-

derful,  a bright green color

near the top and gradually

turning into a beautiful

sparkling white as the water

neared the bottom.

After taking two pic-

NIAGARA FALLS

tures of this enchanting sight we went down to the base of the
falls. From there we could get an idea of the great height of
the falls as the water came tumbling down, the mist obscuring
all the surrounding falls. I ventured almost under the falling
water and was drenched to the skin. The water wet and spoiled
35 post cards I had in my shirt pocket besides a pretty picture
I had of the falls. While at the base of the falls Hap took a
picture of me on a large rock at the water's edge.

CHAPTER FIVE

The 70th Day       (Cont.)

E.Pembroke,New York to Buffalo,New York.

The American Falls was about 1,000 feet wide with a drop of about
165 feet. The Horseshoe or Canadian Falls was about 2,500 feet
wide with a drop about 10 feet less than the American Falls.

After some time at the base of the falls we came back to
the top and walked down to the steel arch bridge above the falls
and Hap took a picture of the bridge. On the far side of the
bridge was a large pipe about 15 feet in diameter out of which
was shooting a great quantity of water at tremendous speed. This
was what furnished the power for the Niagara Power Company.

Later we went up to the top and walked over nearer the
Canadian Falls on a bridge over part of them.The falls were a
beautiful sight and I hated to leave them. We could see across
into Canada which was at war. Before leaving I took a picture of
some of the power plants.

We had a nice train ride back to Buffalo and I enjoyed the
trip very much. Upon our arrival there we found a place to stay
at the DeLuxe Hotel at 75¢ for the both of us.

In the evening we went to a motion picture theatre where we
saw a war picture, then turned in about 10:45 P.M.


END OF CHAPTER FIVE.

CHAPTER SIX

BUFFALO,NEW YORK TO CHICAGO,ILLINOIS.

September 6th,1915      The 71st Day      (Monday)

Buffalo,New York to Farnham,New York.

We were sleeping soundly when a band playing in the street
below woke us up. We looked out the window and there was a parade

MAIN STREET

SAVINGS BANK

NIAGARA SQUARE

TEMPLE OF MUSIC

BUFFALO,
NEW YORK

CITY HALL

marching down the street. Then we remembered that this was Labor
Day so we dressed in a hurry as we wanted to see the activities.

We had breakfast of beans and hamburger. This close to the
Canadian border we often got their money in change. This restaurant man refused to accept it and Hap had to go out and exchange
it so he could pay for his breakfast. We watched the parade in
front of the City Hall. This was a three story building constructed of a light colored stone and had a high tower with four
way clocks. "Votes for Women" was one of the principal floats
in the parade.

We went to the Temple of Music, it was in this building
that President McKinley was assassinated on September 6th,1901
just 14 years to the day before we were there. A large reception

CHAPTER SIX

The 71st Day        (Cont.)

Buffalo,New York  to  Farnham,New York.

was being held for him while he was attending the Pan-American
Exposition. The assassin was captured, convicted and executed.

We next visited Niagara Square and right in the center of
it was a McKinley Monument. It was a tall obelisk resting on a
large pedestal with pools and decorated with figures of lions.

We left Buffalo about noon after getting our bikes out of
the 'Newspaper' garage and there was no charge for keeping them.
After leaving the city we rode past the plant of the Lackawanna
Steel Co. In this town there were identical  houses on both
sides of the streets all joined together as one continuous
structure about a quarter of a mile long. It was quite a sight
and there were several children on every doorstep.

We had lots of tire trouble and I got a big puncture in my
front tire. We stopped and asked a small boy to get us a sandwich. He ran home and when he came back he said we should come
over to his house. We went with him and the lady gave each of us
three sandwiches, two cups of tea and some cookies. Hap repaired
the tire and I took their name and address so that I could thank
them again when we got home.

For 16 miles out of Buffalo there was a fine brick pavement.
We rode along beautiful Lake Erie, it seemed almost like an ocean,
it was so large, and to think we would ride its entire great
length. Fifteen miles out of Buffalo we stopped and looking back,
saw the city in the dim distance. When I realized how far we had
gone in so short a time, I began to realize what a vast distance

## CHAPTER SIX

The 71st Day        (Cont.)

Buffalo,New York to Farnham,New York.

we were covering on our trip.

We were soon beyond the good road and ahead of us the road was dirt and very dusty from the automobiles and wagons. It started to rain when we were at Evans Center and the road was now mud and water. We stayed in Evans Center for about two hours to wait out the rain. While there we ate our evening meal of crackers and cheese. It was nearly dark when I left this town and Hap was not far behind. The road by now was in terrible shape and we had a hard time riding as it was a fight all the way to keep going in the deep mud and water.

After about five miles of this we reached the town of Farnham and got permission to sleep in a barn. While going out of the farmer's yard to get my bike I fell down a deep hole filled with water. We went to bed about 9:30 wet clothes and all.

CHAPTER SIX

BUFFALO,NEW YORK TO CHICAGO,ILLINOIS.

September 7th,1915    The 72nd Day        (Tuesday)

Farnham,New York to Ripley,New York.

Up early after a good sleep in the barn. School was starting in St.Paul that day and here we were a thousand miles from
home. No doubt my Mother was very much disturbed because we
were not home for the opening of school.

I stopped at a school house for a drink of water and in
about a minute there were at least fifty children around me.
They wanted to know all about our trip and one said he **was going**
to make a trip like ours when he grew up.

Hap had not arrived yet as he had two punctures which delayed him. All day long we had been riding along the shore of Lake
Erie. The lake and other scenery was beautiful and we enjoyed the
days run very much in spite of the fact that the roads were poor.

We rode through several small towns including Fredonia and
Westfield where we sold a few cards. We reached Ripley,N.Y. in
the evening and sold several cards. We got permission to sleep
in a barn then went to a show to see a movie.

We went back to the house where we had made arrangements
to sleep in the barn. The people came out to meet us and said we
could sleep in the house. Of course we were more than happy to
sleep in a bed for a change.

We visited with the people in the evening and they were very
much interested in our trip. We then went to bed in a comfortable
bed.

## CHAPTER SIX

### BUFFALO,NEW YORK TO CHICAGO,ILLINOIS.

September 8th,1915     The 73rd Day     (Wednesday)

Ripley,New York to  Girard,Pennsylvania.

We had a good sleep in a real bed and the people woke us at
7:30. The Baptists were having a convention in Ripley and a minister of that group was also staying at the same house. When we
sat down at the table he led us in prayer and then we enjoyed an
excellent breakfast. After
a short visit, we thanked
our host and were on our
way.

About three miles be-
yond Ripley we came to the
Pennsylvania State line. I
stopped and looked back at
the State we had just left.
I had sort of a feeling of

STATE STREET

4 MILE CREEK

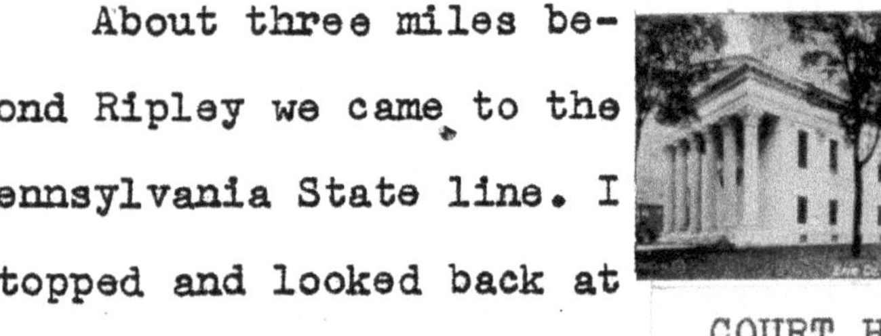

COURT HOUSE

BLOCK HOUSE

ERIE, PENNSYLVANIA

sadness leaving the great State of New York where we met so many
kind and helpful people and saw so many things of interest.

We stopped at a roadside stand and bought peaches and grapes.
After visiting with two girls for a few minutes we continued on
our way. Hap was having a great deal of tire trouble resulting
in delay after delay. In spite of this we enjoyed the ride.

We continued along the shore of Lake Erie and reached Erie
about 2 P.M. We had lunch of hamburger steak and we each bought
a pie at a bakery. The girls in town were very friendly and several stopped to talk. Hap changed his rear inner tube and then

CHAPTER SIX

The 73rd Day     (Cont.)

Ripley,New York to   Girard,Pennsylvania.

we went up to the Continental Rubber Co. and after talking to
the man for some time and explaining we were in a bad way as
far as tires were concerned he said he would give each of us a
tire to try out. They were good $5.00 Vitalic tires and we were
to advise him how they stood up. The tires served us well and
we so advised him when we reached home. They were better on the
poor roads than the cheaper tires we had been using.

Before leaving Erie we visited the Anthony Wayne Block
House, the Court House and of course we walked down State St.

Erie was a large city with a population of about 80,000.
It had a fine harbor on Lake Erie and there was some manufacturing in the city. East of Erie was an important grape growing area which we passed through on our way into the city. The
Wolverine, the first iron ship on the Great Lakes was built there
in 1843. The 'Niagara' flagship of Perry's fleet which scored a
victory over the British in 1813 was sunk following the coming
of peace. The ship was raised in 1913 and after being rebuilt and
equipped it was anchored at the public dock and maintained as a
historical exhibit.

We continued on our way through a cattle and poultry rais-
ing area to N.Girard. We had our evening meal there of hamburger
sandwiches and apple pie. We decided to spend the night in N.
Girard and in looking around we noticed a band stand in the city
park, which we figured would be a good place to sleep. It was a

CHAPTER SIX

The 73rd Day        (Cont.)

Ripley, New York to    Girard, Pennsylvania.

two story affair with the band stand on the second floor. The
first floor was entirely enclosed and as the door on the lower
level was locked there was no way to get up to the second level.
We managed to borrow a ladder and climbed up and found a trap
door leading to the lower level. I descended on the inside ladder to the lower level. It was pitch dark down there, I found
the exit door but it was locked so I went up on the inside ladder and came down on our outside ladder.

We got permission to put our bikes in a garage for safe-
keeping. After one more climb up into our "Robinson Crusoe" house,
we pulled the ladder up and were secure in our home for the night.
Hap slept on the trap door and I was soon fast asleep on the
floor in another part of the abode.

Girard was a quiet town with many retired people living
there. It somewhat resembled an old New England settlement.
There was a beautiful Soldiers and Sailors Monument with a round
marble shaft, located on the Main Street.

## CHAPTER SIX

### BUFFALO, NEW YORK TO CHICAGO, ILLINOIS.

September 9th, 1915      The 74th Day      (Thursday)

Girard, Pennsylvania to N. Kingsville, Ohio.

Up at 7:45, we let the ladder down and took our gear down and returned the ladder to the owner. We had breakfast, got our bikes and while on the main street I sold 50¢ worth of cards to a Norwiegan. This was a better than usual sale for me.

We stopped for a few minutes at both East and West Springfield where we sold a few cards. Two miles beyond these towns I reached the Ohio State Line, I waited there for Hap to arrive.

Now the East was behind us, it had been a wonderful trip in the Eastern States. We had met so many kind and helpful people, we had seen so many places of historical interest, not to mention great cities like Philadelphia, New York and Boston. I have always felt that this was the most interesting part of the trip. From now on we will be doing our riding in the Middle West and this too was very rewarding.

The first city we came to in Ohio was Conneaut with a population of about 8,000. It had a fine harbor transshipping much coal and ore. The coal was shipped Northwest and

CONNEAUT HARBOR

the ore went to steel mills to the East in Pennsylvania and New York. We had to pay 1¢ toll to cross a bridge into Conneaut and while there we sold a few cards. I won a half pound box of candy for 5¢ and then spent 20¢ trying to win another. Hap also won candy but dont know how much it cost him.

## CHAPTER SIX

The 74th Day          (Cont.)

Girard,Pennsylvania to N.Kingsville,Ohio.

During the morning while coming down a steep grade my brake failed to work and as I was going too fast to make a sharp turn at the bottom I was sent crashing over rocks, sticks and rubbish at the side of the road. Keeping my seat with difficulty I finally got stopped and back on the road safely none the worse for the experience.

We soon came to Amboy about three miles beyond Conneaut. We decided to go swimming in Lake Erie at this town. We went over to the lake, took off our outer clothing, we had bathing suits for underwear so they served as usual when we went swimming.

We spent the afternoon and evening swimming and fooling around in the water. It was nearly dark when we left with our 'underwear' still wet. We had gone about a mile when Hap realized that he had left his pack on the beach. I waited for him to return but it took him some time as it was a sand road.

We rode four miles after dark to the town of N.Kingsville and the first thing we did was to get a can of beans for supper. We easily found a place to sleep on the floor of a private garage. It did not surprise us as we had been so well treated in Ohio on our trip East.

We went to bed about 9 P.M. and the man of the house gave us a Buffalo robe to sleep on.

CHAPTER SIX

BUFFALO,NEW YORK TO CHICAGO,ILLINOIS.

September 10th,1915     The 75th Day     (Friday)

N.Kingsville,Ohio to East Cleveland,Ohio.

Our host woke us at 5:30, no doubt that was when he got up
for his daily chores. We didn't want to get up so early but of
course we did. Hap repaired a puncture in my front tire.

We left about 6:30 and rode six miles to Ashtabula where I
had a breakfast of two dishes of oatmeal and a whole 5¢ pie. It
was a city of about 20,000 and is located at the mouth of the
Ashtabula River. It was an important shipping point on Lake Erie.

We sold a few cards but didn't stay long as we were anxious
to be on our way. Beyond Ashtabula we had five miles of macadam
road, the balance to Painesville was gravel and clay. Between
Ashtabula and Geneva there were foot paths at the side of the road
and we rode on them wherever possible. We soon reached Geneva,
this being the third Geneva we had been in on the trip i.e.
Geneva,Wisconsin, Geneva,N.Y. and Geneva,Ohio.

After leaving Geneva we rode
18 miles without a stop and reached
Painesville about 1:30 P.M. We had
covered 33 miles during the morning in spite of the fact that the
road was not too good, being sandy

MAIN STREET

PAINESVILLE,     COURT HOUSE
OHIO

in places. We stopped for a rest and a bite to eat. After eating
we continued on to the vicinity of East Cleveland where we decided to spend the night. We had trouble finding a place to pitch
our tent but finally found a vacant area and put up our tent about

CHAPTER SIX

The 75th Day      (Cont.)

N.Kingsville,Ohio to East Cleveland,Ohio.

50 feet from the waters edge of Lake Erie. We were about 30 feet
above the water with nothing between us and the lake so it was
a pleasant place to be. There were two adjacent trees and we supported the tent between them.

After getting organised for the night, we went in swimming,
and while in the water noticed occasional flashes of lightning.
We didn't stay in the water very long and back at the tent we
hung our wet bathing suits (our underwear) on the tent ropes to
dry. We drove the tent stakes down better as we anticipated a
storm.

We were soon asleep when all of a sudden the storm hit. A
terrific wind off the lake was blowing against us and it was
pouring down rain. There was no protection between us and the
lake so we felt the full fury of the storm. We leaped out of bed
to save the tent and it took all our strength to keep it from
blowing away. The rain was coming down by the bucketful and the
tent leaked like a sieve. After a while when it calmed down
some we went to bed soaking wet.

Note: We saw many horse drawn wagons and buggies on the
road today.

CHAPTER SIX

BUFFALO,NEW YORK TO CHICAGO,ILLINOIS.

September 11th,1915       The 76th Day      (Saturday)

East Cleveland,Ohio to Elyria,Ohio.

When we woke up in the morning the wind was still blowing a
little but the rain had stopped. We went outside the tent to get
our underwear (bathing suits) and bath towels but they were no-
where in sight. It looked like we were in for trouble without our
underwear. We started out to look for them and at last found
them scattered far and near. Some were nearly a block away but
eventually we found all of our belongings so we avoided a bad
situation.

On the way into the city of Cleveland we stopped at the
Goodrich Agency and they gave us road guides for the entire rest
of the trip home. They were very nice about it and gave us information about the roads and the best ones to take. We stopped at

a store and
bought milk and
Zu Zu ginger
snaps for break-
fast. We were
soon down town

LUNA PARK          PUBLIC SQUARE                    EUCLID AVE

CLEVELAND,OHIO

on Euclid Avenue which was a very busy street in the heart of the
business district. We sent souvenir cards home from the Post Office.

The St. Paul cards we expected to get here had not arrived
and as our supply of cards was running out, I wrote home to have
them send us some at a designated city on our way west. We didn't
have any trouble selling a few cards in the downtown area.

CHAPTER SIX

The 76th Day      (Cont.)

East Cleveland,Ohio to Elyria,Ohio.

The Public Square with the wide streets and the many tall buildings was very impressive. Superior Avenue, Euclid Avenue and Huron Road were fine wide streets.

Cleveland was one of the largest cities in the United States and was a large steel producing city. It is located on Lake Erie and the Cuyahoga River.

We did not spend much time in Cleveland as we were anxious to be on our way. We passed the remains of a large truck at the side of the road that had been more or less destroyed by fire. We stopped at a farm house and asked to buy some apples but of course they gave us all we wanted.

We kept going and as the road for the last few miles to Elyria was brick we soon reached the city. An interesting sight in Elyria was so-called "Cheapside" there were many horse drawn vehicles on the street and parked at the side of the road. We ate our evening meal consisting of hamburgere,

BROAD STREET
ELYRIA,OHIO

beans and cookies. We stopped to look at a racing automobile and a crowd soon collected, thinking we had come in with it.

It was getting dark but we started out, a policeman on the corner of Broad and Middle Avenue wished us good luck and we proceeded in the dark. We had several narrow escapes from  automobiles so we stopped at a farm house about two miles west of town and got permission to sleep in the barn and the farmer gave

CHAPTER SIX

The 76th Day      (Cont.)

East Cleveland,Ohio to Elyria,Ohio.

us a canvas to sleep on. Later when I asked him for a drink of
water, he gave each of us a pint bottle of rich milk.

All the way from Buffalo to Cleveland we had been riding
along the shore of Lake Erie but west of Cleveland the road no
longer followed the shore so we wont see the lake again until
we get to Toledo.

Elyria is lo-
cated eight miles
south of the lake
on the Black Riv-
er. The river
furnishes water
power for the
many industries
located there.

Theodore Dreiser in his book "A Hoosier Holiday" tells about
an automobile trip he made from New York City to Indiana. He rode
over the same road that we did, between Buffalo and Elyria and at
about the same time that we did.He speaks of long stretches of
poor roads and the difficulty they had getting through. If they
were so bad for an automobile you can well imagine what they
were like for bicycles.

## CHAPTER SIX

### BUFFALO, NEW YORK TO CHICAGO, ILLINOIS.

September 12th,1915     The 77th Day        (Sunday)

Elyria,Ohio to Norwalk,Ohio.

I woke up at 5 but felt a little under the weather so stayed in bed for awhile. Hap woke up before long so we both got up and put our gear on the bikes.We ate in a restaurant and were ready to be on our way. We reached Oberlin at noon so stopped for lunch. Hap repaired a puncture I had and then we moved on as this being a College town things were high-priced.

Oberlin is where Oberlin College is located, understand that this was the first college in the United States to adopt a co-education policy. The city was a nice residential community and understand that it was a station on the "Underground Railway" prior to the Civil War.

We passed the college buildings on our way out of town and had two miles of good concrete road. Then the road was poor macadam again for the next fifteen miles. We stopped at Wakeman long enough to sell a few cards and about eight miles from Norwalk we were back on a good road.

We got to Norwalk about 5 P.M. We had now completed a great circle. It was here on the trip East that we turned Southeast to Akron, Pittsburgh, Philadelphia, New York City and Boston. Now coming West by way of Albany, Buffalo, Cleveland and Elyria and once again Norwalk, the great circle was completed.

I immediately recognized the place as a town we had stayed overnight in on the trip East. We ate supper in the same restaurant as before and then sold some cards in the business area.

## CHAPTER SIX

The 77th Day        (Cont.)

Elyria,Ohio to Norwalk,Ohio.

We visited with the residents for awhile and decided to camp in the same spot where we had camped before. We set up camp with the aid of a lantern we borrowed from the same man who let us use his lantern on our previous stop. A young man stopped by and offered to take us out to a restaurant for supper but we had already had something to eat so had to pass it up.

We bought and ate so many roasted marshmallows that we both felt rather sick. While roasting our marshmallows a newspaper reporter stopped by to get the information on our trip for the local paper. The people remembered us and were very nice and very much interested in the trip. I roasted a few marshmallows for the small boy who still had the baby alligator as before. During the evening a man came over and told us "fish" stories for about an hour. Another man came over and brought us a pitcher of ice water, everyone was so friendly. The same little boy who sold popcorn came around again, he had shown us the place to camp on our trip East. He left and soon came back with ice cream for us, which was quite a treat.

It was just like getting home after a long absence to be in this friendly city again and we certainly appreciated it. We went to bed, after several warnings to beware of snakes, which was the same warning we had on our previous stay.

## CHAPTER SIX

### BUFFALO, NEW YORK TO CHICAGO, ILLINOIS.

September 13th,1915     The 78th Day     (Monday)

Norwalk,Ohio to Hessville,Ohio.

We were up at eight, the snakes didn't bother us that night for which we were thankful. We packed our gear, went to the business district and after selling two or three cards we had breakfast. We then canvassed the stores and sold a few more cards.

We were now ready to leave Norwalk. From here to South Bend, Indiana, a distance of 180 miles, we will be traveling on the same road we used on our trip East. This part of the trip proved very interesting as we got to meet and say hello to the many people who had helped us along the way on our trip East. As we rode along we recognized the many things we had seen before and we came to the short stretch of concrete road where we had raced.

We stopped at Monroeville to sell cards and I bought a roll of tape for tire repairs. At Bellevue we got a drink of water at the same fountain as before and where Hap had taken a picture of me before.

MAIN STREET
BELLEVUE,OHIO.

At Clyde we had marshmallow sundaes, remembering how good they were as we had some there before on our way East. I wrote home from Fremont and we stopped at the same place in Hessville where we had been given so many cherries on our stop before. The people had a store and we bought beans and cookies for our evening meal. The lady gave us bread and tea to go with our meal. (J.H.Melious,General Merchandise) She told us of a good place to sleep at a farm house near by. Taking her suggestion we called

CHAPTER SIX

The 78th Day       (Cont.)

Norwalk,Ohio to Hessville,Ohio.

on the farmer and he said we were quite welcome to sleep in the
barn (John Reed, R.F.D. Route 1, Lindsey,Ohio). It certainly
was a pleasure to travel across Ohio, the people were so kind
and friendly.

We found it too hot to sleep in the barn so we spread our
blankets under a tree and slept there. My clothes were much the
worse for wear and while I was busy mending them the farmer came
out and visited for a short time.

We talked for a long time about the trip and the possibility
of organizing a bicycle club when we got home.

It was cool out under the tree and we finally went to sleep.

## CHAPTER SIX

### BUFFALO,NEW YORK TO CHICAGO,ILLINOIS.

September 14th,1915       The 79th Day     (Tuesday)

Hessville,Ohio to Sylvania,Ohio.

Up at 6. I dreamt that I was home in bed and when I woke up I was surprised to find that I was under a tree in far off Ohio.

The farmer invited us for breakfast and after cleaning up we sat down to a good home cooked meal. After breakfast I did some more mending of my worn clothing.

After thanking the Reeds we were on our way going over the same hot, dusty roads that we had been on going East. We stopped at Woodville where I bought tape for tire repairs, got a shave and sold seven cards. Hap repaired my rear tire puncture and we were off and running.

It was unusually hot and the Sun,reflected by the hot, white macadam nearly blinded us. We were getting pretty hot and thirsty so we stopped at a farm house for a drink of water. While there the farmer gave us several apples. We moved on and were soon in Toledo. We went to the Post Office to write home and I received mail from there.



The cards we had forwarded from Cleveland did not arrive due to insufficient postage. I sent the postage and asked them to send the cards to us at South Bend,Indiana. I wrote to the Principal of the high school in St.Paul explaining why I would be late for the opening of school. I only had 28 cards left to last until we reached South Bend. This was not enough so at Toledo we each bought cards at the 5 and 10¢ store at 6 for 5¢ and then went out in front of the store and sold them at 5¢ each.

CHAPTER SIX

The 79th Day        (Cont.)

Hessville,Ohio to Sylvania,Ohio.

This was not the first time we ran out of cards and did the same thing. A man came up to me and said, " How are you hikers?" We told him we were riding bikes, this surprised him as people didn't take long bike trips at that time.

We visited awhile and he told me of many of his experiences while hiking. We went to a small lunch room for our noon meal of hamburger steak and chocolate pie.

In the afternoon we did some sightseeing around Toledo, then headed West to Sylvania, a very small community. A resident said we could sleep in his barn, so we went to his house and sat out in the yard taking it easy. I read the letter from my Mother again, she was very much concerned about me being so late for school. She suggested that we take the train part way home.

In the first place, we didn't have the money and in the second place, we had undertaken a round trip bicycle trip and we were not about to change our plans come what may. We would complete the trip exactly as planned, otherwise we felt the whole thing would be a failure.

We had supper at the house and then had a long visit in the evening. The people were very much interested in trip and the two daughters of these people asked many questions about it.

After our pleasant evening we said good night and went to bed in the hay loft about 9:30.

CHAPTER SIX

BUFFALO,NEW YORK TO CHICAGO,ILLINOIS.

September 15th,1915     The 80th Day     (Wednesday)

Sylvania,Ohio to Stryker,Ohio.

Up at 7 and had a good breakfast at the farmer's house.
( Thomas Whittaker, Box 42, Sylvania No. 2,Ohio ) . After a short
visit we left and rode 10 miles to Caragher against a strong
wind which made riding rather difficult. We stopped to rest there.

At Swanton we sold a few cards and had an ice cream Sundae
before leaving. At Delta we went to the newspaper in regard to
an article previously put in the paper on our trip East. We
stopped at Wauseon where I took a picture of a school house. At

Archbold we met
a man who was on
the same trolley
with us coming
from Coney Island
in New York City.

We stopped
at Stryker  and
looked for a
place to spend

A SCHOOL HOUSE ALONG THE WAY

the night. We got two offers to sleep in barns so we took our
choice. All day long we had been riding through the area where
the farmers had huge red barns, extending from Toledo to Bryan,
Ohio.

## CHAPTER SIX

The 80th Day        (Cont.)

Sylvania,Ohio to Stryker,Ohio.

The barns usually have the farmer's name on them. We had not seen any other place like it.

We had fish for supper at a restaurant and afterwards went to a movie to see, "Behind the Screens". It was a good movie and we enjoyed it. We visited with the farmers for a while and then went to bed shortly after nine. We could hear the rats running around the barn but we were too tired to let it bother us. If all goes well we should reach Indiana some time tomorrow. Once again we had found the people of Ohio very friendly and helpful.

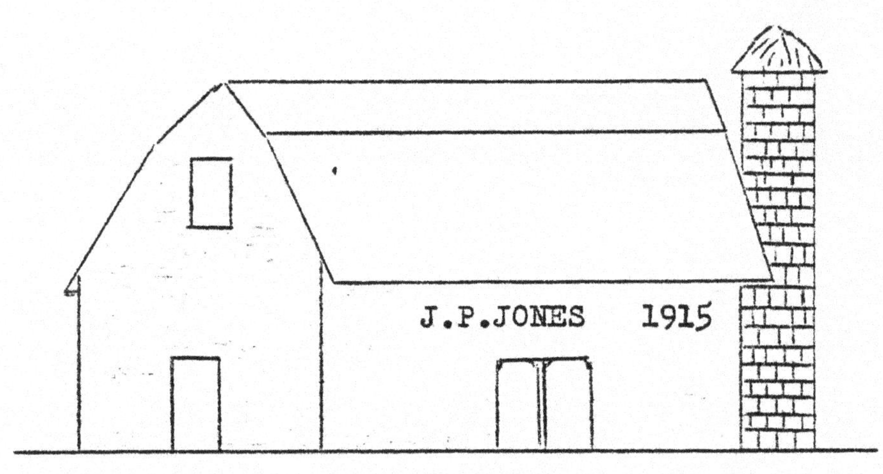


A TYPICAL LARGE RED BARN OF OHIO

## CHAPTER SIX

### BUFFALO,NEW YORK TO CHICAGO,ILLINOIS.

September 16th,1915     The 81st Day     (Thursday)

Stryker,Ohio to Sedan,Indiana.

Up at 8 and packed our gear. The barn we were in was a huge one with a silo at one end. As usual in this area it was painted red with the owners name painted on the side. I made a sketch of one  of these barns with the owners name on it.

The farmer invited us for breakfast which was a typical farm meal with plenty to eat and good farm cooking which we enjoyed. We visited with these people for some time so got a late start for our days ride.

It was only eight miles to Bryan,Ohio and when we got there the first thing we did was to call on Mrs. Flinn. She was the lady who had been so kind to us when we stopped

COURT HOUSE
BRYAN, OHIO

there on our trip East. She was glad to see us and of course we enjoyed visiting with her again. Later we bought real ice cream at 20¢ a quart. I bought oil for the bike and a small boy gave me an oil can which came in handy.

We left shortly, facing a strong wind from the West and by 1 P.M. we had only made about 8 miles. We were now only about 8 miles from the Indiana line so we hurried on as we were anxious to get there. I reached Edgerton,Ohio ahead of Hap so waited for him to catch up. We called on Mr. Krill at his furniture store. He came out to see us and was very much interested in our trip and asked many questions about it. The water pump and the bench were still out in front of the store just as they were before.

## CHAPTER SIX

The 81st Day      (Cont.)

Stryker,Ohio to Sedan,Indiana.

On our trip East Hap was feeling sick that morning and he rested on the bench for about an hour until he felt better.

We were soon headed West again and I reached Indiana first. I wrote my name on the boundary marker and when he arrived we shook hands, Hap in Ohio with me in Indiana. He took my picture, I was half in Ohio and half in Indiana.

At Butler,Indiana we went to a cider mill. The owner gave each of us a cup, took us over to a barrel of cider and said "Help yourself, Boys" and believe me, we did.

We bought something to eat at Waterloo and it was nearly dark when we left there. It was raining before long so we went to a farm house between Sedan and Corunna. The farmer gave us permission to sleep in the barn but the rain stopped so we slept in a wagon box in the yard instead. We did a little so-called singing before going to sleep.

CHAPTER SIX

BUFFALO,NEW YORK TO CHICAGO,ILLINOIS

September 17th,1915      The 82nd Day      (Friday)

Sedan,Indiana to Goshen,Indiana.

We were up at 7:30 and were soon packed up and ready to go. Our first stop was Kendallville and about that time my coaster brake failed. Hap repaired it and after selling a few cards we had breakfast. We rode through Brimfield and stopped at Wawaka. We met a man there who was very unfriendly, one of the few times this happened to us. We next came to Ligonier and were once more on the Lincoln Highway. Between Benton and Goshen there was a long detour on a very poor road. This delayed us some just as it had on our trip East.

McCRAY  PLANT
KENDALLVILLE

MAIN ST.LIGONIER

At Goshen we sold some cards and as it was getting late we decided to spend the night there. After eating we got permission to sleep in a summer kitchen in town. A summer kitchen is a small detached building for

MAIN ST.GOSHEN

cooking in hot weather. We visited with some people from Minneapolis and then went to the movies. I sold 25¢ worth of cards to one man and he said there had been an article in the local newspaper about our arrival in New York City. I wonder what they thought about the article in the 'New York World' newspaper. We went to bed in the summer kitchen about 10 P.M. We were glad to be in out of the weather and it was a nice change from sleeping in barns.

CHAPTER SIX

BUFFALO,NEW YORK TO CHICAGO,ILLINOIS.

September 18th,1915    The 83rd Day      (Saturday)

Goshen,Indiana to Elkhart,Indiana.

I was up at 8 and looked out the window, it looked so much like rain that I didn't wake Hap. When he got up at 9 o'clock it was raining hard. We sat in the summer kitchen hoping it would stop but it kept raining harder and harder. We didn't have any-thing to eat so we waited not wanting to get soaking wet.

After a while it let up a little so I went to a store and bought a can of beans and an apple pie. When I got back,the lady of the house brought us a pot of coffee, a large plate of bread, meat, butter, jelly and apple jam, so we had a good breakfast after all. The rain continued all morning and at noon she in-vited us into the house for lunch. We visited with these kind people (Daniel Granger) for a long time while waiting out the storm. The rain stopped about 3:30 so we prepared to leave.

We rode and walked to Elkhart over terrible roads deep in mud and water. The going was slow and we didn't get to Elkhart until 6 P.M.We had enough of those roads for one day so we de-cided to stay in Elkhart. We only made about 12 miles that day.

We canvassed the stores and sold a few cards. A man who stopped to talk to us told us we could sleep in his barn and gave us directions how to get there. We went to the place but no one was home so we left our gear and bikes on the back porch and went down town to a movie. The show was, "Sent from Headquarters" Anita Stewart was the leading lady and we thought she was a fine

CHAPTER SIX

The 83rd Day      (Cont.)

Goshen,Indiana to Elkhart,Indiana.

actress. There were two short movies in addition, "The Slavey
Student" and "Mustang Pete". I could better appreciate good
acting after seeing how they make them and under what circum-
stances as we saw at the Lubin Studio in Philadelphia. Elkhart
was a lively city on a Saturday night. There were many people
on the street and we sold a few cards after the show.

We went back to the house where our gear and bikes were,
but the house was dark as the people had gone to bed. We tried
to arouse them by knocking on the door and after a long wait the
man came to the door. He said they didn't know anything about
our staying there but that we could sleep in the yard. Hap went
to sleep in a wagon and I spread the tent on the ground under
a tree where I slept.

Elkhart is located where the Elkhart and St.Joseph Rivers
join. There were several band instrument factories located there
as well as other factories. It was a fairly large city of perhaps
20 or 25,000 inhabitants. The city was settled in the early
1830s.

CHAPTER SIX

BUFFALO,NEW YORK TO CHICAGO,ILLINOIS.

September 19th,1915     The 84th day     (Sunday)

Elkhart,Indiana to Rolling Prairie,Indiana.

I woke up at about 8 but as Hap was still asleep I brought my diary up to date. I packed my gear and then aroused Hap so we could get going. I checked my finances and found I had 90¢ so I felt pretty flush.

It looked like rain again but I hoped it didn't so we could make some distance. We had breakfast in Elkhart, I had scrambled eggs, pancakes and oatmeal. The road to Mishawaka was in very poor shape and was rough going. While in Mishawaka we met several members of the local bike club and had a nice visit with them.

We went on to South Bend but this being Sunday the Post Office was closed so we couldn't get the cards we had forwarded from Cleveland. We ate lunch at the Burger Lunch Room, sold a few cards and then continued on our journey. We had to take a detour because of the awful condition of the famous Lincoln Highway. About four miles beyond South Bend my chain came off and broke eight spokes in my rear wheel. After that the chain came off at every revolution of the wheel. I put on another chain but it was so loose it slipped over the front sproket now badly worn. Hap took a link out of the chain and we were once more on our way. We rode through New Carlisle without stopping and continued on to Rolling Prairie where we stopped to get oil. We tried to get a man to open his store but nothing doing, we were unable to get anyone to accommodate us. A woman who ran a

CHAPTER SIX

The 84th Day        (Cont.)

Elkhart,Indiana to Rolling Prairie,Indiana.

boarding house refused to sell us a sandwich and said we would
have to buy a full meal or nothing. A man with her said, "Don't
sell them anything." For some unknown reason most of our trouble
with people was in Indiana, however we met mostly kind and helpful people there as well as in the balance of the States we
visited.

We finally found a store open and bought tuna, bananas and
cookies for supper. While we were eating our meal on the church
steps the Minister came by and after visiting awhile he told us
we could sleep in his barn. We 'sang' songs for about an hour
in the hay loft before going to sleep.

We only made 42 miles that day due to poor roads most of
the way.

CHAPTER SIX

BUFFALO,NEW YORK TO CHICAGO,ILLINOIS.

September 20th,1915    The 85th Day     (Monday)

Rolling Prairie,Indiana to 8 Miles W.of Michigan City,Indiana.

Up at 8. Hap sewed up a large hole in his trousers then amused himself by jumping into the hay from a board some distance above. We were about ready to leave when Hap stepped up to pet a horse, when suddenly it turned its head and hit him in the face. It nearly knocked him over, he was white as a sheet and that is probably the last time he will ever pet a horse. Rolling Prairie was a small town and there were many Indians living there.

We hadn't gone very far when I ran over a snake, I went back and killed it as it was badly injured. It started to rain and we stopped to help a man put the top up on his Ford.

We went into a barn to get out of the rain and the farmer gave us several apples. We passed the time by playing "knife baseball" while waiting for the rain to stop. When it stopped we started out but after about six miles it rained again. We got permission to wait in a barn during the rain, which soon stopped.

FRANKLIN ST.     POST   OFFICE     S.S. ROOSEVELT
MICHIGAN CITY,INDIANA

We continued on and when we reached Michigan City it was drizzling. We left our bikes at a Ford Agency, washed and went about the business of selling cards. Before long it was raining hard so we went to the 5 and 10¢ store to buy some tape to wrap

CHAPTER SIX

The 85th Day        (Cont.)

Rolling Prairie,Indiana to 8 Miles W.of Michigan City,Indiana.
around my badly worn shoe.

We waited out the rain in the 5 and 10¢ store and when it
stopped we went to a lunch wagon and each had an egg sandwich.
They beat the eggs in a cup,let the grease get real hot in the
pan and put the eggs in. It makes the eggs fluffy and they were
very good. While we were eating it started to pour real hard.

There was a fire in town and I got good and wet going to
see it. I tried to get my shoes repaired but they were too far
gone. I'll have to buy a second hand pair if and when I get the
money. Michigan City,Indiana was a city of 20 or 25,000, and is
located on the shore of Lake Michigan in the heart of the Indiana
sand dunes.

We continued West late in the day after the rain stopped.
The road was macadam and there were large puddles of water in
the road which we had to ride through. About 8 miles West of
Michigan City we struck the worst muddy road we had encountered
anywhere East of Chi-
cago. It was dark and
we had to walk so we
looked for and found
a barn to sleep in. We
could hear the rats
running around the
barn not two feet from

LAKE MICHIGAN

us. It had been a cold day with the rain and a cold wind.

## CHAPTER SIX

### BUFFALO, NEW YORK TO CHICAGO, ILLINOIS.

September 21st,1915     The 86th Day     (Tuesday)

8 Miles W.of Michigan City,Indiana to Chicago,Illinois.

"THE MIDNIGHT RIDE THROUGH CHICAGO TO THE DOWNTOWN LOOP"

Up at 9. We had a fine place to sleep, hay on all sides
with a small entrance through the hay. It had been rather cold
but by stacking hay over us we were comfortable and warm. I put
on my new socks but as the soles of my shoes were about gone I
was just about walking in my stocking feet. Before we left
the farmer gave each of us a nice red apple to take along.

We were on our way, facing an icy N.W. wind. We had to walk
most of the way in deep mud but after about two miles of this we
came to a good stone road. This speeded things up and we were
soon in Porter where we sold a few cards and bought rolls and
pie for breakfast. I taped up my rear tire and we were off and
running. We rode for several miles without stopping and then my
rear tire blew out. We stopped at a little store near Calumet
Park and Hap put on my new Vitalic tire on the rear. This was the
tire given me by the rubber company in Erie,Pennsylvania. At this
point the cyclometer on Hap's bike registered 3,056 miles.

We talked to some girls for awhile and then moved on as the
Sun was shining and we wanted to ride while the riding was good.
We hadn't gone very far when I had a puncture in my front tire.
Hap repaired it and we continued on to East Gary, reaching there
about 4 P.M. All day long we had been riding through the Indiana
Sand Dune country with the vast areas of pure white sand.

We went up to see H.S.Weisskopl who had given us a meal on

## CHAPTER SIX

The 86th Day          (Cont.)

8 Miles W. of Michigan City,Indiana to Chicago,Illinois.

our trip East. When he saw us coming he ran out and shook hands
and was very glad to see us. He called his wife to come home and
she also seemed glad to see us. They insisted that we stay for
supper and she cooked a fine meal of hamburgers, potatoes, bread,
coffee, cake and apple butter. It was a welcome relief from the
meals we had recently.

We left about 5:45 P.M. It was nearly dark when we left
Gary and after oiling the bikes at a garage we moved on. It was
soon dark but this Indiana road was smooth stone and as it was
perfectly level we rode mile after mile without stopping. There
was a full moon so it wasn't too bad riding without lights on
the bikes. It was cold with a chill North wind blowing. We had
to walk a short distance where the road was torn up and then we
came to one of the finest roads we had encountered on the entire
trip. It was smooth as glass and perfectly level, we could see
lights ahead and kept going,not knowing where for sure.

On both sides of the road was a small lake and we had a
clear view on both sides for miles. Now and then we saw pure
white sand extending for miles on either side of the road. There
was little if any traffic on the road and we rode on unmolested.
At places the water was close to the road and had it been a
little higher the road would have been flooded.

It was 7:50 by the village clock when we reached East
Chicago,Indiana but we decided to go on into downtown Chicago,
still 20 miles away.

CHAPTER SIX

The 86th Day (Cont.)

8 Miles W. of Michigan City,Indiana to Chicago,Illinois.

I bought a little 10¢ lantern and Hap bought oil at a
garage. We visited with a number of girls and then went down
to a medicine show in town. In those days traveling peddlers of
patent medicines put on shows in the small towns to sell their
wares. I lit my little red lantern and a great many people came
over to where I was to see what was going on. Literally hundreds of men, women and children followed me into the street
when I started away and surrounded me on all sides. About that
time a couple of kids yelled, "fight fight". Then the crowd
grew larger and Hap managed to get away but I was stuck in the
middle of things.

One kid touched me on the back and said, "Well, I can say
I touched him anyway". In a second or two the entire crowd was
doing the same thing and repeating the same phrase. For a while
I didn't know if I'd get out of there alive or not. I had a hard
time getting away but I sure was glad when I did.

We started out, the light went out immediately but we left
anyway at 8:40 P.M. It was a little after 9 P.M. when we crossed
the line into Illinois with Indiana now behind us. It was 9:30
when we pulled into the East Side, 9:50 P.M. when we reached
South Chicago. We stopped for a cup of coffee and put on our
coats as it was getting cold. We came into the City of Chicago
on South Chicago Avenue and branched off on Cottage Grove Ave.
We went over about half a mile to look up a friend of Hap, he
was not at home so we continued on.

CHAPTER SIX

The 86th Day        (Cont.)

8 Miles W. of Michigan City,Indiana to Chicago,Illinois.

    We went over to Michigan Avenue and about at 20th Street
my little light went out. While lighting it a man lost his hat,
I retrieved it for him and got a cigar for my trouble. We talked
to several policemen on the way in but none of them stopped us
and they wished us luck.

    It was 12:41 A.M. by the electric clock on Michigan Avenue
when we reached Washington Boulevard in the Loop area. We put our
bikes in a garage on the other side of the river, stopped at a
restaurant for a bite to eat, then located a place to spend the
night in a cheap 25¢ hotel on West Madison St. There was not a
soul on the street so we turned in about 1:40 A.M.

MICHIGAN AVE.          COLISEUM
    (BY MOONLIGHT)
CHICAGO,ILLINOIS


END OF CHAPTER SIX

CHAPTER SEVEN

CHICAGO,ILLINOIS TO SAINT PAUL,MINNESOTA.

September 22nd,1915      The 87th Day      (Wednesday)

At Chicago,Illinois.

Up at 9:30. I brought my diary up to date then we went out for breakfast. We went to the garage to get our bikes and they charged us 10¢ for keeping the two bikes over night.

We took the bikes to the Mead Cycle Co. and they said they would put them in first class shape at no charge to us. They were very nice about it and said they would handle it as a rush job so we wouldn't be unduly delayed. They asked us to write a testimonial for them and I was very glad to do so in view of the fine way they had treated us.

We walked around the downtown area most of the day, visiting some of the large department stores and sightseeing generally. I got mail from St.Paul and wrote home, telling them that we were coming home by way of Dubuque,Iowa as planned. We talked to a motorcycle rider who was making a short trip in Illinois. A soldier stopped to talk and tried to get us to join the Army but we were not interested.

We moved to a different cheap hotel and I went there about 4 P.M. to work on my diary and read my mail again. This was a very cheap hotel, the room was about 5 ft. by 7 ft. The walls were painted green and were constructed of galvanized iron and the ceiling was common chicken wire. Half of a window let in what light there was, the other half of the window was in Hap's room. There was a dirty curtain hanging at the window and every- thing was covered with dust. The furnishings of the room were

CHAPTER SEVEN

The 87th Day     (Cont.)

At Chicago,Illinois.

an iron bed with a dirty red cover on it, a small compartment
for clothes and a small stool. There was an electric light hanging down from the ceiling and covered with dust. The sheets on
the bed as well as the floor were clean, I hoped I would be able
to sleep under those conditions. I was down to my last five
cents so couldn't do anything about it. There was a metal strip
about 8 inches long attached to the key to prevent its being
carried away inadvertently.

Hap came back shortly and we went out to sell some cards.
I got coffee and a roll with my last five cents. We walked down
Michigan Avenue and sold a few cards, then on State St. and
Madison Ave. I sold 25¢ worth to one man. On the way back to the
hotel we had coffee and pie costing each of us five cents. We
stopped at a barber shop and got shaved at 10¢ each. Our hotel
was located on Madison Avenue at Des Plaines Street not far from
the Loop. We went to bed before long in our "sumptuous" quarters.

CHAPTER SEVEN

CHICAGO,ILLINOIS TO SAINT PAUL,MINNESOTA.

September 23rd,1915      The 88th Day      (Thursday)

At Chicago

We slept good in spite of the unpleasant surroundings. We bought cookies for breakfast and then went to the Post Office but no mail for us. We decided to go to the library and walked down Michigan Avenue(sometimes referred to as Michigan Boulevard). We were stopped by a policeman who told us we would have to get off the Avenue as no advertising was allowed there. We took our signs off and continued on our way to the Library. Hap left about 1 P.M. and I stayed there until about 2:15 P.M.

On my way back to the hotel I bought some cookies for lunch and ate them as I walked along. Found a note from Hap in which he said he would be back at 6 P.M. I waited there for him and he showed up promptly at 6. Hap had quite a story to tell. He said while walking down the street he was stopped by two detectives who took him to the Police Station. He was questioned at length about what he was doing in Chicago. He told them about our trip and that we were leaving town the next morning as soon as we could get our bikes from the Mead Cycle Co. who were making repairs on them. They wanted to know where we were staying and with that they let him go.

We walked around the downtown area in the evening, taking in the bright lights and watching the crowds. We got a bite to eat and went back to the hotel. The Salvation Army was playing music just below our window and after listening to them for awhile we went to bed.

CHAPTER SEVEN

The 88th Day      (Cont.)

At Chicago, Illinois.

While waiting at the hotel for Hap I wrote a testimonial
for the Mead Cycle Company as they had asked me to do. It is
shown below:


                                        September 23,1915


Mead Cycle Co.,

Washington Street Bridge,

Chicago, Illinois.

Gentlemen:-

After riding two of your Crusader wheels half way across
the continent and back we are satisfied that your bicycles are
all right and all that you claim for them. Starting from St.Paul
Minn. on June 28th,1915 we rode to Chicago over poor country
roads. From Chicago we went to New York via Pittsburgh and
Philadelphia. We returned to Chicago by way of Boston and Buffalo.
Upon our arrival at Chicago we had covered 3,106 miles, the
wheels holding up fine under the strain. We were well treated by
the Mead Cycle Co.

                              Signed

                        Leon Schroeder


The above letter appeared in the Mead Cycle Co's advertising
for a number of years afterward.

CHAPTER SEVEN

September 24th,1915    The 89th Day      (Friday)

Chicago,Illinois to 15 miles W. of Elgin,Illinois.

It looked like rain when we got up in the morning but we
wanted to get out of Chicago as soon as possible, regardless. I
looked out the window and there on the opposite side of the
street were two policemen watching the hotel. We went for breakfast
with the two cops not far behind, they waited and then followed
us to the Mead Cycle Co. When they saw us come out with the bikes
they left. It seemed odd to us, with all the crime and criminals
in Chicago that they would assign two cops to watch a couple of
suntanned high school boys who were riding bicycles across the
country. We felt that they could put them to better use, but then,
that was Chicago. I presented the testimonial I had written and
the Mead Co. seemed pleased with it.

The bikes were ready, the Mead Co. replaced all worn parts.
I got a new chain, pedals, sprocket, hanger, hand grips, new
back wheel including a new coaster brake, new seat and a new tire
on front. Hap got a new frame,pedals, chain, hand grips, sprocket,
hanger, wrench and new tire on front. They certainly treated us
fine and we greatly appreciated it for now we were in good shape
for the balance of the trip.

We went to the Goodrich Agency and got a road guide to Elgin
and one for the Lincoln Highway across Illinois. After getting
our bikes we went West on Jackson Boulevard to Racine St. We then
went over on Van Buren St. to look up a Dr. Scott who was a relative of my Mother. He was not in his office so we came back to
Jackson Boulevard, sold a few cards and continued our journey.

CHAPTER SEVEN

The 89th Day        (Cont.)

Chicago,Illinois to 15 miles W. of Elgin,Illinois.

About 7 miles out we came to a fork in the road, we decided
to go by way of Elgin, Rockford and Galena to Dubuque, Iowa instead of following the Lincoln Highway by way of Clinton which

ELGIN
ILLINOIS

CHICAGO ST.

HIGH SCHOOL

ELGIN WATCH CO.

would have been farther. At Elgin we saw the Elgin Watch factory.
We visited other points of interest including the City Hall. The
city is located on the Fox River with watches a principal product.

After leaving the city we rode over the North Road of the
Elgin Race Course. We saw the tree that race driver Wishart hit
when he was killed in 1914. There was a large gash in the tree
where he hit and we saw the yard where his car ended up. The
track was oiled, had several sharp turns and was $8\frac{1}{2}$ miles long.

About 11 miles west of Elgin we asked a farmer if we could
sleep in his barn, he refused so we continued on. We came to a
one room country school house and as it was late at night, very
cold and with rain threatening we stopped to see if we could sleep
there. We found it open and brought our bikes inside. I laid
down in an aisle between two rows of seats and Hap laid on a bench.
He nearly fell off the bench and then he too, slept on the floor.

CHAPTER SEVEN

CHICAGO,ILLINOIS TO SAINT PAUL,MINNESOTA.

September 25th,1915    The 90th Day    (Saturday)

15 miles w.of Elgin,Illinois to Rockford,Illinois.

I was up at 5:30 A.M., I did some sewing on my worn clothes and had a hard time getting Hap up. We looked around at the things of interest and were ready to leave at 6:30. We looked out the window to see if all was clear and as no one was around we moved out. We left everything just as we found it and were glad to get out safely. The school teacher probably never knew that there had been visitors over night.

CITY HALL
ELGIN, ILL.

We lost no time getting away from there and at the first town we came to we each got a quart of milk at 5¢ a quart, also cookies which we had for breakfast. I sold fifty cents worth of cards at Marengo. I now had 75¢ and felt pretty flush. I sent a card home and then rode down the main street of the town. The street was not paved and there were a number of horse drawn vehicles on the street. Marengo was a small town with a population of about fifteen hundred.

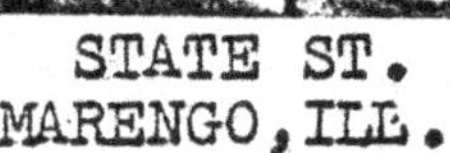

STATE ST.
MARENGO, ILL.

STATE ST.
BELVIDERE, ILL.

We stopped at Belvidere to sell some cards but didn't stay there long. It was somewhat larger than Marengo with a population of several thousand.

STATE ST.
TRANSFER CORNER
ROCKFORD, ILL.

CHAPTER SEVEN

The 90th Day      (Cont.)

15 miles W. of Elgin, Illinois to Rockford, Illinois.

It started to rain when we reached Rockford so decided to spend the night there. We met some teen age boys and they said we could sleep in their tent. They had a large 10 ft. x 18 ft. tent in the back yard where they lived down near the gas house. We unloaded our bikes and gear there and the boys gave us a ride back to town in their Ford. We ate supper and went to a 5¢ motion picture show, then walked back to the tent in the rain. There were two beds in the tent, Hap and I slept in one and two of the boys slept in the other. The third boy slept in the house.

It poured something fierce during the night and the tent started to leak. Hap got a little wet but we were given a rubber blanket to put over us and we kept dry the balance of the night.

Rockford is located on the Rock River and at the time we were there had a population in excess of 50,000. It was a large industrial city with many factories.

CHAPTER SEVEN

CHICAGO,ILLINOIS TO SAINT PAUL,MINNESOTA.

September 26th,1915     The 91st Day          (Sunday)

Rockford,Illinois to Evarts,Illinois.

It was drizzling when we got up about ten O'clock, we packed
our gear and got ready for the days run. The people invited us
for breakfast and it was a good home cooked meal.(S.D.Palmer, 601
Pleasant St.) They were very much interested in the trip and
bought eight cards.

Note::

During World War One, when I was in the Army and stationed at Camp Grant near Rockford, I spent a Sunday with these
people and enjoyed visiting with them again.

We spent the morning at their house and left about noon when
the rain stopped, after thanking them for their kindness. It was
very cold, the road was good for a few miles, then we came to a
dirt road that was in terrible condition. The road was nothing
but mud and water, we had to walk and push the bikes through deep
mud. At times we walked at the side of the road in the tall wet
weeds and grass. Part of the way we could ride between the barb
wire fence and the line of telegraph poles, but it was a tight
squeeze, but it was walking through the mud and water eighty
percent of the time.

We stopped at the little town of Seward to get something to
eat. It was just like being cut off from the rest of the world
in this town, no traffic, no tourists and most of the residents
in the general store.

CHAPTER SEVEN

The 91st Day        (Cont.)

Rockford,Illinois to Evarts,Illinois.

We soon continued our journey in the cold, wintry weather
and the muddy road. At times the mud guards would become packed
with mud and we would have to dig it out with our fingers or
with a stick if available. The wheels would not turn until the
mud was removed. The road was so bad we decided to ride on the
railroad tracks. We rode six miles on the track and it was the
longest six miles on the trip. It was one continuous bump, bump,
bump as we rode over the railroad ties.

It was nearly dark and icy cold when we got to the small
town of Evarts. This was a very small town, not even on the map.
We finally found a place to stay with a German family and they
were very friendly. They invited us for a good German supper,
we certainly appreciated a good meal after our hard days ride
in the cold and through the mud and water and over the railroad
cross ties. After eating we sat down in their nice warm house
and visited for a long time. An auctioneer was a guest in the
house and we enjoyed listening to him. We were invited to stay
over night and we went to sleep in a nice clean,comfortable bed
in the house.

CHAPTER SEVEN

CHICAGO,ILLINOIS TO SAINT PAUL,MINNESOTA.

September 27th,1915     The 92nd Day      (Monday)

Evarts,Illinois to Lena,Illinois.

We had breakfast with these people and then visited for
about an hour while waiting for it to stop raining.

We headed out and it was very cold so we were glad we had
coats with us. The road was in terrible shape, mud and more mud
and we walked most of the way to Ridott. Beyond there the road was
impassable for a bike so we went on the railroad tracks the balance
of the way to Freeport. It took us 2½ hours to go the 7 miles as
we had to walk most of the way. We sold cards and ate lunch there.
Hap repaired my tire resulting in further delay.

We planned to go to Dubuque by way of Galena which was the
best and shortest way. We were advised that we could not get
through that way as the whole country around Galena was flooded
and the roads were closed. This would mean we would have to detour up through Wisconsin and then come back down to Dubuque,
missing Galena. The distance was greater but the worst part would
be that we would be on country roads in very poor condition.

Freeport was a city of about 15,000. It is located on the
Pecatonica River and was the trading center of a dairying and
farming district. There was also considerable manufacturing in
the city. Freeport was the site of a debate between Abraham
Lincoln and Stephen Douglas over the slavery question. A large
boulder marked the spot where this famous debate took place.

After leaving Freeport the road was in fair shape for five

CHAPTER SEVEN

The 92nd Day          (Cont.)

Evarts,Illinois to Lena,Illinois.

miles and then we came to a place where the water was two to
three feet deep over the road for a distance of about 50 feet.
We had to wade through, holding the bikes up out of the water, we
were soaking wet which added to our discomfort.

We came to the place where the Galena road turned off so
from there on we were on the detour. After another 5 miles on the
muddy road we went on the railroad track to Lena, walking most of
the way. We had not been able to make many miles each day due to
the condition of the roads.

It was nearly dark when we reached Lena,we sold a few cards
then had a meal of rolls, bread, pop and cheese. We got permission to sleep in a barn and the man took down some straw for us
to sleep on. It was cold so we made our beds by sleeping on half
of the tent and covering up with our blanket and half the tent.


A BICYCLE TRIP OF LONG AGO.

September 28th,1915    The 93rd Day       (Tuesday)

Lena,Illinois to Shullsburg,Wisconsin.

Up at 10, it was cloudy but we hoped it wouldn't rain again
during the day. On this day we had been on the trip for three
months and were still about four hundred miles from home.

The road was oiled the five miles to Waddams and was in good
condition. I sold 25¢ worth of cards to a storekeeper and we had
breakfast of cookies and beans. Waddams is on high ground and it
was downhill to the Apple River, a distance of 2 or 3 miles.

CHAPTER SEVEN

The 93rd Day        (Cont.)

Lena,Illinois to Shullsburg,Wisconsin.

We continued by road to Nora and while it was not easy going, the road had dried up a little.While at Nora we climbed to the top of a windmill and had a good view of the surrounding country side.

When we left Nora I went by road and Hap rode on the rail-road tracks. I beat him to Warren by about half a mile and when he caught up we sold a number of cards. I was about out of cards and Hap let me barrow 10 cards from him as he still had plenty.

We left Warren at 3:30 after buying beef sandwiches for lunch. About two miles beyond this town we crossed over into Wisconsin, this being the second time we had been in that state on the trip.

MAIN ST.
WARREN,ILL.

It was clearing up some in the West, this cheered us up as we hadn't seen the Sun since Saturday noon.The road was drying up some and was not as bad as those we had been on recently, but it was still muddy. Hap tried to get through a muddy place by riding in an automobile rut and in the process he fell and landed in the black mud on his face. He got up, covered with mud from head to foot. Five miles East of Shullsburg the road was im-passible and we had to walk all the rest of the way through the mud and water. At last the sky was clear but by now it was nearly dark. We had been wading through mud and water way above our shoe tops. The mud and water came through the holes in the soles of my badly worn shoes, my feet were soaking wet and very uncomfortable.

CHAPTER SEVEN

The 93rd Day          (Cont.)

Lena,Illinois to Shullsburg,Wisconsin.

At long last we came to a sign that said, '3 miles to Shullsburg'at which point we stopped to scrape out the mud lodged between the wheels and mudguards. This prevented the wheels from
turning and while on these muddy roads we had to free the wheels
many times in this manner. We walked most of the next two miles
and then the road was macadam the last mile to the town.

When we reached Shullsburg the bikes were covered with mud,
it was so thick we could hardly see the spokes and the bikes were
a sight to behold. We were also covered with mud from head to
feet, I was so tired from the hard work on the road and so hungry
I could hardly stand. We went at once to a lunch room, we each
got coffee, six rolls each, a 15¢ can of shrimp and some cookies.

After eating we sold some cards and I won a 35¢ box of
candy for 5¢, then I spent another nickel trying to win another.
Hap failed to win one for his 5¢ so we shared the box I won. We
were very tired and set about finding a place to sleep. Some
young boys found a place for us in a small shed. Hap slept on a
couch and I was on a folding cot that ripped every time I moved.
It finally gave way entirely and I slept on the floor the balance
of the night.

### CHAPTER SEVEN

### CHICAGO,ILLINOIS TO SAINT PAUL,MINNESOTA.

September 29th,1915     The 94th Day     (Wednesday)

Shullsburg,Wisconsin to Dubuque,Iowa.

We were up at 8:45 and the lady of the house brought us some coffee, bread and apple sauce for our breakfast.

Shullsburg was a town of about a thousand population. There were streets in the town with names such as Truth, Happy, Peace and Faith. West of the town there had been many lead mines, some of which had long been abandoned. We went to the business district and sold a number of cards, I won a lunch basket for a nickel and as I had no use for it, I gave it to a workman we met.

We had some pretty steep hills to climb west of Shullsburg and were soon in the lead mining area of Southwest Wisconsin. We passed through the town of Lead Mine and next came to Benton which was a typical min- ing town. We saw several lead mines on our way to Hazel Green, and while there we sold some cards.

CLEVELAND MINE
HAZEL GREEN,WIS.

We reached E.Dubuque,Illinois about 4:15 P.M. and saw several railroad tunnels on the way. We crossed the Mississippi River on a toll bridge to Dubuque,Iowa, the twelfth State on our journey. I went at once to the

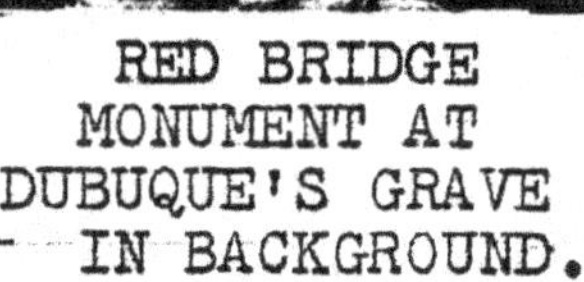

RED BRIDGE
MONUMENT AT
DUBUQUE'S GRAVE
IN BACKGROUND.

Post Office and received a supply of cards from home, also my winter cap and several letters. Hap arrived shortly but his cards forwarded from South Bend had not arrived. I sent some local cards home and bought a pair of shoes for $2.50 and also a pair of socks.

CHAPTER SEVEN

The 94th Day        (Cont.)

Shullsburg,Wisconsin to Dubuque,Iowa.

My family knew some people in Dubuque by the name of Briggs so we called on them. We arrived at 6 O'clock just in time to sit down to a good home cooked meal. After eating we had the house to ourselves as the people went to a show having previously purchased the tickets. We spent the evening reading and after visiting a while with the Briggs after they returned home we went to bed in a warm, comfortable bed.

The residential area of Dubuque is on high bluffs overlooking the business section and the river. From there three states can be seen, Iowa, Illinois and Wisconsin.

Dubuque is located on the Mississippi River opposite the State line between Illinois and Wisconsin on the other side of the river. In the early days it was the center of a lead mining district, in fact some of the mines were still operating when we were there. The city is named for Julien Dubuque. He probably was the first white man to settle permanently in the area of the present city.

DUBUQUE, IOWA
TIMES-JOURNAL
OCTOBER 1, 1915

## TRAVEL ALL SUMMER; ARE USING BICYCLES

**PAIR OF YOUTHS HAVE TROUBLESOME TRIP TO DUBUQUE FROM CHICAGO.**

**PUSH BICYCLES FROM GALENA**

**Roads in Such Condition Between Chicago and Dubuque That They Had to Walk Most of the Way—Going to St. Paul.**

Harwood Temple and Leon Schroeder, of St. Paul, arrived in Dubuque Wednesday morning on bicycle from Chicago on their way to their home in St. Paul. They are returning home from New York and Boston. The young men left Dubuque by way of the Hawkeye Highway. They left St. Paul for New York early in the spring.

The young men arrived in Dubuque pushing their bicycles about 11 o'clock Wednesday morning, coming over the Grant Highway from Chicago. They and their bicycles were covered with mud. They said that they were forced to push the wheels a greater part of the way from Chicago to Dubuque. They left New York on June 28 and have covered over three thousand miles. They have been actually traveling sixty-nine days.

When they arrived in Dubuque they had no intention of staying here any length of time, but said they were so tired from their riding and walking that they were forced to rest several hours. They left Dubuque Wednesday evening about 7 o'clock and expect to arrive in St. Paul in less than a week, unless they meet with another hard rain.

CHAPTER SEVEN

CHICAGO,ILLINOIS TO SAINT PAUL,MINNESOTA.

September 30th,1915    The 95th Day      (Thursday)

Dubuque,Iowa to Guttenberg,Iowa.

Up at 8. We had a good breakfast with pancakes and jelly.
We visited awhile and then got ready to leave, the Briggs wanted
us to stay another day but we were anxious to be on our way. We
left at 10:30 and Mrs. Briggs gave us several apples, pie, cookies and crackers to take along.

We rode down the long hill to the business district and Hap
had a tire blowout on the way. I got a shave while Hap was putting on his new Vitalic tire that was given him at Erie,Penn.

We climbed some hills out of Dubuque and I ran over a snake
on the way. As we rode along we saw many corn fields flattened
by the storm and a great deal of debris along the road. We ate

our lunch in Durango, a small town on
the Maquoketa River. We continued on to
the town of Rickardsville where we stopped to rest in a park. While there we
played with a tame fox that a man was
exercising and we came away with all our
fingers. We continued on through Holy

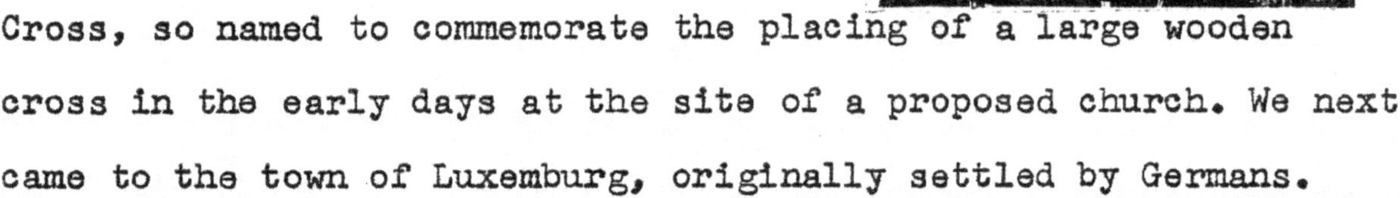

Cross, so named to commemorate the placing of a large wooden
cross in the early days at the site of a proposed church. We next
came to the town of Luxemburg, originally settled by Germans.

From there we headed North and there were many steep hills
and we had to walk up most of them. I came to a fork in the road,
it was not marked and I took the wrong road. I stopped before long
and asked for directions and then cut across the fields to get

CHAPTER SEVEN

The 95th Day         (Cont.)

Dubuque,Iowa to Guttenberg,Iowa.

back on the right road. When Hap came along he saw my tire marks
in the mud so he went on the wrong road. He went about a mile
before finding out he was on the wrong road and had to come back.

I came down a steep hill about a mile long into the town of
Millville on the Turkey River. While waiting for Hap I bought
candy and cookies to hold me over until we got to Guttenberg. Hap
didn't show up so I started out. There was a long steep hill out
of Millville and I had to walk most of the way to the top.It was
getting dark and by the time I reached the turnoff to Guttenberg
it was pitch dark. It was pretty risky going down the long hill
into the town but I made it safely.

I went to the Post Office and talked to the girl working
there. My paternal Grandmother lived in Guttenberg and we lived
there when I was three to six years old so there were many people
to look up. I saw Addie Jacobs and then went to my Grandmother's
house. She was at home as well as my Aunt Annie and my Uncle Baldwin of St.Paul was visiting for the day. Their dog was very friendly, almost too friendly, as I had trouble getting away from him.

After visiting a while I went out looking for Hap who had
not arrived yet. I soon saw him riding down the main street and
we went back to the house. Grandma and Aunt Annie prepared supper
for us, we enjoyed it a lot as we were tired and hungry. After a
long visit we went to bed on the lounge in the parlor.

Guttenberg was a town of 15oo to 2ooo inhabitants and is located on the Mississippi River, there were many people of German
ancestry living there.

CHAPTER SEVEN

The 95th Day        (Cont.)

Dubuque,Iowa to Guttenberg,Iowa.

My Grandfather, James Schroeder, had been Postmaster in Guttenberg for many years until he died in 1907. My Grandmother then became Postmistress until 1913 when Wilson was President.

My Grandfather was one of those who met in Ripon,Wisconsin before the Civil War in connection with the founding of the present Republican Party.

WE LIVED HERE    1900-1903

MISS. BAKER
MY TEACHER

I WAS IN THE LST GRADE AT THIS SCHOOL

CHAPTER SEVEN

CHICAGO,ILLINOIS TO SAINT PAUL,MINNESOTA.

October 1st,1915     The 96th Day     (Friday)

At Guttenberg and then to Garnavillo,Iowa.

Uncle Baldwin left for St. Paul and we got up to see him off. We had a good home-cooked breakfast and then we rode up and down the main street and had quite an audience of school children.

I wrote home, bought a film and then went out to see Uncle Alex but he was out fishing so missed him. I called on Mr.James but he too was away from home. I had better luck calling on the Duffins and had a nice visit with them. My next visit was to the Wolters who still lived in the same house next door to where we formerly lived. After a nice visit with them I took a picture of Mr. and Mrs. Wolters and their daughter Cecilia. When we left Mrs. Wolters gave us some apples to take along. Before leaving Cecilia played the harp for us and later the Edison Phonograph. I took a picture of the house we had lived in and then Hap and I went over to the park along the river. The park and town were on high ground about 50 feet above the river. In the park was an old cannon mounted on a stone foundation. Hap took a picture of me sitting on the cannon, we locked our bikes and went down to the river.

THE WOLTERS

THE OLD CANNON

## CHAPTER SEVEN

The 96th Day      (Cont.)

At Guttenberg,Iowa and then to Garnavillo,Iowa.

We waded in to look for clams, I finally found one which I opened but there was no pearl inside.

We went up near the button factory and saw a large pile of clam shells with holes in them, cut out to make the buttons. It was about noon so went back to my Grandmother's house for lunch. After eating I took a picture of her in front of the house.

We then went out to the cemetery and I found my father's grave with the aid of a Mrs. Roda. My father died when I was three years old and I had not seen his grave since 1903 when we moved away from Guttenberg. I bought some flowers at a nearby store and put them on his grave and then took a picture of the Schroeder burial plot.

MY GRANDMOTHER IN HER YARD

THE SCHROEDER BURIAL PLOT
MY FATHER'S GRAVE WITH THE FLOWERS

We went back to town and called on Mrs. Chase for a nice visit. We decided we better be on our way so went back for our gear, bid my Grandmother and Aunt good-bye and headed out. We stopped at Uncle Alex's house and found him home this time.

CHAPTER SEVEN

The 96th Day      (Cont.)

At Guttenberg,Iowa and then to Garnavillo,Iowa.

We went to the canning factory to see my boyhood friend,
Herald Duffin, son of Doctor Duffin. We got acquainted with a
young fellow and he showed us through the plant, which proved
very interesting. He told us that they were moving to St.Paul
shortly and that he would enter Johnson High School about the
time we reached home.

It was getting late so we left shortly and rode to Garnavillo. I wrote home and Hap wrote to South Bend to have his
cards forwarded. While in the Post Office a lady gave us half
a loaf of bread, a cup of jelly, two buns and four doughnuts.
We bought some cookies, rolls and beans to go with the food the
lady gave us for our supper.

After eating we looked for a place to sleep. We asked a man
if we could sleep in his barn, he said no but said he could arrange it so we could sleep in the fire station. He called the
Mayor of the town and he said we could. We visited for a while
and it turned out that he used to go to lodge with my Grandfather. We soon went to bed on the floor of the fire station.

We had now accomplished all we set out to do on the trip
and were anxious to get home after a most wonderful Summer of
adventure.

CHAPTER SEVEN

The 96th Day      (Cont.)

At Guttenberg,Iowa and then to Garnavillo,Iowa.


VIEWS OF GUTTENBERG,IOWA

FRONT ST.

GUTTENBERG
AND THE
MISSISSIPPI RIVER

CEMETERY

FRONT STREET BUSINESS SECTION

CHAPTER SEVEN

CHICAGO,ILLINOIS TO SAINT PAUL,MINNESOTA.

October 2nd,1915     The 97th Day     (Saturday)

Garnavillo,Iowa to Ossian,Iowa.

I slept fine last night in the fire station. When I got up
I brought my diary up to date while sitting in the Council Room
which was in the same building as the fire station. We ate breakfast there, consisting of the food the lady gave us in the Post
Office.

We rode to Monona as the roads were in fair shape. We stopped to get some food and then continued on to Postville. It
started to rain on the way so we continued on into the town and
put our bikes under cover. We waited awhile but it continued to
rain so we decided to move on. The road by now was too muddy to
ride on so we went on the Milwaukee Railroad tracks instead of
the road. It was pretty rough riding on the ties, so when it got
dark we walked the last mile and a half to Ossian.

We sold a few cards and ate our supper. We then started out
in search of a place to spend the night. The first farmer we
asked gave us permission to sleep in his barn.

The nights were getting colder and colder and very often it
rained during the night so whenever possible we tried to get a
place to sleep indoors.

The area through which we traveled during the day was mainly a dairying country and much cheese and butter was produced.

CHAPTER SEVEN

CHICAGO,ILLINOIS TO SAINT PAUL,MINNESOTA.

October 3rd,1915      The 98th Day       (Sunday)

Ossian,Iowa to Cresco,Iowa

Up at 9 A.M.We ate breakfast consisting of ham sandwiches and coffee. We continued on to Calmar, walking part of the way on the railroad tracks. The last four miles to Calmar were clay roads and we managed to ride on them. I reached this town ahead of Hap and while waiting for him I watched them tear down the remains of a fair. When Hap arrived we sold some cards and went to a lunch room and had ham sandwiches and cookies. While eating it started to pour so we waited there for it to stop raining.

When the rain stopped we continued our journey. The road was good for a short distance out of town and beyond the road was deep mud and water so we walked and pushed the bikes most of the way.

It started to pour when we were half a mile from the nearest farm house, we got soaked and nearly froze tramping through the mud and water. I reached Ridgeway ahead of Hap and while waiting a man in a store gave me six 5¢ dishes of ice cream for a total of 5¢. I didn't have any trouble eating all of them.

Hap arrived and we left at 4:20 P.M. for Cresco, nine miles away. We had to go on the railroad tracks as the road was impassable, and we had to walk most of the way. It was soon dark and pretty dangerous walking on the tracks but we kept going. It was cold and windy and it seemed as if we would never get there. At last we saw the lights of Cresco and this gave us a

CHAPTER SEVEN

The 98th Day        (Cont.)

Ossian,Iowa to Cresco,Iowa.

lift so we proceeded with renewed vigor. It seemed ages before
we finally made it.

We rode up and down the main street for awhile and then
stopped at a lunch room (Cafe Freeburn) for our evening meal. I
had a ham sandwich and coffee and while eating, a newspaper reporter asked about the trip for the local
paper. He was very friendly and bought a card,
paying me 25¢ for it.

All of a sudden all the lights in town
went out, everything was in total darkness.

MAIN STREET
CRESCO,IOWA

They lit candles in the restaurant and it was about an hour before the lights came back on.

We soon found a place to sleep in a barn and had a large
Russian Wolfhound for a bed fellow. The man brought us blankets
so we would be warm and comfortable.

We would reach Minnesota the following day and in leaving
Iowa wish to say how kind and friendly the people of that State
had been, giving us every assistance possible.

CHAPTER SEVEN

CHICAGO,ILLINOIS TO SAINT PAUL,MINNESOTA.

October 4th,1915     The 99th Day    (Monday)

Cresco,Iowa to Taopi,Minnesota.

We were up at 9 after a good nights sleep. It was cold in the barn and we hated to get out of our warm bed in the hay. We could hear the wind howling outside but we had to leave the barn and face it. We thanked the people and went downtown to eat.

After selling a few cards we started our journey. There was a bitter cold N.W.wind blowing and we had to face it. It started to rain and we just about froze but we buttoned up our light suit coats which were all we had and I pulled down my ear flaps. We continued on in the rain and cold but progress was slow. We eventually reached Bonair where we bought some cookies made in St.Paul. At 11:55 A.M. we were still sitting in the store, we could hear the wind howling outside and the noise made by the high wind in the trees.

We started out but it took a lot of nerve to go out and face it. We went through Lime Springs stopping long enough to have an article put in the paper. We continued on to Chester, the last town we would be in,in Iowa.

AT THE IOWA*MINN.LINE
COLD  WET  MUDDY

Three miles North of Chester we crossed the line into Minnesota, our home State. Hap took a picture of me at the State line, and we continued on to Le Roy,Minnesota. We had trouble selling cards

CHAPTER SEVEN

The 99th Day        (Cont.)

Cresco,Iowa to Taopi,Minnesota.

there and one of the places where I tried to sell was a real
estate office and the man gave me a half hour lecture but I
don't remember what it was all about.

We started in the direction of St.Paul, there were puddles
of water standing in the road but other than that the road was in
fair shape and we were able to ride on it. It was pretty cold
riding even with our coats on but we kept going and reached Taopi
about dusk. We stopped at a store for food and the owner told us
about a restaurant in the center of town and suggested we go there
to eat. We rode down on the sidewalk as the street was muddy and
had no trouble finding the place. We each got a cup of coffee
and a ham sandwich. When the man found out about our trip he gave
each of us another sandwich and said he had read about us in the
St.Paul paper. After our lunch we ventured out in the cold to
look for a place to sleep. We met a man who said we could sleep
in the lumber yard. He told us where it was and that he would
meet us there after awhile. We sold some cards and then rode down
to the place. We didn't go in as there was a big dog in the yard,
who didn't take kindly to our presence. The dog barked so loud
that the town Constable came down to see what all the commotion
was about. He offered to let us sleep in the town jail, so we
thanked our lumber yard friend and told him we were going to sleep
in the town lock-up.

We walked down to the jail with the Constable and he was very
friendly. He lit a light for us, asked our names and asked us to

CHAPTER SEVEN

The 99th Day       (Cont.)

Cresco,Iowa to Taopi,Minnesota.

write to him when we got home. With that he left us, bidding us good night and wishing us a good sleep.

After he left we had time to look the place over and see what a small town jail was like. We were in a small building about 15 feet by 30 feet and it was used as a fire station as well as for a jail. The cells were in the rear of the building and the fire department in front. It was some jail, each of the two cells had two beds, one above the other. Each bed consisted of an iron shelf attached to the wall and when not in use they folded up against the wall. There was a chain at each end to hold them in a horizontal position when let down. Each bed had a mattress on it, they didn't look too clean but the Constable said everything was clean. The above arrangement was similar to the jail in Pittsburgh,Pennsylvania where we spent a night. However the jail in Pittsburgh didn't have any mattresses. We were very thankful for the accomodation and were sure that we would make out all right.

CHAPTER SEVEN

CHICAGO,ILLINOIS TO SAINT PAUL,MINNESOTA.

October 5th,1915      The 100th Day      (Tuesday)

Taopi,Minnesota to Owatonna,Minnesota.

Up at 8 and feeling fine as I had a good nights sleep. I slept on one of the cell beds and Hap slept on a mattress on the floor. It seemed great to be so close to home and to think that in a couple of days we would be able to have a nice clean bed to sleep in every night. Also we were only two days away from real home cooked meals every day. This eating of cookies and other make shift meals is nice but give me home cooked meals as a regular diet. Of course I'm not forgetting the many fine meals we received on the road but there were many times when we ate what we could buy at the store.

Our wonderful Summer adventure was about over and I intended to make the most of the short time remaining. I just hoped that it didn't snow before we got home. We rode to the town of Adams for breakfast, the roads were in fair shape but we nearly froze riding against a cold N.W.wind. We have had such a great time that I was a little sorry that it was so near over.

We bought cookies for breakfast, canvassed the town and sold a few cards. There were many Swedes around these southern Minnesota towns and one we talked to said, "You bane taking a long ride, yah". He then proceeded to tell us that we were a long way from St.Paul.

Rose Creek was the next town and I arrived first, as usual. That is the way we planned it as Hap had all the equipment to make tire repairs and I would be in a bad way if I had a puncture

CHAPTER SEVEN

The 100th Day      (Cont.)

Taopi,Minnesota to Owatonna,Minnesota.

when I was way behind him.

We rested awhile and talked to a young fellow sitting on
the pool room steps eating peanuts. They looked so good we bought
some to eat on the way. We stopped at a fountain for a drink of
water and as it was getting late in the morning we continued on
our way. We ate peanuts as we rode and reminded each other of
the many wonderful experiences we had on the trip. It was nice
to know that we had ridden about 500 miles farther than from
New York to San Francisco, and St.Paul still about a hundred
miles away. We reached Austin at 1:30 P.M.

The roads were good coming into the city
but part of the way we rode on the sidewalk
which was even better.

Austin was a nice clean city of about
10,000 population with well paved streets.
The city is located on both banks of the Cedar River, The Hormel
food products plant is located there.

MAIN STREET
AUSTIN,MINN.

It seemed just like home to see all the automobiles with
Minnesota license plates. Most of the people we talked to thought
we were just starting out for New York. When we told them we had
been there and were on our way home, they just shook their heads
in disbelief. We went to a lunch room and ate a big meal after
washing up and getting that half inch of dirt off. The people in
Austin were very friendly and we enjoyed our visit. When leaving
Austin we bought souvenier cards to send to relatives and friends.

CHAPTER SEVEN

The 100th Day       (Cont.)

Taopi,Minnesota to Owatonna,Minnesota.

Before long Austin was far behind, the roads were very good, the Sun was shining and it was not too cold. In places the road was lined with large,beautiful trees on both sides and the ride was very enjoyable.

We reached Blooming Prairie late in the afternoon and stopped to rest after our non-stop ride from Austin. We sold a few cards and a storekeeper gave me some cards to sell as my stock was getting exceedingly low. It was late when we left this town, which was a small collection of houses on the prairie.

We wanted to get to Owatonna that day so we rode 22 miles without a stop, by then it was dark and we rode the last 13 miles to Owatonna after dark. We didn't have lights so we used the whistle code we agreed on at the start of the trip to signal each other. At last we saw the lights of the city and we were glad we had made the run safely. It was 8 P.M. when we reached Owatonna after going down the long hill leading into the city.

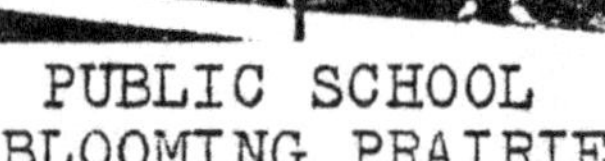

PUBLIC SCHOOL
BLOOMING PRAIRIE

N.CEDAR ST.
OWATONNA,MINN.

There were ornamental lights on the business street which was why they called N.Cedar Street the "White Way".

We went to a bakery for our meal, and thought we would starve waiting for them to prepare it, it took so long. The steaming hot meal we finally got was very good and included very good pie.

CHAPTER SEVEN

The 100th Day        (Cont.)

Taopi,Minnesota to Owatonna,Minnesota.

I went to a drug store where I could write to the St.Paul
newspaper and tell them that we would arrive at the St.Paul Court
House at three P.M. on Thursday October 7th,1915. Hap argued
about it as he thought it might rain the next day and slow us up.
In spite of his objection I didn't change the letter, I felt
that we should chance it, who knows, it might rain for a week. I
sent cards home and to several of my friends telling them when
to expect us.

About 9:15 P.M. we went in quest of a place to sleep, we
went out in the country nearby to look for a barn. It looked
like we were out of luck as many of the farmers had gone to bed
and others turned us down. It was pretty discouraging as I was
tired after our long ride that day.

We entered another farmer's yard but were stopped by a large
growling dog, we managed to get by him and went up to the back
door of the house. During the brief time between our knock and
the opening of the door by the farmer's wife we wondered how we
would be received. It was rather late and there was not a single
light in a farmhouse as far out in the country as we could see.

I asked the lady if we could sleep in the barn and an 'icy'
no came out of the next room where the farmer was smoking a pipe
and reading a newspaper. We were not to be defeated so easily,
the situation being what it was. However we retreated to the yard,
talking continually and trying to get the owner to change his mind.

CHAPTER SEVEN

The 100th Day        (Cont.)

Taopi,Minnesota to Owatonna,Minnesota.

We were followed into the yard by the farmer and his wife
and they began to warm up a bit. Using all the diplomacy I
could muster, the farmer was finally won over to our side with
the aid of his wife who was more or less on our side from the
start and didn't think we should have to sleep in the cold barn.

In a few minutes we were headed in the direction of the
large barn, the farmer leading the way with a lantern. We put
our bikes in the barn out of the weather, then passed between
rows of cows of all colors and the farmer showing us the way.
Hap got to the loft first and I threw our blankets up to him.
The farmer held the lantern until I climbed the ladder, then left
saying good night and all was quiet. We made our beds in the dark
and put hay over us as it was cold in the barn. Believe me, we
were thankful for a place to sleep that night. Thus ended a long,
hard day, we rode fifty four miles during the day.

CHAPTER SEVEN

CHICAGO,ILLINOIS TO SAINT PAUL,MINNESOTA.

October 6th,1915    The 101st Day       (Wednesday)

Owatonna,Minnesota to Farmington,Minnesota.

First thing in the morning the farmer came into the barn and
told us to get up and come to the house for breakfast. We told him
we would be right down and after fooling around in the hay,we
dressed. It is fun sleeping in a barn loaded with hay, we covered
ourselves with about four feet of it to keep warm during the night.

To hear the big rats nibbling under us was exciting, but to
have them run over us, sometimes across our faces was even more
so, I used to think they might nibble our toes, but by now we
were used to them and didn't mind sharing the barn with them.

The crickets kept up their chirping as they jumped from place
to place, sometimes landing on us. We felt quite at home by now
with all the bugs, crickets and large rats. It didn't bother us
anymore to even wake up and find a large spider right over us.

Hap said it looked like rain so we decided to hurry. The
farmer called us again so we rushed down, made our way between
the rows of cows and watched the animals eat while we loaded our
gear. We had a good hearty breakfast and they said they had read
about us in the paper. They told us that the paper said we had
already arrived home. We thanked the people and were on our way.

We didn't waste any time as it looked like rain. In order
to get home when we said we would, we would have to ride this day
come rain, snow or high water. We came to a sign post stating
that it was 57 miles to St.Paul. I was very excited knowing that
in a couple of days I would be home and back in school.

CHAPTER SEVEN

The 101st Day        (Cont.)

Owatonna,Minnesota to Farmington,Minnesota.

The road was gravel and in pretty good shape. We crossed a
little stream at Clinton Falls and stopped at Medford for re-
freshments. We went to the creamery but failed to get any free
milk as the natives told us we could.

We reached Faribault at noon, and went to the Post Office
and re-
ceived our
long ex-
pected
cards from

CENTRAL AVENUE

SCHOOL
FOR THE DEAF
FARIBAULT,MINNESOTA

SHATTUCK
MILITARY SCHOOL

Shrewsbury,Mass. which we should have received at Cleveland,Ohio.
I now had 100 cards to last me just one day. I wrote to my Mother
and told her we would come in on the Robert St. Bridge so that
we could ride through the business district on our way to the
Court House.

We canvassed the business area to sell cards, when it started
to rain hard, then let loose and came pouring down. We went into
every store on the main street as we were anxious to sell as many
cards as possible because I had a hundred and Hap had 225 left.
We had a good meal in a restaurant and talked to many people who
said they had read about us in the St.Paul papers.

We left Faribault in the rain but before we had gone very
far Hap refused to go on in the rain. I decided to continue so
I wrapped my half of the tent over me for protection to try to
get to Northfield in the downpour. After leaving Faribault I rode

CHAPTER SEVEN

The 101st Day        (Cont.)

Owatonna,Minnesota to Farmington,Minnesota.

mile after mile in the rain without stopping. I must have looked

odd with the tent over me but I kept reasonably dry.

I reached Dundas about 3:40 P.M. and as the rain had about

stopped, I took the tent off, rolled it up and put it on the bike.

Hap was not in sight so I went on alone to Northfield,arriving

safely but more or less covered with mud.

While waiting for Hap I got a haircut and sent

some cards home.

NORTHFIELD,MINN.

Hap arrived shortly, we sold some cards,

ate at a restaurant and visited with some students from St.Olaf

College. We left Northfield at 5:30 on our last big run for the

day, about 15 miles. The road was in poor shape but it was a

pleasure riding in the rain when we were so close to our goal.

It was getting dark, Hap was way ahead but I soon caught

up to him. The road was getting worse all the time from the heavy

rain and was sloppy and muddy. It was soon pitch dark and Hap was

now way behind me and failed to answer my whistle signals. The

heavy rain continued and I once again covered myself with the tent.

It was cold and dreary and black as ink and I nearly got hit

by automobiles three or four times. The road now had large puddles

of water on it and I was covered with mud and was cold and wet.

This day had been plain awful but we had to get to Farmington

that night, regardless.

All of a sudden a clamp on the tent got caught on a spoke of

my rear wheel, and as I was wrapped up in the tent, I was sent

CHAPTER SEVEN

The 101st Day          (Cont.)

Owatonna,Minnesota to Farmington,Minnesota.

headlong into a large puddle of muddy water, with the tent, bike
and all. I picked my muddy self up, forgetting that I was hurt
more or less and completely drenched.

I didn't cover myself with the tent again as I rode on,as I
was as wet as I could get anyway. Before long I saw the lights
of Farmington far ahead and it looked like we would make it, thank
goodness. I reached Farmington about 8 P.M. but Hap was not there
yet as the last I knew of him he was far behind me.

It was still raining hard so I put my bike in a livery stable
doorway while waiting for him. At 8:20 he had not arrived and I
was getting nervous about him. If he failed to show up before long
I would go out in the country looking for him but decided to wait
a little longer before going.

At 8:30 I was told that he was in town and now to find him.
Before long I saw him riding down the street, I asked him what
happened and he said he got stalled in the rain.

I went out to sell cards while Hap got a shave. I sold $1.25
worth of cards, canvassing about every store in town. We ate at a
restaurant and then I got a shave and after cleaning up, I felt
much better.

We decided to sleep in a hotel but had a hard time finding
one. We finally located one and paid 35¢ each for a room. I paid
Hap the 25¢ I owed him for the cards he let me have and we were
now square. While selling cards I went into a bakery and the lady
asked if I had a picture of Johnson High School in St.Paul as her

CHAPTER SEVEN

The 101st Day        (Cont.)

Owatonna,Minnesota to Farmington,Minnesota.

son used to go there. Come to find out her son had been in the
same physics class with me the previous year.

I won two, half pound boxes of candy on a punch board for
25¢ and Hap won two for 95¢. We each ate a box of candy in bed
and saved the others for our Mothers.

This was to be our last night on the trip. We were sorry
that the trip was so near over, but we realized that it was for
the best, as it was getting too cold, especially at night to live
out this way. I wrote in my diary that I had the best time of my
life on the trip but that St. Paul  and home were good enough for
me.

I wondered how we would be received at the Court House
the following day. I wondered if only three people would be down
to welcome us home as was the case when we left on what seemed
to most people an impossible trip. I was so excited about getting
home I couldn't go to sleep for a long time.

We rode 46 miles that day in spite of the heavy rains and
the terrible condition of the road.

CHAPTER SEVEN

CHICAGO,ILLINOIS TO SAINT PAUL,MINNESOTA.

October 7th,1915  The 102nd Day     (Thursday)

<u>THE LAST DAY OF THE JOURNEY</u>

Farmington,Minnesota to Saint Paul,Minnesota.

This day we would reach home. We jumped out of bed with a great deal of vim. I slept good that night in our hotel room and we were dressed in a jiffy. We were soon ready for our last ride on our wonderful trip.

We ate breakfast and I called on Milton Shafer, the son of the woman in the bakery and who I knew at Johnson High School the year before. His father got him out of bed to see me and had a nice visit talking about school.

Hap changed his front tire and put on his new casing. It was very cold and we just about froze, so we warmed up at the stove in the livery stable. It looked and felt like it might begin to snow, we hoped not, at least not until after we got home.

We each bought a pair of canvas gloves and after canvassing the stores we hadn't visited before, we were ready to begin our last 24 miles to St.Paul.

We were off with a shout, down the main street on the sidewalk, Hap nearly ran into the town constable who turned to look after the speeding traveler. Just then I came riding by and missed him by about six inches. I stopped to say goodby to Shafer and the cop ran up and grabbed me, I think he was on the verge of putting me in the calaboose. He made me get off the sidewalk and ride in the muddy street, and was not very friendly about it. We were full of pep and reached Rosemount at 11:20 a.m.

CHAPTER SEVEN

The 102nd Day      (Cont.)

Farmington,Minnesota to Saint Paul,Minnesota.

We were now only 16 miles from our goal.

At Rosemount I sold 25¢ worth of cards to a grocer and
found out that the clerk in the store lived just a block from
where I lived in St.Paul. He told us that there had been a half
page article about us in the previous Sunday St.Paul paper. We
ate a whole pie in a restaurant and then bought a morning St.
Paul paper and there was an article in it about our arriving at
3 P.M. on October 7th  at the St.Paul Court House.

We were on our way in a few minutes, leaving behind the last
good sized town we would be in on our long trip. We had been in
about a thousand cities and towns in the twelve states we had visited. The roads were good and we soon reached Westcott, it was at
this town where we said good-by to Lawrence Zachrison on our trip
East. It was at this place that we took the road to Cannon Falls
on our way East. It was now only 10 miles to St.Paul and only
12:45 P.M. so we had plenty of time to make it to the Court House
by 3P.M.

We spent some time in the railroad station as we were ahead
of schedule and left a little after 1 P.M. We were getting pretty
excited about being so close to home. We saw a sign on a high hill,
"6 miles to St.Paul" and then in the dim distance we saw the white
dome of the State Capitol. A moment later the Cathedral loomed up
before us, I can not describe the way I felt when I first saw
those buildings which meant home to me. People who travel in foreign countries must feel the same way when they first see the

## CHAPTER SEVEN

The 102nd Day        (Cont.)

Farmington,Minnesota to Saint Paul,Minnesota.

Statue of Liberty in New York Harbor after a long absence.

We were soon in West St.Paul and when we were near the High

Bridge we saw Colby and Carl Temple on a motorcycle coming out

to meet us. We said hello and shook hands, it was great to see

someone we knew again. They left and went back 

to the Court House to tell the people there

that we would arrive at 3 P.M. as planned.

STATE CAPITOL

It was a little after two so waited at

the store near the bridge. At 2:25 P.M.we started

down the street for the Robert Street Bridge over

the Mississippi River. It was now snowing a little, 

little did we think when we left St.Paul that it

would be snowing when we got home, however it soon

stopped and the Sun came out.

CATHEDRAL

We reached the Robert Street Bridge at twenty minutes to

three so we stopped in a warehouse to kill time. At about ten

minutes to three we crossed the bridge, rode 

down Robert Street to Seventh Street. We

turned on Seventh Street riding slowly

through the business district. At Seventh

COURT HOUSE

and Wabasha we turned left on Wabasha Street

and were only three blocks from our goal. When we were half way

between Fifth and Fourth Streets the crowd on the Court House

steps and vicinity saw us and came running down to greet us.

We were snowed under by a deluge of questions and were

## CHAPTER SEVEN

The 102nd Day       (Cont.)

The End of the Journey at Saint Paul, Minnesota.

shaking hands on all sides. When we left Saint Paul there were

three people to see us off and now on our return home there were

three hundred people at the Court House to welcome us. There were

reporters, photographers and the Mayor of Saint Paul to see us

home. When we reached the Court House the cyclometer on Hap's

bike registered 3,627.3 miles.

I wanted to say hello to all my friends but in the excite-

ment I missed many of them. With so much commotion I also failed

to say hello to my four year old sister, Dorothy, and she looked

up at Mother and said, "Tell Leon I'm here".

After about fifteen minutes of hand shaking in front of the

Court House we were ushered up to the Mayor's Office (Winn Powers)

and he came up to us, shook hands and said, "You had some trip".

We were then taken into the Mayor's private office and the St.

Paul Dispatch newspaper photographer took a flash light picture

of us with the Mayor. I was shaking hands with

him in the picture which appeared in the morn-

ing paper the next day. We spent the next ten

minutes talking to the reporters.

HOME
1010
FAIRMOUNT AVE.

We went down stairs, talked to some of

our friends who were still there. Then Hap

and I mounted our trusty bikes and headed for home. On the way

we stopped to say hello to the man I worked for on Saturdays to

CHAPTER SEVEN

The 102nd Day       (Cont.)

The End of the Journey at Saint Paul,Minnesota.

earn part of the money for the trip.We rode the rest of the way
on Summit Avenue. I shook hands with Hap at his home on Lincoln
Avenue and then I continued on home.

Thus ended our 102 day, 3,627 mile bicycle trip, Saint Paul
to Chicago, Pittsburgh, Philadelphia, New York City and Boston
and return by way of Albany, Buffalo, Cleveland, Toledo, Chicago,
Dubuque,Iowa and Saint Paul,Minnesota.

We either rode our bikes or walked every foot of the way.
We did not accept a ride of any kind or at any time on the entire
trip.


THE END.


COPYRIGHT 1980
BY
LEON W. SCHROEDER

# $100,000 FLATS TO BE BUILT BY WOMAN

## Contract Is Let for Two Structures at Grand and Lexington Avenues.

Contracts for the immediate construction of two apartment buildings to cost $100,000 were let yesterday by Mrs. Nadine Rosenstein, 152 South Lexington avenue.

The buildings will be erected at Grand and Lexington avenues. The Realty Service company, 713 Pioneer Building, will have charge of the construction.

### Will Be Three Stories.

The building will be of brick and concrete, three stories in height, and containing nineteen apartments each. The apartments will consist of three and four rooms each, with bath and kitchenette.

### Work to Start Soon.

Work on the structures will be started within a few days. The buildings are expected to be ready for occupancy by February 1.

Mrs. Rosenstein has owned the property for some time.

## CHALLENGE STILL STANDS.

### No One Tries to Claim Forfeit Posted in Defense of Equity.

If any one has accepted the challenge of M. C. Merchant of Ellendale and claimed the $1,000 he posted as forfeit to the one who could prove that the Equity Co-operative exchange of St. Paul has ever received one car of grain that has not been accounted for to the shipper, no report of it has reached St. Paul.

# A Great Light

## FOR

# Little Money

Friday and Saturday. Open Saturday until 9 P. M.

We have just received 500 new imported Fringe Lights in amber, silver and green just like cut.

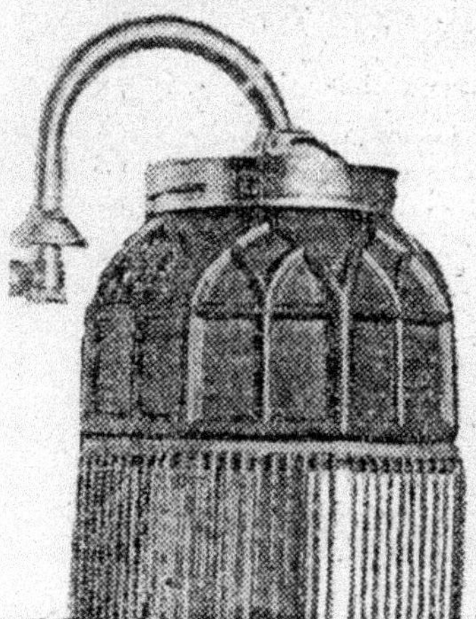

# SCHOCH

## Free Apples
Half peck of apples with an order of 50c or over. ASK FOR THEM.

**Buy Pasteurized Butter Is Advice of State Dairy and Food Commissioner** —Issues Warnings to Consumers—Germs Are Killed By Heat—Prevents High Acid Cream Being Used, Which Assures More Wholesome Products. "If you would have pure, wholesome butter on your dinner table, buy butter made from pasteurized cream." This is the advice given people of Minnesota by John McCabe, assistant dairy and food commissioner, who said it is desirable that a law be passed at the 1917 session of the Legislature compelling pasteurization of milk and cream that is to be made into butter.

## Use Schoch's "Golden Crown

Pasteurized Butter," the highest grade butter made. Costs a little more than ordinary brands, but worth the difference. There are imitations, but only one genuine "Golden Crown Pasteurized," which is sold only by us.

## The Apple Season Is Here

### Eat More Apples!
A car of orchard packed Apples—new, clean, sanitary barrels. Many fine varieties, including Greenings, Wealthies, Otters, Wolf Rivers, McMans, Haas, Plum Ciders, etc.

**10 Pounds for 17c. BARREL............ $1.90**

### Black Prince Grapes
Extra quality dark California grapes. Very sweet. Large Square Basket..... **23c**

### Concord Grapes
A carload of fancy Michigan Concords just unloaded and on sale today at ........... **25c**
Basket (6¾ lbs net.)

### Tokay Grapes
Beautiful Flaming Tokays, the finest of the season, worth 60c...................... **25c**
Large Square Basket.

### Italian Blue Plums
Don't fail to buy your Plums now to put up. Last car now on sale.

- Large market basket or crate (tight pack) ........... **65c**
- Large square basket ......................... **20c**
- ½-large basket crate ...................... **79c**

### Peaches
Fine, juicy Colorado, Utah and California Elbertas at far less than their value. Peach crate.... **58c**

### Kieffer Pears
A carload of good sound Kieffers in bushel baskets, on sale at, Bushel Basket.. **87c**

### Jonathan Apples
A car of extra fancy, long-keeping Jonathans in bu. bkts. Bushel bkt.. **$1.25**

**Blueberries** Box ................10c / 16-box case .......$1.58

Fancy Japanese Persimmons, each... 10c
Bananas, dozen ...........10c & 15c
Seckel Pears, basket ................ 20c
**Sweet Potatoes, 11 lbs.......25c**
New Grapefruit, Isle of Pines, each..10c
Lemons, dozen ......................10c
Cooking Apples, 10 lbs.............17c
Fresh shipment of Wild Plums.
**New Cranberries, 2 lbs or 3 lbs 25c**
(1 lb sugar free.)
**Pink Melons** Crate, 12s, 15s and 18s ......... **40c**
4 for 10c.
**Sweet Rockyford Melons ..... 8 for 25c**
California Quinces, dozen........... 20c
New Dates.................. } **3 pkgs. 25c**
New Figs....................
**Popcorn** Shelled, 3 pkgs......... 25c / On the cob, 6 lbs........ 25c
Sweet Corn—Evergreen and Country Gentleman.
Ground Cherries, lb...............12½c
Fresh Lima Beans, lb...............35c
Tomatoes, basket ..................10c
Brussels Sprouts, quart box.........25c
Oyster Plants, bunch................ 5c
Tomatoes—Yellow Plum, 10 lbs.......35c
Kale—Large bunch .................. 5c
Citron Melons for pickling, each......10c
Hubbard Squash ....................10c
Fresh Parsley Roots, 3 bunches...... 10c
Large Boiling Onions, 3 bunches...... 5c
Green Bell Peppers, dozen...........10c
**Eggs, dozen ..........22c**
**Butter** Extra Daily, lb ........... **25c**

## Cash Cane Sugar Offers

| | |
|---|---|
| 100 lbs $4.85<br>24 lbs $1.00 | With $5.00 order or over of other goods. |
| 100 lbs $5.00<br>23 lbs $1.00 | With $4.00 order or over of other goods. |
| 100 lbs $5.10<br>22 lbs $1.00 | With $3.00 order or over of other goods. |
| 100 lbs $5.08<br>21 lbs $1.00 | With $1.00 order or over of fresh fruit. |
| 100 lbs $5.15<br>20 lbs $1.00 | With $1.00 order or over of other goods. |

**Honey** New White Clover—Comb................... **18c**

### CANNED FISH SPECIALS.
Fish Flakes, Burnham & Morrill's, regular 15c ..................... **12c**
Clams—Doxsee's minced, can ........ 10c
Clam Chowder, Burnham's, 3 cans... 25c
No. 1 Tall Alaska Red Salmon, can...15c
No. ½ flat Chinook Salmon..........12½c
Regular 50c Izumi Crab Meat........ 39c
Creole Dinner, 3 cans............... 25c
Hot Tamales, can .................. 10c
Chili Con Carne, can............... 10c

### Friday's Salt Fish Specials.
New Alaska Herring, 3 for........... 10c
Fat Breakfast Mackerel, 3 for........ 25c
Large Norway Herring, 3 for......... 10c
Norway Herring, 10-lb pail.........$1.10

### FRIDAY'S FRESH FISH.
Fresh Bulk Oysters, quart..........40c
Fresh Frogs' Legs, 2 doz.......... 25c
Pickerel, 3 lbs ...................25c
Sunfish, lb .......................10c

# Boy Cyclists, Waxing Flush in Fields Afar, Pedal Home For Fatted Calves

**H**ARWOOD TEMPLE and Leon Schroeder, St. Paul youths, who cycled to New York City and return, being welcomed by Mayor Powers yesterday afternoon, when they delivered a reply to his message to Mayor Mitchel of New York.

# Cry Wrung From Mother Heart, "Why Didn't You Buy New Pants," Greets Wanderers at Gates of St. Paul's City Hall.

"**W**HY didn't you buy a pair of pants?" A matter-of-fact question, perhaps, but it concealed a great emotion. Addressed to a pair of sunburned youths who had jumped off their bicycles before the Wabasha street entrance of the City Hall, it marked these travelers' return from a far pilgrimage at 3:02 o'clock yesterday afternoon.

### WANDERS IN LANDS AFAR.

Full many a mile, to-wit, 3,627.3 miles, according to the cyclometer on one front wheel—had they wandered through distant lands. Week after week, month after month, rolled by; and, except for occasional telegrams and a letter every few days, these young adventurers had been given up as lost, and mourned as dead, by all who held them dear.

### Cry Wrung From Heart.

So it was Mrs. Baldwin Schroeder of 1010 Fairmount avenue who cried out thus to one survivor, her 18-year-old son Leon, instead of fainting upon his neck. She restrained herself with a mighty effort, even after Mrs. Cora I. Temple of 758 Lincoln avenue had fervently kissed her son Harwood, 17 years old, the last remaining member of the adventuring company and had asked him plainly if he didn't look fine.

### Rises to Great Crisis.

But when a chronicler of crises had set forth to Mrs. Schroeder that her self-constraint left a chasm in a thrilling incident, and that no movie mother would have failed to fold her long-lost offspring to her bosom, she answered, smiling bravely, "Well, if Mrs. Temple did, I suppose I have to." Then she hunted up Leon in the crowd and kissed him without warning.

And the pants—there have been more comely trousers, less mud-stained and less informally creased. But the real significance, the poignant soul throb—ah, yes, indeed!

### Receive Official Salute.

Mrs. Temple's mother was there also—Mrs. M. L. Walker, and John, who was the brother of Leon, and Florence, his sister. With these and with several friends the boys presented themselves before Mayor Powers to receive the official salutation, "You had some trip!"

### Far Away and Back Again.

On their way to the remote East, as the pilgrims recounted, they had traveled through La Crosse, Madison, Chicago, Cleveland, Pittsburgh, Philadelphia, New York City, Boston, Albany, Buffalo, Cleveland again, Chicago, Dubuque and Farmington.

### Cook Spuds "and Things."

They carried a tent in two sections; also blankets and cooking utensils. While their eyes were fixed upon the dawn, as it were, they cooked potatoes and things by the roadside.

But as they started toward Boston they found the arid steppes so full of suburban homes that camp fires burned the lawns, and, besides, it was just about as cheap to buy refreshment for man and wheel at the vine-clad inns on Main street.

In many a strange tongue, but especially in Pennsylvania Dutch, were they welcomed by the honest peasantry to shelter within the barn and to a share of bread and meat. But by selling postcard pictures of St. Paul scenes at an average price of one nickel they garnered $150 and paid all of their expenses.

The lord mayor's warrant under the great seal assured them respect and protection in every land.

### Mitchell's Aid Helps 'Em.

His honor's great and good friend, Mayor Mitchell of New York, had fared afar with his men-at-arms, but his clerk provided a parchment script that was held in fear even by the gentlemen of the road.

Miraculously, they escaped all wounds, albeit their tires suffered sorely. Their machines, re-equipped twice at the makers' expense, broke never at all.

### Wax Fat as They Pedal.

Despite much rainy weather, though the roads were good beyond Chicago, no cold afflicted them nor other sicknesses. At the hour of parting, June 28, each weighed by the steelyard 135 pounds. Leon fell almost sick of overmuch eating and lost two pounds, but his weight is 139 now, and that of Howard has waxed great at 150.

In the kingdom of New York fared they one red-lettered day, full seventy-three miles, and the days of their travel were three score and seventeen.

### "Not Without Honor."

Their honest tongues maintain the green lettered legend on white oilcloth and their wallets, "St. Paul to New York and return." Yet it was in the borders of their own country, over against Farmington, that they first heard the jibe, "Aw, whatcher givin' us?" For so it ever haps.

## Husband Busy So Wife Builds Home

"My husband is too busy so I am building our new home," said Mrs. William Niksch, 1263 James street, who applied for a building permit at the City Hall yesterday.

She displayed a thorough familiarity with the house, the construction and various dimensions.

Her husband is a foreman at the White Enamel Refrigerator company.

Through Pullman car, Chicago to Norfolk, Va., via Pennsylvania lines to

## EPILOGUE

On October 8th, the morning after I reached home I reported to Johnson High School. There had been so much publicity about the trip that the teachers knew why I was late. They welcomed me, asked about the trip and suggested that I give a talk about my experiences later on, and this I did. All went well until I went to my English class. The teacher said, "why are you so late, you are supposed to enter school at the beginning of the semester". I told her I couldn't report on time as I was out of the city. She said, "that is no excuse for starting school a month late". She then asked my name and when I told her, she said, "Oh, your the bicycle rider" and all was well.

I was about a month late but I received passing grades in all my subjects for the six week report card period. The teachers probably thought that I learned more on the trip than would have been the case had I been in school. Being late for school was one of the things that bothered my Mother but it all turned out for the best. As far as I know Hap was also treated in the same manner at Central High School where he went to school.

The trip was a very rewarding experience and we learned a great deal from it. One of the things that meant a great deal to me was the fact that we saw, first hand, so many things of historical interest concerning the early days of this country. It was also of great interest to see so many large cities as well as the many small towns we visited.

I have mentioned some states in particular where the people were unusually friendly and helpful but as a matter of fact we received unusually kind and helpful treatment in all the twelve

<u>EPILOGUE</u>

states that we visited.

If it had not been for the help of so many people, buying post cards, giving us an occasional meal or a place to sleep, the trip would not have been possible, as we were without money to pay our way. For ten years afterwards, each year at Christmas time I sent greetings to a great many of the people who had helped us.

There were many things to be thankful for on the trip and one of the most important was the fact that we did not get sick on the way. What with riding so many times in the rain and being wet to the skin (we didn't have raincoats) and going to bed wet and sleeping on the damp, some times wet ground. It was remark-able that we didn't become seriously ill. The only trouble we had along those lines was to feel a little under the weather on one or two mornings. This did not delay us any and I think it was due more to our diet than to the weather.

Another thing for which we were thankful, what with all our riding at night without lights we didn't once get hit by a car although we did have some narrow escapes.

JOHNSON
HIGH SCHOOL

To say it all in a few words: We learned what a great and beautiful country we live in and that it is inhabited by a kind and hospitable people.

San Carlos, Calif. 94070
1980

# St. Paul to New York and Ba

### BY HARVEY B. FULLER, JR.

IN these swift moving times that keep pace with automobile and aeroplane, motorcycle and motor boat, the once laureled bicycle is relegated to the dim background along with the urbane sedan chair and the sociable stage coach of antiquity. It was but a couple of decades ago when all the world wheeled by on bicycle paths, talking of handle-bars and forks, sprockets and saddles—terminology long since obsolete. But this summer the bicycle has had a resurrection, a renaissance—at least in the hearts of two enterprising St. Paul boys.

Harwood Temple, 758 Lincoln avenue, and Leon Schroeder, 1010 Fairmount avenue, juniors at Central high school, wanted to see the country, after the manner of those who are possessed with a youthful wanderlust. Their summer vacation afforded the time but fortune afforded only means sufficient for their bicycles and the limited equipment they could carry. Their determination afforded the principal contribution to their expedition. Temple and Schroeder left the St. Paul Court House at 6 A. M., June 28, and have just returned. In the three months of continual daily riding they have covered a distance of about 3,500 miles and have visited the principal cities between here and New York.

### In Quest of Adventure.

Ulysses and Marco Polo, Stanley and Scott, in their happy adventuring grounds, must beam on these lads. The spirit of the big adventurers finds true hearts in these plucky young followers of the gleam. With modern means of transportation reducing time and distance, as well as romance, to a minimum, there is something heroic, epic, in such a pilgrimage as Temple and Schroeder have successfully made. It is gratifying to know that in these somewhat effete, sophisticated times there are those of the rising generation who are willing to forego the easy, soft, upholstered life. It takes courage, perseverance and endurance to go half way across the continent, and, back, by none other than your own muscular power.

The route over which the boys made their long trip lay through the following cities: La Crosse, Madison, Chicago, Valparaizo, Akron, Toledo, Pittsburgh, Philadelphia, New York, New Haven, Boston, Worcester, Albany, Syracuse, Buffalo, Erie, Cleveland, South Bend, Chicago and Dubuque. Every mile of this circuit they covered on their wheels, not once yielding to any opportunity for a "lift." Their stops in the various cities were of necessity brief, but allowed them time to see the most important "sights."

### Carried Knapsacks and Luggage on Wheels.

Temple and Schroeder carried their entire baggage and equipment on their wheels. A tent in which they camped on the road over night was divided into two parts, each boy carrying half. Each one also carried a knapsack loaded with necessary articles; and on the bars of their wheels were strapped a blanket and raincoat. It was only in the larger cities where they put up in hotels. With a complete outfit of tools they were able to make necessary repairs on their bicycles. At Chicago, both ways, they had their wheels overhauled and were presented with new tires by the company whose make of bicycle they were riding.

Before leaving St. Paul the boys secured from Mayor Powers a letter of introduction "to whom it may concern." With this "passport" the bicyclists were duly accredited and their credentials always acknowledged. We have read much of late of trade boosting tours, but they have little on what Temple and Schroeder have accomplished, proportionately, in the way of advertising St. Paul. Pinned to each knapsack was a large square pennant with the slogan, "St Paul to New York," printed in big white capitals against a dark background. Furthermore the boys took with them, or had forwarded to them at different points, some 2,000 picture

post cards, displaying the attractions of St. Paul. These they sold everywhere on the way at 5 cents apiece, making a generous profit on the wholesale price of half a cent which they paid. The sale of these St. Paul views was the only source of income, except for a small amount of pocket money to start with, upon which the boys had to rely. Their expenses were reduced to a minimum as they camped out in their tents most of the nights or slept in barns or vacant houses. Occasionally some generous and admiring farmer would treat them to a bed in his own house. In a number of towns along the way the newspapers gave considerable publicity to their exploit. They were well received everywhere, and in many instances were the recipients of kindness and assistance.

### Letters Home Form Log of Journey.

The letters which Temple and Schroeder have written to their families in St. Paul have served as an interesting log of their trip. The following, from a letter written soon after their departure, recounts experiences that characterized their traveling:

"We are now 435 miles from St. Paul, and so far have had no accidents or misfortunes outside of a few blowouts and punctures, but none of them have stopped up on the road more than twenty minutes at the longest. The first night we stopped and camped on a man's lawn at Cannon Falls. He gave us a horse blanket to sleep on and a lantern, and we put the wheels in his barn. The postcards sell like hot cakes. We just sell to fellows along the road who inquire about the trip.

"Tuesday we had a big dinner, and we cooked meat, potatoes and everything over a wood fire. Could you arrange to send some home-cooked oatmeal? We have often wished we had some since we left.

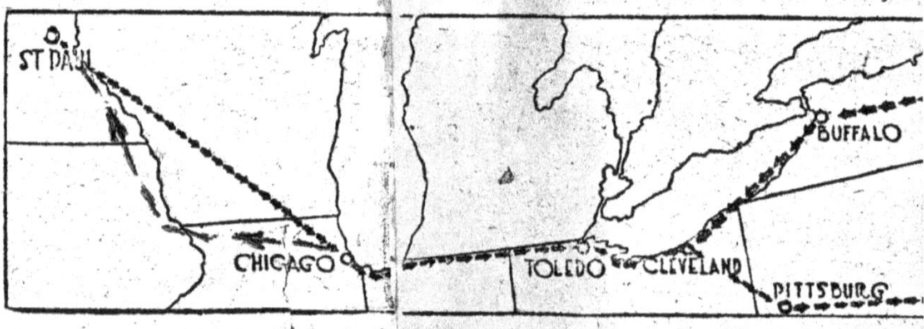


The route covered by Temple and Schroeder

3,627 Miles

# ack on Bikes; Local Lads Cover 3,500 Miles

Leon Schroeder (left) and Harwood Temple.

We have seen a lot of country since leaving St. Paul. We never go into a large town but what we are met by reporters who demand facts and ask us how we do it. All the people think we are wonderful, and look up to us. In all the little towns we get our names in the paper and we are going to have our pictures in the Madison papers. The people all along are very good to us. The wear and tear on the bicycles is something awful but we never get tired ourselves to amount to anything. The first couple of days the knapsacks were pretty heavy, but now they seem to weigh very little. We consume enormous amounts of oil and the wheels have to be gone over every night. Tomorrow we are going to push on to Chicago, where we stay one day and after that we push on to New York. Don't worry about us, we are getting along in great shape."

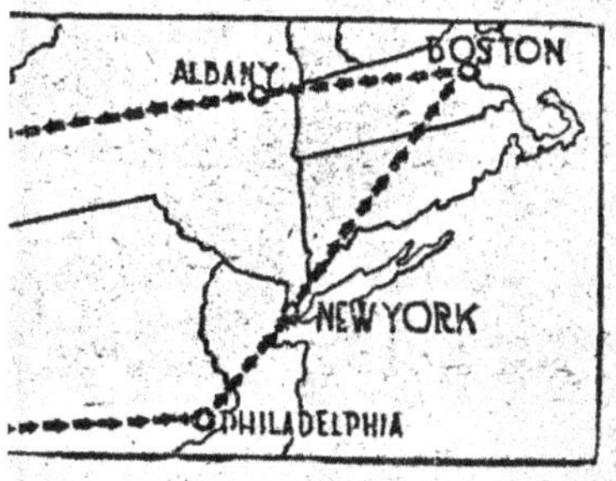


## Average About Fifty-five Miles a Day.

From Chicago they wrote briefly:

"We arrived this noon and are feeling fine. Took the bicycles to the manufacturers and they are going to overhaul them and give us new tires free. We never felt better before in our lives and we sleep like a couple of logs. We average about 55 miles per day on the road. We are often invited to eat at people's houses. We are staying at a hotel in Chicago. It is a wonderful city. We have seen more in the last two weeks than we've ever seen before in our lives."

From York, Pa., came the advice that:

"We are over the mountains now and will have good roads all the rest of the way to New York. We toured the battlefield of Getttysburg, and it was quite a sight, but a great deal too much to tell about in a letter. We went through a large building containing an enormous painting of the big battle known as the 'Cyclorama.' We slept in a barn last night because it was raining and the ground was too damp."

Their impression of the Quaker City was summed up briefly:

"Philadelphia is almost as big as Chicago, but it hasn't got the tall buildings. They have subways and elevated trains here that are just as good as in Chicago. St. Paul has got better street cars than we have seen so far."

Temple and Schroeder celebrated their arrival in New York August 9 by sending home the following triumphant telegram: "Arrived in New York 5 P. M. Actual riding, 33 days. Delayed by rains and tire trouble. Feeling fine. Will return via Boston and Buffalo."

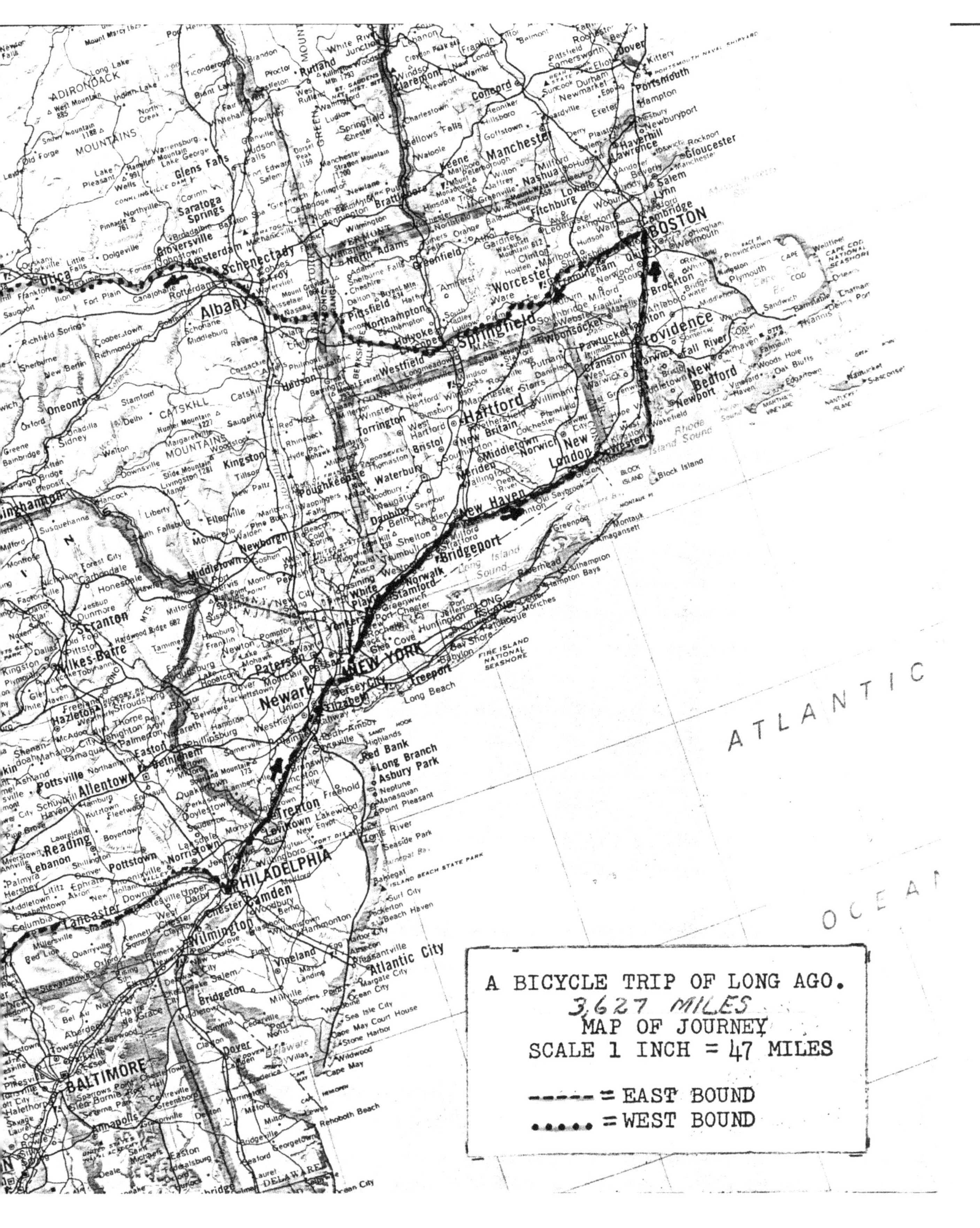

A BICYCLE TRIP OF LONG AGO.
3,627 MILES
MAP OF JOURNEY
SCALE 1 INCH = 47 MILES
------ = EAST BOUND
..... = WEST BOUND

A  BICYCLE  TRIP  OF  LONG  AGO.

BY

LEON W. SCHROEDER


TWELVE TYPEWRITTEN COPIES OF THE STORY.

THIS IS COPY NUMBER _7_


COPYRIGHT 1980
BY
LEON W. SCHROEDER


ALL RIGHTS TO THIS STORY OR ANY PART OF IT, INCLUDING

REPRODUCTION IN ANY FORM, ARE RESERVED BY THE AUTHOR.

To my daughter Judith & Family

For whatever it is worth, I have told this story just as it was.

Leon W. Schroeder
October 7, 1980

www.ingramcontent.com/pod-product-compliance
Lightning Source LLC
Chambersburg PA
CBHW040139110726
48005CB00018B/2587